Fourth Edition

Exploring Social Life

Readings to Accompany
ESSENTIALS OF SOCIOLOGY:
A DOWN-TO-EARTH APPROACH

Edited by
James M. Henslin
Southern Illinois University, Edwardsville

Boston ■ New York ■ San Francisco
Mexico City ■ Montreal ■ Toronto ■ London ■ Madrid ■ Munich ■ Paris
Hong Kong ■ Singapore ■ Tokyo ■ Cape Town ■ Sydney

Executive Editor: Jeff Lasser
Series Editorial Assistant: Lauren Macey
Senior Marketing Manager: Kelly May
Editorial Production Service: Omegatype Typography, Inc.
Manufacturing Buyer: Debbie Rossi
Electronic Composition: Omegatype Typography, Inc.
Cover Administrator: Kristina Mose-Libon

For related titles and support materials, visit our online catalog at www.pearsonhighered.com.

Between the time website information is gathered and then published, it is not unusual for some sites to have closed. Also, the transcriptions of URLs can result in typographical errors. The publisher would appreciate notification where these errors occur so that they may be corrected in subsequent editions.

Library of Congress Cataloging-in-Publication Data

Exploring social life : readings to accompany Essentials of sociology:
a down-to-earth approach / [edited by] James M. Henslin. — 4th ed.
      p.   cm.
  Includes bibliographical references and index.
  ISBN-13: 978-0-205-63306-7 (pbk.)
  ISBN-10: 0-205-63306-4 (pbk.)
  1. Sociology.   I. Henslin, James M.
  HM586.E97 2009
  301—dc22

                                                          2008036034

Printed in the United States of America

10 9 8 7 6 5 4 3   12 11 10

Contents

Preface

It is gratifying to see that students and instructors alike have responded so favorably to *Essentials of Sociology: A Down-to-Earth Approach.* Since many instructors want to give their students the opportunity to read original sociological research, I have designed this brief anthology as a companion for *Essentials of Sociology.* Because the readings follow the text's outline chapter for chapter, they are incorporated easily into the course. In keeping with the *Essentials* theme, there is a single reading for each chapter. The exception is the inclusion of a reading on human sexuality for those who incorporate this topic into their course.

This fourth edition has seven new selections. I hope you enjoy reading them as much as I did in locating them. As always, a reading can have several subthemes. This allows an article to be incorporated into a different chapter than the one I have assigned it, or to be included in the course even though a particular chapter is not assigned.

Also in keeping with the *Essentials* theme, I will keep this preface brief. If you have any suggestions for the next edition of this reader, please let me know. As always, I look forward to hearing from you.

Jim Henslin
henslin@aol.com

The Sociological Perspective

All of us, at least to some degree, want to understand social life. If nothing else, we want to understand why people react to us as they do. We may want to know why some people boast and tell lies, while others undergo personal hardship in order to tell the truth. These are important questions, and they affect our everyday lives. So do issues on a much broader scale, such as why certain types of jobs are drying up around us, why we need more and more education to get a good job, why so many marriages break up, why people are prejudiced, why people are marrying later, or why cohabitation, which most people used to consider shameful, is now so common. Then, too, there is the question of why nations go to war despite the common sentiment that war is evil and should be avoided.

The tool that sociology offers in our quest for understanding is called *the sociological perspective* (also known as *the sociological imagination*). Basically, the sociological perspective means that no behavior or event stands in isolation. Rather, it is connected to other events that surround it. To understand any particular behavior or event, we need to view it within the context in which it occurs. The sociological perspective sensitizes us to the need to uncover those connections.

Back in the 1950s and 1960s, sociologist C. Wright Mills noted that world events were coming to play an increasingly significant role in our personal lives. More than ever, this is so today. What transpires in other countries—even on the other side of the globe—has profound effects on our own lives. An economic downturn in Japan or Europe, for example, pinches our economy—and may force us to put our lives on hold. When China and India undergo rapid industrialization and their people strive for higher standards of living, the additional pressure on the world's resources drives up the cost of the goods we buy and threatens our domestic industries. When jobs are hard to get—or we can get only low-paying jobs—we may decide that it is better to postpone getting married—no matter how much we are in love. Very reluctantly, we may even determine that it is prudent to move back in with our parents. Similarly, if our country goes to war in some far-off region, perhaps in a country we hadn't even heard of before, many people's lives are disrupted, some even shattered.

Economies surge, then tumble. Empires grow to a peak of power, then overreach and decline. Wars come and go, not only leaving behind their dead and mutilated but also becoming a strange and unwelcome intruder in our lives. The Internet appears, changing the way we do business, and even the way we communicate, do our homework, and, for some of us, how we make dates and meet our husbands and wives. What once were luxuries come to be considered as necessities. Even morals change, and what was once considered wrong comes to be accepted as an ordinary part of everyday life.

Such events form a shaping context that affects us profoundly. They affect both the ways we look at the world and how we see ourselves. Our aspirations—and our other "innermost" desires—do not originate within us. Instead, if we view them from the sociological perspective, we see that they are transplanted inside us. The social origin of these transplantings, though, ordinarily remains beyond our field of vision. We tend to perceive only what we experience directly—our feelings, our interactions, our friendships, our problems. The shaping context of these vital forces in our lives, we perceive but dimly.

In short, we cannot understand our lives merely by looking inside ourselves—at our own abilities, emotions, desires, or aspirations. Nor is it sufficient to consider only our family, friends, associates, or even our neighborhood or the social institutions such as school and church that influence us. Although they are important, we have to also consider a world far beyond our immediate confines, a broader world that is becoming increasingly significant for our everyday lives.

All these factors—our personal feelings, our everyday interactions, and events around the globe—come together in *the sociological perspective*. Learning to see ourselves and others from this perspective is a fascinating journey, certainly an intriguing and promising aspect of our introduction to sociology.

To begin our journey, we open this anthology with a selection that has become a classic in sociology. Peter Berger invites you to consider the excitement of exploring social life and beginning to view it from the sociological perspective. We follow this opening article with a reading by Napoleon Chagnon, who recounts his fascinating adventure with a tribe in South America. In the third selection, Gwynne Dyer examines techniques that the U.S. Marine Corps uses to transform ordinary young men into soldiers who will not hesitate to kill when the order is given. In the fourth article, Helene Lawson and Kira Leck analyze one of the many ways that technology is changing our ideas, norms, and practices, the Internet's impact on dating. Together, these first four selections can give you a taste of sociology, hopefully whetting your appetite for the other articles that follow.

Invitation to Sociology

Peter L. Berger

introduction

To grasp the *sociological perspective* is to see the social world in a new light. As your angle of vision changes, no longer do things look the same. As you peer beneath the surface of human relationships, the taken-for-granted may take on an unfamiliar hue as other realities begin to emerge. For example, if you place the sociological lens on something as familiar as friendship, you will find that rather than being a simple matter, friendship is based on complex rights and obligations. As you analyze friendship, the implicit under-standings on which it is based will begin to emerge. You will make visible its reciprocal obligations (how social debts accumulate when your friend does something for you that you are expected to repay). Although seldom stated, these implicit understandings provide the background that rules the relationship. Violate them and you risk severing the friendship.

Uncovering realities that lie beneath the surface and attaining a different under-standing of social life are part of the fascination of sociology. Regardless of a sociologist's topic—whether as common and familiar as friendship or as uncommon and unfamiliar as people who kill for money (Reading 6)—as Peter Berger points out in this selection, the sociologist's overriding motivation is curiosity, a desire to know and discover more about some aspect of social life.

Thinking Critically

As you read this selection, ask yourself:

1. What is the difference between a sociologist and a pollster?

2. What does Berger mean by saying "Statistical data by themselves do not make sociology"?

3. What does Berger mean when he says that "an invitation to sociology is an invitation to a special kind of passion"?

It is gratifying from certain value positions (including some of this writer's) that sociological insights have served in a number of instances to improve the lot of groups of human beings by uncovering morally shocking conditions or by clearing away collective illusions or by showing that socially desired results could be obtained in more humane fashion. One might point, for example, to some applications of sociological knowledge in the penological practice of Western countries. Or one might cite the use made of sociological studies in the Supreme Court decision of 1954 on racial segregation in the public schools. Or one could look at the applications of other sociological studies to the humane planning of urban redevelopment. Certainly the sociologist who is morally and politically sensitive will derive gratification from such instances. But, once more, it will be well to keep in mind that what is at issue here is not sociological understanding as such but certain applications of this understanding. It is not difficult to see how the same understanding could be applied with opposite intentions. Thus the sociological understanding of the dynamics of racial prejudice can be applied effectively by those promoting intragroup hatred as well as by those wanting to spread tolerance. And the sociological understanding of the nature of human solidarity can be employed in the service of both totalitarian and democratic regimes. . . .

One image [of the sociologist is that of] a gatherer of statistics about human behavior. . . . He* goes out with a questionnaire, interviews people selected at random, then goes home [and] enters his tabulations [into computers]. . . . In all of this, of course, he is supported by a large staff and a very large budget. Included in this image is the implication that the results of all this effort are picayune, a pedantic re-statement of what everybody knows anyway. As one observer remarked pithily, a sociologist is a fellow who spends $100,000 to find his way to a house of ill repute.

This image of the sociologist has been strengthened in the public mind by the activities of many agencies that might well be called parasociological, mainly agencies concerned with public opinion and market trends. The pollster has become a well-known figure in American life, inopportuning people about their views from foreign policy to toilet paper. Since the methods used in the pollster business bear close resemblance to sociological research, the growth of this image of the sociologist is understandable. . . . The fundamental sociological question, whether concerned with premarital petting or with Republican votes or with the incidence of gang knifings, is always presumed to be "how often?" or "how many?" . . .

Now it must be admitted, albeit regretfully, that this image of the sociologist and his trade is not altogether a product of fantasy. . . . [A good] part of the sociological enterprise in this country continues to consist of little studies of obscure fragments of social life, irrelevant to any broader theoretical concern. One glance at

*Some classic articles in sociology that are reprinted in this anthology were written when "he" and "man" were generic, when they referred to both men and women. So it is with "his," "him," and so on. Although the writing style has changed, the sociological ideas have not.

the table of contents of the major sociological journals or at the list of papers read at sociological conventions will confirm this statement. . . .

Statistical data by themselves do not make sociology. They become sociology only when they are sociologically interpreted, put within a theoretical frame of reference that is sociological. Simple counting, or even correlating different items that one counts, is not sociology. There is almost no sociology in the Kinsey reports. This does not mean that the data in these studies are not true or that they cannot be relevant to sociological understanding. They are, taken by themselves, raw materials that can be used in sociological interpretation. The interpretation, however, must be broader than the data themselves. So the sociologist cannot arrest himself at the frequency tables of premarital petting or extramarital pederasty. These enumerations are meaningful to him only in terms of their much broader implications for an understanding of institutions and values in our society. To arrive at such understanding the sociologist will often have to apply statistical techniques, especially when he is dealing with the mass phenomena of modern social life. But sociology consists of statistics as little as philology consists of conjugating irregular verbs or chemistry of making nasty smells in test tubes.

Sociology has, from its beginnings, understood itself as a science. . . . [T]he allegiance of sociologists to the scientific ethos has meant everywhere a willingness to be bound by certain scientific canons of procedure. If the sociologist remains faithful to his calling, his statements must be arrived at through the observation of certain rules of evidence that allow others to check on or to repeat or to develop his findings further. It is this scientific discipline that often supplies the motive for reading a sociological work as against, say, a novel on the same topic that might describe matters in much more impressive and convincing language. . . .

The charge that many sociologists write in a barbaric dialect must . . . be admitted. . . . Any scientific discipline must develop a terminology. This is self-evident for a discipline such as, say, nuclear physics that deals with matters unknown to most people and for which no words exist in common speech. However, terminology is possibly even more important for the social sciences, just because their subject matter *is* familiar and just because words *do* exist to denote it. Because we are well acquainted with the social institutions that surround us, our perception of them is imprecise and often erroneous. In very much the same way most of us will have considerable difficulty giving an accurate description of our parents, husbands or wives, children or close friends. Also, our language is often (and perhaps blessedly) vague and confusing in its references to social reality. Take for an example the concept of *class*, a very important one in sociology: There must be dozens of meanings that this term may have in common speech—income brackets, races, ethnic groups, power cliques, intelligence ratings, and many others. It is obvious that the sociologist must have a precise, unambiguous definition of the concept if his work is to proceed with any degree of scientific rigor. In view of these facts, one can understand that some sociologists have been tempted to invent altogether new words to avoid the semantic traps of the vernacular usage.

Finally, we would look at an image of the sociologist not so much in his professional role as in his being, supposedly, a certain kind of person. This is the image of the sociologist as a detached, sardonic observer, and a cold manipulator of men. Where this image prevails, it may represent an ironic triumph of the sociologist's own efforts to be accepted as a genuine scientist. The sociologist here becomes the self-appointed superior man, standing off from the warm vitality of common existence, finding his satisfactions not in living but in coolly appraising the lives of others, filing them away in little categories, and thus presumably missing the real significance of what he is observing. Further, there is the notion that, when he involves himself in social processes at all, the sociologist does so as an uncommitted technician, putting his manipulative skills at the disposal of the powers that be.

This last image is probably not very widely held. . . . The problem of the political role of the social scientist is, nevertheless, a very genuine one. For instance, the employment of sociologists by certain branches of industry and government raises moral questions that ought to be faced more widely than they have been so far. These are, however, moral questions that concern all men in positions of responsibility. . . .

How then are we to conceive of the sociologist? In discussing the various images that abound in the popular mind we have already brought out certain elements that would have to go into our conception. . . .

The sociologist, then, is someone concerned with understanding society in a disciplined way. The nature of this discipline is scientific. This means that what the sociologist finds and says about the social phenomena he studies occurs within a certain rather strictly defined frame of reference. One of the main characteristics of this scientific frame of reference is that operations are bound by certain rules of evidence. As a scientist, the sociologist tries to be objective, to control his personal preferences and prejudices, to perceive clearly rather than to judge normatively. This restraint, of course, does not embrace the totality of the sociologist's existence as a human being, but is limited to his operations *qua* sociologist. Nor does the sociologist claim that his frame of reference is the only one within which society can be looked at. For that matter, very few scientists in any field would claim today that one should look at the world only scientifically. The botanist looking at a daffodil has no reason to dispute the right of the poet to look at the same object in a very different manner. There are many ways of playing. The point is not that one denies other people's games but that one is clear about the rules of one's own. The game of the sociologist, then, uses scientific rules. As a result, the sociologist must be clear in his own mind as to the meaning of these rules. That is, he must concern himself with methodological questions. Methodology does not constitute his goal. The latter, let us recall once more, is the attempt to understand society. Methodology helps in reaching this goal. In order to understand society, or that segment of it that he is studying at the moment, the sociologist will use a variety of means. Among these are statistical techniques. Statistics can be very useful in answering certain sociological questions. But statistics does not constitute sociology. As a scientist, the sociologist will have to be concerned with the exact significance of the terms he is using. That is, he will have to be careful about terminology. This does not have to mean that he must invent a new language of his own, but it does mean that he cannot naively use the language of everyday discourse. Finally, the interest of the sociologist is primarily theoretical. That is, he is interested in understanding for its own sake. He may be aware of or even concerned with the practical applicability and consequences of his findings, but at that point he leaves the sociological frame of reference as such and moves into realms of values, beliefs and ideas that he shares with other men who are not sociologists. . . .

[W]e would like to go a little bit further here and ask a somewhat more personal (and therefore, no doubt, more controversial) question. We would like to ask not only what it is that the sociologist is doing but also what it is that drives him to it. Or, to use the phrase Max Weber used in a similar connection, we want to inquire a little into the nature of the sociologist's demon. In doing so, we shall evoke an image that is not so much ideal-typical in the above sense but more confessional in the sense of personal commitment. Again, we are not interested in excommunicating anyone. The game of sociology goes on in a spacious playground. We are just describing a little more closely those we would like to tempt to join our game.

We would say then that the sociologist (that is, the one we would really like to invite to our game) is a person intensively, endlessly, shamelessly interested in the doings of men. His natural habitat is all the human gathering places of the world, wherever men come together. The sociologist may be interested in many other things. But his consuming interest remains in the world of men, their institutions, their history, their passions. And since he is interested in men, nothing that men do can be altogether tedious for him. He will naturally be interested in the events that engage men's ultimate beliefs, their moments of tragedy and grandeur and ecstasy. But he will also be fascinated by the common place, the everyday. He will know reverence, but this reverence will not prevent him from wanting to see and to understand. He may sometimes feel revulsion or contempt. But this also will not deter him from wanting to have his questions answered. The sociologist, in his quest for understanding, moves through the world of men without respect for the usual lines of demarcation. Nobility and degradation, power and obscurity, intelligence and folly—these are equally *interesting* to him, however unequal they may be in his personal values or tastes. Thus his questions may lead him to all possible levels of society, the best and the least known places, the most respected and the most despised. And, if he is a good sociologist, he will find himself in all these places because his own questions have so taken possession of him that he has little choice but to seek for answers.

It would be possible to say the same things in a lower key. We could say that the sociologist, but for the grace of his academic title, is the man who must listen to gossip despite himself, who is tempted to look through keyholes, to read other people's mail, to open closed cabinets. Before some otherwise unoccupied psychologist sets out now to construct an aptitude test for sociologists on the basis of sublimated voyeurism, let us quickly say that we are speaking merely by way of analogy. Perhaps some little boys consumed with curiosity to watch their maiden aunts in the bathroom later become inveterate sociologists. This is quite uninteresting. What interests us is the curiosity that grips any sociologist in front of a closed door behind which there are human voices. If he is a good sociologist, he will want to open that door, to understand these voices. Behind each closed door he will anticipate some new facet of human life not yet perceived and understood.

The sociologist will occupy himself with matters that others regard as too sacred or as too distasteful for dispassionate investigation. He will find rewarding the company of priests or of prostitutes, depending not on his personal preferences but on the questions he happens to be asking at the moment. He will also concern himself with matters that others may find much too boring. He will be interested in the human interaction that goes with warfare or with great intellectual discoveries, but also in the relations between people employed in a restaurant or between a group of little girls playing with their dolls. His main focus of attention is not the ultimate significance of what men do, but the action in itself, as another example of the infinite richness of human conduct. So much for the image of our playmate.

In these journeys through the world of men the sociologist will inevitably encounter other professional Peeping Toms. Sometimes these will resent his presence, feeling that he is poaching on their preserves. In some places the sociologist will meet up with the economist, in others with the political scientist, in yet others with the psychologist or the ethnologist. Yet chances are that the questions that have brought him to these same places are different from the ones that propelled his fellow-trespassers. The sociologist's questions always remain essentially the same: "What are people doing with each other here?" "What are their relationships to each other?" "How are these relationships organized in institutions?" "What are the collective ideas that move men and institutions?" In trying to answer these questions in specific instances, the sociologist will, of course, have to deal with economic or political matters, but he will do so in a way rather different from that of the economist or the political scientist. The scene that he contemplates is the same human scene that these other scientists concern themselves with. But the sociologist's angle of vision is different. When this is understood, it becomes clear that it makes little sense to try to stake out a special enclave within which the sociologist will carry on business in his own right. There is, however, one traveler whose path the sociologist will cross more often than anyone else's on his journeys. This is the historian. Indeed, as soon as the sociologist turns from the present to the past, his preoccupations are very hard indeed to distinguish from those of the historian. However, we shall leave this relationship to a later part of our considerations. Suffice it to say here that the sociological journey will be much impoverished unless it is punctuated frequently by conversation with that other particular traveler.

Any intellectual activity derives excitement from the moment it becomes a trail of discovery. In some fields of learning this is the discovery of worlds previously unthought and unthinkable. This is the excitement of the astronomer or of the nuclear physicist on the antipodal boundaries of the realities that man is capable of conceiving. But it can also be the excitement of bacteriology or geology. In a different way it can be the excitement of the linguist discovering new realms of human expression or of the anthropologist exploring human customs in faraway countries. In such discovery, when undertaken with passion, a widening of awareness, sometimes a veritable transformation of consciousness, occurs. The universe turns out to be much more wonder-full than one had ever dreamed. The excitement of sociology is usually of a different sort. Sometimes, it is true, the sociologist penetrates into worlds that had previously been quite unknown to him—for instance, the world of crime, or the world of some bizarre religious sect, or the world fashioned by the exclusive concerns of some group such as medical specialists or military leaders or advertising executives. However, much of the time the sociologist moves in sectors of experience that are familiar to him and to most people in his society. He investigates communities, institutions and activities that one can read about every day in the newspapers. Yet there is another excitement of discovery beckoning in his investigations. It is not the excitement of coming upon the totally unfamiliar, but rather the excitement of finding the familiar becoming transformed in its meaning. The fascination of sociology lies in the fact that its perspective makes us see in a new light the very world in which we have lived all our lives. This also constitutes a transformation of consciousness. Moreover, this transformation is more relevant existentially than that of many other intellectual disciplines, because it is more difficult to segregate in some special compartment of the mind. The astronomer does not live in the remote galaxies, and the nuclear physicist can, outside his laboratory, eat and laugh and marry and vote without thinking about the insides of the atom. The geologist looks at rocks only at appropriate times, and the linguist speaks English with his wife. The sociologist lives in society, on the job and off it. His own life, inevitably, is part of his subject matter. Men being what they are, sociologists too manage to segregate their professional insights from their everyday affairs. But it is a rather difficult feat to perform in good faith.

The sociologist moves in the common world of men, close to what most of them would call real. The categories he employs in his analyses are only refinements of the categories by which other men live—power, class, status, race, ethnicity. As a result, there is a deceptive simplicity and obviousness about some sociological investigations. One reads them, nods at the familiar scene, remarks that one has heard all this before and don't people have better things to do than to waste their time on truisms—until one is suddenly brought up against an insight that radically questions everything one had previously assumed about this familiar scene. This is the point at which one begins to sense the excitement of sociology.

Let us take a specific example. Imagine a sociology class in a Southern college where almost all the students are white Southerners. Imagine a lecture on the subject of the racial system of the South. The lecturer is talking here of matters that have been familiar to his students from the time of their infancy. Indeed, it may be that they are much more familiar with the minutiae of this system than he is. They are quite bored as a result. It seems to them that he is only using more pretentious words to describe what they already know. Thus he may use the term "caste," one commonly used now by American sociologists to describe the Southern racial system. But in explaining the term he shifts to traditional Hindu society, to make it clearer. He then goes on to analyze the magical beliefs inherent in caste tabus, the social dynamics of commensalism and connubium, the economic interests concealed within the system, the way in which religious beliefs relate to the tabus, the effects of the caste system upon the industrial development of the society and vice versa—all in India. But suddenly India is not very far away at all. The lecture then goes back to its Southern theme. The familiar now seems not quite so familiar any more. Questions are raised that are new, perhaps raised angrily, but raised all the same. And at least some of the students have begun to understand that there are functions involved in this business of race that they have not read about in the newspapers (at least not those in their hometowns) and that their parents have not told them—partly, at least, because neither the newspapers nor the parents knew about them.

It can be said that the first wisdom of sociology is this—things are not what they seem. This too is a deceptively simple statement. It ceases to be simple after a while. Social reality turns out to have many layers of meaning. The discovery of each new layer changes the perception of the whole.

Anthropologists use the term "culture shock" to describe the impact of a totally new culture upon a newcomer. In an extreme instance such shock will be experienced by the Western explorer who is told, halfway through dinner, that he is eating the nice old lady he had been chatting with the previous day—a shock with predictable physiological if not moral consequences. Most explorers no longer encounter cannibalism in their travels today. However, the first encounters with polygamy or with puberty rites or even with the way some nations drive their automobiles can be quite a shock to an American visitor. With the shock may go not only disapproval or disgust but a sense of excitement that things can *really* be that different from what they are at home. To some extent, at least, this is the excitement of any first travel abroad. The experience of sociological discovery could be described as "culture shock" minus geographical displacement. In other words, the sociologist travels at home—with shocking results. He is unlikely to find that he is eating a nice old lady for dinner. But the discovery, for instance, that his own church has considerable money invested in the missile industry or that a few blocks from his home there are people who engage in cultic orgies may not be drastically different in emotional impact. Yet we would not want to imply that sociological discoveries are always or even usually outrageous to moral sentiment. Not at all. What they have in common with exploration in distant lands, however, is the sudden illumination of new and unsuspected facets of human existence in society. This is the excitement and, as we shall try to show later, the humanistic justification of sociology.

People who like to avoid shocking discoveries, who prefer to believe that society is just what they were taught in Sunday School, who like the safety of the rules and the maxims of what Alfred Schuetz has called the "world-taken-for-granted," should stay away from sociology. People who feel no temptation before closed doors, who have no curiosity about human beings, who are content to admire scenery without wondering about the people who live in those houses on the other side of that river, should probably also stay away from sociology. They will find it unpleasant or, at any rate, unrewarding. People who are interested in human beings only if they can change, convert or reform them should also be warned, for they will find sociology much less useful than they hoped. And people whose interest is mainly in their own conceptual constructions will do just as well to turn to the study of little white mice. Sociology will be satisfying, in the long run, only to those who can think of nothing more entrancing than to watch men and to understand things human. . . .

To be sure, sociology is an individual pastime in the sense that it interests some men and bores others. Some like to observe human beings, others to experiment with mice. The world is big enough to hold all kinds and there is no logical priority for one interest as against another. But the word "pastime" is weak in describing what we mean. Sociology is more like a passion. The sociological perspective is more like a demon that possesses one, that drives one compellingly, again and again, to the questions that are its own. An introduction to sociology is, therefore, an invitation to a very special kind of passion.

The Fierce People

Napoleon Chagnon

introduction ■ ■ ■ ■

The many cultures of humans are fascinating. Each human group has its own culture, whether an urban gang in the United States or a tribe in the jungles of South America. Like an envelope, our culture encloses us into a particular area of life, directing our thoughts, behaviors, and perceptions. It sets boundaries and dictates what is significant and insignificant. It provides the rules for how we should interact with one another. Culture also provides the framework from which we view life. Understand a people's culture, and you come a long way to understanding why they think, feel, and act as they do.

Understanding and appreciation are two different things. To understand a group does not necessarily mean that you appreciate it. Understanding might help, but not necessarily. In this selection, Napoleon Chagnon recounts his harrowing stay with the Yąnomamö, a tribe in South America. As you read this selection, you will see how uncomfortable he was during his lengthy fieldwork.

Thinking Critically

As you read this selection, ask yourself:

1. Why didn't Chagnon develop an appreciation for the way of life of the Yąnomamö?

2. Why was Chagnon so stingy with his food—and so reluctant to accept food from others?

3. How does the culture of the Yąnomamö compare with your own culture? Be sure to compare gender relations (relationships among men and women).

The Yąnomamö Indians live in southern Venezuela and the adjacent portions of northern Brazil. Some 125 widely scattered villages have populations ranging from 40 to 250 inhabitants, with 75 to 80 people the most usual number. In total numbers their population probably approaches 10,000 people, but this is merely a guess. Many of the villages have not yet been contacted by outsiders, and nobody knows for sure exactly how many uncontacted villages there are, or how many people live in them.

By comparison to African or Melanesian tribes, the Yąnomamö population is small. Still, they are one of the largest unacculturated tribes left in all of South America.

But they have a significance apart from tribal size and cultural purity: The Yąnomamö are still actively conducting warfare. It is in the nature of man to fight, according to one of their myths, because the blood of "Moon" spilled on this layer of the cosmos, causing men to become fierce. I describe the Yąnomamö as "the fierce people" because that is the most accurate single phrase that describes them. That is how they conceive themselves to be, and that is how they would like others to think of them.

I spent nineteen months with the Yąnomamö during which time I acquired some proficiency in their language and, up to a point, submerged myself in their culture and way of life. The thing that impressed me most was the importance of aggression in their culture. I had the opportunity to witness a good many incidents that expressed individual vindictiveness on the one hand and collective bellicosity on the other. These ranged in seriousness from the ordinary incidents of wife beating and chest pounding to dueling and organized raiding by parties that set out with the intention of ambushing and killing men from enemy villages. One of the villages was raided approximately twenty-five times while I conducted the fieldwork, six times by the group I lived among. . . .

This is not to state that primitive man everywhere is unpleasant. By way of contrast, I have also done limited fieldwork among the Yąnomamö's northern neighbors, the Carib-speaking Makiritare Indians. This group was very pleasant and charming, all of them anxious to help me and honor bound to show any visitor the numerous courtesies of their system of etiquette. In short, they approached the image of primitive man that I had conjured up, and it was sheer pleasure to work with them. . . .

My first day in the field illustrated to me what my teachers meant when they spoke of "culture shock." I had traveled in a small, aluminum rowboat propelled by a large outboard motor for two and a half days. This took me from the Territorial capital, a small town on the Orinoco River, deep into Yąnomamö country. On the morning of the third day we reached a small mission settlement, the field "headquarters" of a group of Americans who were working in two Yąnomamö villages. The missionaries had come out of these villages to hold their annual conference on the progress of their mission work, and were conducting their meetings when I arrived. We picked up a passenger at the mission station, James P. Barker, the first non-Yąnomamö to make a sustained, permanent contact with the tribe (in 1950). He had just returned from a year's furlough in the United States, where I had earlier visited him before leaving for Venezuela. He agreed to accompany me to the village I had selected for my base of operations to introduce me to the Indians. This village was also his own home base, but he had not been there for over a year and did not plan to join me for another three months. Mr. Barker had been living with this particular group about five years.

We arrived at the village, Bisaasi-teri, about 2:00 P.M. and docked the boat along the muddy bank at the terminus of the path used by the Indians to fetch their drinking water. It was hot and muggy, and my clothing was soaked with perspiration. It clung uncomfortably to my body, as it did thereafter for the remainder of the work. The small, biting gnats were out in astronomical numbers, for it was the beginning of the dry season. My face and hands were swollen from the venom of their numerous stings. In just a few moments I was to meet my first Yąnomamö, my first primitive man. What would it be like? I had visions of entering the village and seeing 125 social facts running about calling each other kinship terms and sharing food, each waiting and anxious to have me collect his genealogy. I would wear them out in turn. Would they like me? This was important to me; I wanted them to be so fond of me that they would adopt me into their kinship system and way of life, because I had heard that successful anthropologists always get adopted by their people. I had learned during my seven years of anthropological training at the University of Michigan that kinship was equivalent to society in primitive tribes and that it was a moral way of life, "moral" being something "good" and "desirable." I was determined to work my way into their moral system of kinship and become a member of their society.

My heart began to pound as we approached the village and heard the buzz of activity within the circular compound. Mr. Barker commented that he was anxious to see if any changes had taken place while he was away and wondered how many of them had died during his absence. I felt into my back pocket to make sure that my notebook was there and felt personally more secure when I touched it. Otherwise, I would not have known what to do with my hands.

I looked up and gasped when I saw a dozen burly, naked, filthy, hideous men staring at us down the shafts of their drawn arrows! Immense wads of green tobacco were stuck between their lower teeth and lips making them look even more hideous, and strands of dark-green slime dripped or hung from their noses. We arrived at the village while the men were blowing a hallucinogenic drug up their noses. One of the side effects of the drug is a runny nose. The mucus is always saturated with the green powder and the Indians usually let it run freely from their nostrils. My next discovery was that there were a dozen or so vicious, underfed dogs snapping at my legs, circling me as if I were going to be their next meal. I just stood there holding my notebook, helpless and pathetic. Then the stench of the decaying vegetation and filth struck me and I almost got sick. I was horrified. What sort of a welcome was this for the person who came here to live with you and learn your way of life, to become friends with you? They put their weapons down when they recognized Barker and returned to their chanting, keeping a nervous eye on the village entrances.

We had arrived just after a serious fight. Seven women had been abducted the day before by a neighboring group, and the local men and their guests had just that morning recovered five of them in a brutal club fight that nearly ended in a shooting war. The abductors, angry because they lost five of the seven captives, vowed to raid the Bisaasi-teri. When we arrived and entered the village unexpectedly, the Indians feared that we were the raiders. On several occasions during the next two hours the men in the village jumped to their feet, armed themselves, and waited nervously for the noise outside the village to be identified. My enthusiasm for collecting ethnographic curiosities diminished in proportion to the number of times such an alarm was raised. In fact, I was relieved when Mr. Barker suggested that we sleep across the river for the evening. It would be safer over there.

As we walked down the path to the boat, I pondered the wisdom of having decided to spend a year and a half with this tribe before I had even seen what they were like. I am not ashamed to admit, either, that had there been a diplomatic way out, I would have ended my fieldwork then and there. I did not look forward to the next day when I would be left alone with the Indians; I did not speak a word of their language, and they were decidedly different from what I had imagined them to be. The whole situation was depressing, and I wondered why I ever decided to switch from civil engineering to anthropology in the first place. I had not eaten all day, I was soaking wet from perspiration, the gnats were biting me, and I was covered with red pigment, the result of a dozen or so complete examinations I had been given by as many burly Indians. These examinations capped an otherwise grim day. The Indians would blow their noses into their hands, flick as much of the mucus off that would separate in a snap of the wrist, wipe the residue into their hair, and then carefully examine my face, arms, legs, hair, and the contents of my pockets. I asked Mr. Barker how to say "Your hands are dirty"; my comments were met by the Indians in the following way: They would "clean" their hands by spitting a quantity of slimy tobacco juice into them, rub them together, and then proceed with the examination.

Mr. Barker and I crossed the river and slung our hammocks. When he pulled his hammock out of a rubber bag, a heavy, disagreeable odor of mildewed cotton came with it. "Even the missionaries are filthy," I thought to myself. Within two weeks everything I owned smelled the same way, and I lived with the odor for the remainder of the fieldwork. My own habits of personal cleanliness reached such levels that I didn't even mind being examined by the Indians, as I was not much cleaner than they were after I had adjusted to the circumstances.

So much for my discovery that primitive man is not the picture of nobility and sanitation I had conceived him to be. I soon discovered that it was an enormously time-consuming task to maintain my own body in the manner to which it had grown accustomed in the relatively antiseptic environment of the northern United States. Either I could be relatively well fed and relatively comfortable in a fresh change of clothes and do very little fieldwork, or, I could do considerably more fieldwork and be less well fed and less comfortable.

It is appalling how complicated it can be to make oatmeal in the jungle. First, I had to make two trips to the river to haul the water. Next, I had to prime my kerosene stove with alcohol and get it burning, a tricky procedure when you are trying to mix powdered milk and fill a coffee pot at the same time: the alcohol prime always burned out before I could turn the kerosene on, and I would have to start all over. Or, I would turn the kerosene on, hoping that the element was still hot enough to vaporize the fuel, and not start a small fire in my palm-thatched hut as the liquid kerosene squirted all over the table and walls and ignited. It was safer to start over with the alcohol. Then I had to boil the oatmeal and pick the bugs out of it. All my supplies, of course, were carefully stored in Indian-proof, ratproof, moisture-proof, and insect-proof containers, not one of which ever served its purpose adequately. Just taking things out of the multiplicity of containers and repacking them afterward was a minor project in itself. By the time I had hauled the water to cook with, unpacked my food, prepared the oatmeal, milk, and coffee, heated water for dishes, washed and dried the dishes, repacked the food in the containers, stored the containers in locked trunks and cleaned up my mess, the ceremony of preparing breakfast had brought me almost up to lunch time.

Eating three meals a day was out of the question. I solved the problem by eating a single meal that could be prepared in a single container, or, at most, in two containers, washed my dishes only when there were no clean ones left, using cold river water, and wore each change of clothing at least a week to cut down on my laundry problem, a courageous undertaking in the tropics. I was also less concerned about sharing my provisions with the rats, insects, Indians, and the elements, thereby eliminating the need for my complicated storage process. I was able to last most of the day on *café con leche,* heavily sugared espresso coffee diluted about five to one with hot milk. I would prepare this in the evening and store it in a thermos. Frequently, my single meal was no more complicated than a can of sardines and a package of crackers. But at least two or three times a week I would do something sophisticated, like make oatmeal or boil rice and add a can of tuna fish or tomato paste to it. I even saved time by devising a water system that obviated the trips to the river. I had a few sheets of zinc roofing brought in and made a rain-water trap. I caught the water on the zinc surface, funneled it into an empty gasoline drum, and then ran a plastic hose from the drum to my hut. When the drum was exhausted in the dry season, I hired the Indians to fill it with water from the river.

I ate much less when I traveled with the Indians to visit other villages. Most of the time my travel diet consisted of roasted or boiled green plantains that I obtained from the Indians, but I always carried a few cans of sardines with me in case I got lost or stayed away longer than I had planned. I found peanut butter and crackers a very nourishing food, and a simple one to prepare on trips. It was nutritious and portable, and only one tool was required to prepare the meal, a hunting knife that could be cleaned by wiping the blade on a leaf. More importantly, it was one of the few foods the Indians would let me eat in relative peace. It looked too much like animal feces to them to excite their appetites.

I once referred to the peanut butter as the dung of cattle. They found this quite repugnant. They did not know what "cattle" were, but were generally aware that I ate several canned products of such an animal. I perpetrated this myth, if for no other reason than to have some peace of mind while I ate. Fieldworkers develop strange defense mechanisms, and this was one of my own forms of adaptation. On another occasion I was eating a can of frankfurters and growing very weary of the demands of one of my guests for a share in my meal. When he asked me what I was eating, I replied: "Beef." He then asked, "What part of the animal are you eating?" to which I replied, "Guess!" He stopped asking for a share.

Meals were a problem in another way. Food sharing is important to the Yąnomamö in the context of displaying friendship. "I am hungry," is almost a form of greeting with them. I could not possibly have brought enough food with me to feed the entire village, yet they seemed not to understand this. All they could see was that I did not share my food with them at each and every meal. Nor could I enter into their system of reciprocities with respect to food; every time one of them gave me something "freely," he would dog me for months to pay him back, not with food, but with steel tools. Thus, if I accepted a plantain from someone in a different village while I was on a visit, he would most likely visit me in the future and demand a machete as payment for the time that he "fed" me. I usually reacted to these kinds of demands by giving a banana, the customary reciprocity in their culture—food for food—but this would be a disappointment for the individual who had visions of that single plantain growing into a machete over time.

Despite the fact that most of them knew I would not share my food with them at their request, some of them always showed up at my hut during mealtime. I gradually became accustomed to this and learned to ignore their persistent demands while I ate. Some of them would get angry because I failed to give in, but most of them accepted it as just a peculiarity of the subhuman foreigner. When I did give in, my hut quickly filled with Indians, each demanding a sample of the food that I had given one of them. If I did not give all a share, I was that much more despicable in their eyes.

A few of them went out of their way to make my meals unpleasant, to spite me for not sharing; for example, one man arrived and watched me eat a cracker with honey on it. He immediately recognized the honey, a particularly esteemed Yąnomamö food. He knew that I would not share my tiny bottle and that it would be futile to ask. Instead, he glared at me and queried icily, "Shaki![1] What kind of animal semen are you eating on that cracker?" His question had the desired effect, and my meal ended.

Finally, there was the problem of being lonely and separated from your own kind, especially your family. I tried to overcome this by seeking personal friendships among the Indians. This only complicated the matter because all my friends simply used my confidence to gain privileged access to my cache of steel tools and trade goods, and looted me. I would be bitterly disappointed that my "friend" thought no more of me than to finesse our relationship exclusively with the intention of getting at any locked up possessions, and my depression would hit new lows every time I discovered this. The loss of the possession bothered me much less than the shock that I was, as far as most of them were concerned, nothing more than a source of desirable items; no holds were barred in relieving me of these, since I was considered something sub-human, a non-Yąnomamö.

The thing that bothered me most was the incessant, passioned, and aggressive demands the Indians made. It would become so unbearable that I would have to lock myself in my mud hut every once in a while just to escape from it: Privacy is one of Western culture's greatest achievements. But I did not want privacy for its own sake; rather, I simply had to get away from the begging. Day and night for the entire time I lived with the Yąnomamö I was plagued by such demands as: "Give me a knife, I am poor!"; "If you don't take me with you on your next trip to Widokaiya-teri, I'll chop a hole in your canoe!"; "Don't point your camera at me or I'll hit you!"; "Share your food with me!"; "Take me across the river in your canoe and be quick about it!"; "Give me a cooking pot!"; "Loan me your flashlight so I can go hunting tonight!"; "Give me medicine . . . I itch all over!"; "Take us on a week-long hunting trip with your shotgun!"; and "Give me an axe, or I'll break into your hut when you are away visiting and steal one!" And so I was bombarded by such demands day after day, months on end, until I could not bear to see an Indian.

It was not as difficult to become calloused to the incessant begging as it was to ignore the sense of urgency, the impassioned tone of voice, or the intimidation and aggression with which the demands were made. It was likewise difficult to adjust to the fact that the Yąnomamö refused to accept "no" for an answer until or unless it seethed with passion and intimidation—which it did after six months. Giving in to a demand always established a new threshold; the next demand would be for a bigger item or favor, and the anger of the Indians even greater if the demand was not met. I soon learned that I had to become very much like the Yąnomamö to be able to get along with them on their terms: sly, aggressive, and intimidating.

Had I failed to adjust in this fashion I would have lost six months of supplies to them in a single day or would have spent most of my time ferrying them around in my canoe or hunting for them. As it was, I did spend a considerable amount of time doing these things and did succumb to their outrageous demands for axes and machetes, at least at first. More importantly, had I failed to demonstrate that I could not be pushed around beyond a certain point, I would have been the subject of far more ridicule, theft, and practical jokes than was the actual case. In short, I had to acquire a certain proficiency in their kind of interpersonal politics and to learn how to imply subtly that certain potentially undesirable consequences might follow if they did such and such to me. They do this to each other in order to establish precisely the point at which they cannot goad an individual any further without precipitating retaliation. As soon as I caught on to this and realized that much of their aggression was stimulated by their desire to discover my flash point, I got along much better with them and regained some lost ground. It was sort of like a political game that everyone played, but one in which each individual sooner or later had to display some sign that his bluffs and implied threats could be backed up. I suspect that the frequency of wife beating is a component of this syndrome, since men can display their ferocity and show others that they are capable of violence. Beating a wife with a club is considered to be an acceptable way of displaying ferocity and one that does not expose the male to much danger. The important thing is that the man has displayed his potential for violence and the implication is that other men better treat him with respect and caution.

After six months, the level of demand was tolerable in the village I used for my headquarters. The Indians and I adjusted to each other and knew what to expect with regard to demands on their part for goods, favors, and services. Had I confined my fieldwork to just that village alone, the field experience would have been far more enjoyable. But, as I was interested in the demographic pattern and social organization of a much larger area, I made regular trips to some dozen different villages in order to collect genealogies or to recheck those I already had. Hence, the intensity of begging and intimidation was fairly constant for the duration of the fieldwork. I had to establish my position in some sort of pecking order of ferocity at each and every village.

For the most part, my own "fierceness" took the form of shouting back at the Yąnomamö as loudly and as passionately as they shouted at me, especially at first, when I did not know much of their language. As I became more proficient in their language and learned more about their political tactics, I became more sophisticated in the art of bluffing. For example, I paid one young man a machete to cut palm trees and make boards from the wood. I used these to fashion a platform in the bottom of my dugout canoe to keep my possessions dry when I traveled by river. That afternoon I was doing informant work in the village; the long-awaited mission supply boat arrived, and most of the Indians ran out of the village to beg goods from the crew. I continued to work in the village for another hour or so and went down to the river to say "hello" to the men on the supply boat. I was angry when I discovered that the Indians had chopped up all my palm boards and used them to paddle their own canoes across the river. I knew that if I overlooked this incident I would have invited them to take even greater liberties with my goods in the future. I crossed the river, docked amidst their dugouts, and shouted for the Indians to come out and see me. A few of the culprits appeared, mischievous grins on their faces. I gave a spirited lecture about how hard I had worked to put those boards in my canoe, how I had paid a machete for the wood, and how angry I was that they destroyed my work in their haste to cross the river. I then pulled out my hunting knife and, while their grins disappeared, cut each of their canoes loose, set them into the current, and let them float away. I left without further ado and without looking back.

They managed to borrow another canoe and, after some effort, recovered their dugouts. The headman of the village later told me with an approving chuckle that I had done the correct thing. Everyone in the village, except, of course, the culprits, supported and defended my action. This raised my status.

Whenever I took such action and defended my rights, I got along much better with the Yąnomamö. A good deal of their behavior toward me was directed with the forethought of establishing the point at which I would react defensively. Many of them later reminisced about the early days of my work when I was "timid" and a little afraid of them, and they could bully me into giving goods away.

Theft was the most persistent situation that required me to take some sort of defensive action. I simply could not keep everything I owned locked in trunks, and the Indians came into my hut and left at will. I developed a very effective means for recovering almost all the stolen items. I would simply ask a child who took the item and then take that person's hammock when he was not around, giving a spirited lecture to the others as I marched away in a faked rage with the thief's hammock. Nobody ever attempted to stop me from doing this, and almost all of them told me that my technique for recovering my possessions was admirable. By nightfall the thief would either appear with the stolen object or send it along with someone else to make an exchange. The others would heckle him for getting caught and being forced to return the item.

With respect to collecting the data I sought, there was a very frustrating problem. Primitive social organization is kinship organization, and to understand the Yąnomamö way of life I had to collect extensive genealogies. I could not have deliberately picked a more difficult group to work with in this regard: They have very stringent name taboos. They attempt to name people in such a way that when the person dies and they can no longer use his name, the loss of the word in the language is not inconvenient. Hence, they name people for specific and minute parts of things, such as "toenail of some rodent," thereby being able to retain the words "toenail" and "(specific) rodent," but not being able to refer directly to the toenail of that rodent. The taboo is maintained even for the living: One mark of prestige is the courtesy others show you by not using your name. The sanctions behind the taboo seem to be an unusual combination of fear and respect.

I tried to use kinship terms to collect genealogies at first, but the kinship terms were so ambiguous that I ultimately had to resort to names. They were quick to grasp that I was bound to learn everybody's name and reacted, without my knowing it, by inventing false names for everybody in the village. After having spent several months collecting names and learning them, this came as a disappointment to me: I could not cross-check the genealogies with other informants from distant villages.

They enjoyed watching me learn these names. I assumed, wrongly, that I would get the truth to each question and that I would get the best information by working in public. This set the stage for converting a serious project into a farce. Each informant tried to outdo his peers by inventing a name even more ridiculous than what I had been given earlier, or by asserting that the individual about whom I inquired was married to his mother or daughter, and the like. I would have the informant whisper the name of the individual in my ear, noting that he was the father of such and such a child. Everybody would then insist that I repeat the name aloud, roaring in hysterics as I clumsily pronounced the name. I assumed that the laughter was in response to the violation of the name taboo or to my pronunciation. This was a reasonable interpretation, since the individual whose name I said aloud invariably became angry. After I learned what some of the names meant, I began to understand what the laughter was all about. A few of the more colorful examples are: "hairy vagina," "long penis," "feces of the harpy eagle," and "dirty rectum." No wonder the victims were angry.

I was forced to do my genealogy work in private because of the horseplay and nonsense. Once I did so, my informants began to agree with each other and I managed to learn a few new names, real names. I could then test any new informant by collecting a genealogy from him that I knew to be accurate. I was able to weed out the more mischievous informants this way. Little by little I extended the genealogies and learned the real names. Still, I was unable to get the names of the dead and extend the genealogies back in time, and even my best informants continued to deceive me about their own close relatives. Most of them gave me the name of a living man as the father of some individual in order to avoid mentioning that the actual father was dead.

The quality of a genealogy depends in part on the number of generations it embraces, and the name taboo prevented me from getting any substantial information about deceased ancestors. Without this information, I could not detect marriage patterns through time. I had to rely on older informants for this information, but these were the most reluctant of all. As I became more proficient in the language and more skilled at detecting lies, my informants became better at lying. One of them in particular was so cunning and persuasive that I was shocked to discover that he had been inventing his information. He specialized in making a ceremony out of telling me false names. He would look around to make sure nobody was listening outside my hut, enjoin me to never mention the name again, act very nervous and spooky, and then grab me by the head to whisper the name very softly into my ear. I was always elated after an informant session with him, because I had several generations of dead ancestors for the living people. The others refused to give me this information. To show my gratitude, I paid him quadruple the rate I had given the others. When word got around that I had increased the pay, volunteers began pouring in to give me genealogies.

I discovered that the old man was lying quite by accident. A club fight broke out in the village one day, the result of a dispute over the possession of a woman. She had been promised to Rerebawa, a particularly aggressive young man who had married into the village. Rerebawa had already been given her older sister and was enraged when the younger girl began having an affair with another man in the village, making no attempt to conceal it from him. He challenged the young man to a club fight, but was so abusive in his challenge that the opponent's father took offense and entered the village circle with his son, wielding a long club. Rerebawa swaggered out to the duel and hurled insults at both of them, trying to goad them into striking him on the head with their clubs. This would have given him the opportunity to strike them on the head. His opponents refused to hit him, and the fight ended. Rerebawa had won a moral victory because his opponents were afraid to hit him. Thereafter, he swaggered around and insulted the two men behind their backs. He was genuinely angry with them, to the point of calling the older man by the name of his dead father. I quickly seized on this as an opportunity to collect an accurate genealogy and pumped him about his adversary's ancestors. Rerebawa had been particularly nasty to me up to this point, but we became staunch allies: We were both outsiders in the local village. I then asked about other dead ancestors and got immediate replies. He was angry with the whole group and not afraid to tell me the names of the dead. When I compared his version of the genealogies to that of the old man, it was obvious that one of them was lying. I challenged his information, and he explained that everybody knew that the old man was deceiving me and bragging about it in the village. The names the old man had given me were the dead ancestors of the members of a village so far away that he thought I would never have occasion to inquire about them. As it turned out, Rerebawa knew most of the people in that village and recognized the names.

I then went over the complete genealogical records with Rerebawa, genealogies I had presumed to be in final form. I had to revise them all because of the numerous lies and falsifications they contained. Thus, after five months of almost constant work on the genealogies of just one group, I had to begin almost from scratch!

Discouraging as it was to start over, it was still the first real turning point in my fieldwork. Thereafter, I began taking advantage of local arguments and animosities in selecting my informants, and used more extensively individuals who had married into the group. I began traveling to other villages to check the genealogies, picking villages that were on strained terms with the people about whom I wanted information. I would then return to my base camp and check with local informants the accuracy of the new information. If the informants became angry when I mentioned the new names I acquired from the unfriendly group, I was almost certain that the information was accurate. For this kind of checking I had to use informants whose genealogies I knew rather well: They had to be distantly enough related to the dead person that they would not go into a rage when I mentioned the name, but not so remotely related that they would be uncertain of the accuracy of the information. Thus, I had to make a list of names that I dared not use in the presence of each and every informant. Despite the precautions, I occasionally hit a name that put the informant into a rage, such as that of a dead brother or sister that other informants had not reported. This always terminated the day's work with that informant, for he would be too touchy to continue any further, and I would be reluctant to take a chance on accidentally discovering another dead kinsman so soon after the first.

These were always unpleasant experiences, and occasionally dangerous ones, depending on the temperament of the informant. On one occasion I was planning to visit a village that had been raided about a week earlier. A woman whose name I had on my list had been killed by the raiders. I planned to check each individual on the list one by one to estimate ages, and I wanted to remove her name so that I would not say it aloud in the village. I knew that I would be in considerable difficulty if I said this name aloud so soon after her death. I called on my original informant and asked him to tell me the name of the woman who had been killed. He refused, explaining that she was a close relative of his. I then asked him if he would become angry if I read off all the names on the list. This way he did not have to say her name and could merely nod when I mentioned the right one. He was a fairly good friend of mine, and I thought I could predict his reaction. He assured me that this would be a good way of doing it. We were alone in my hut so that nobody could overhear us. I read the names softly, continuing to the next when he gave a negative reply. When I finally spoke the name of the dead woman he flew out of his chair, raised his arm to strike me, and shouted: "You son-of-a-bitch![2] If you ever say that name again, I'll kill you!" He was shaking with rage, but left my hut quietly. I shudder to think what might have happened if I had said the name unknowingly in the woman's village. I had other, similar experiences in different villages, but luckily the dead person had been dead for some time and was not closely related to the individual into whose ear I whispered the name. I was merely cautioned to desist from saying any more names, lest I get people angry with me.

I had been working on the genealogies for nearly a year when another individual came to my aid. It was Kaobawa, the headman of Upper Bisaasi-teri, the group in which I spent most of my time. He visited me one day after the others had left the hut and volunteered to help me on the genealogies. He was poor, he explained, and needed a machete. He would work only on the condition that I did not ask him about his own parents and other very close kinsmen who were dead. He also added that he would not lie to me as the others had done in the past. This was perhaps the most important single event in my fieldwork, for out of this meeting evolved a very warm friendship and a very profitable informant-fieldworker relationship.

Kaobawa's familiarity with his group's history and his candidness were remarkable. His knowledge of details was almost encyclopedic. More than that, he was enthusiastic and encouraged me to learn details that I might otherwise have ignored. If there were things he did not know intimately, he would advise me to wait until he could check things out with someone in the village. This he would do clandestinely, giving me a report the next day. As I was constrained by my part of the bargain to avoid discussing his close dead kinsmen, I had to rely on Rerebawa for this information. I got Rerebawa's genealogy from Kaobawa.

Once again I went over the genealogies with Kaobawa to recheck them, a considerable task by this time: they included about two thousand names, representing several generations of individuals from four different villages. Rerebawa's information was very accurate, and Kaobawa's contribution enabled me to trace the genealogies further back in time. Thus, after nearly a year of constant work on genealogies, Yąnomamö demography and social organization began to fall into a pattern. Only then could I see how kin groups formed and exchanged women with each other over time, and only then did the fissioning of larger villages into smaller ones show a distinct pattern. At this point I was able to begin formulating more intelligent questions because there was now some sort of pattern to work with. Without the help of Rerebawa and Kaobawa, I could not have made very much sense of the plethora of details I had collected from dozens of other informants.

Kaobawa is about 40 years old. I say "about" because the Yąnomamö numeration system has only three numbers: one, two, and more-than-two. He is the headman of Upper Bisaasi-teri. He has had five or six wives so far and temporary affairs with as many more women, one of which resulted in a child. At the present time he has just two wives, Bahimi and Koamashima. He has had a daughter and a son by Bahimi, his eldest and favorite wife. Koamashima, about 20 years old, recently had her first child, a boy. Kaobawa may give Koamashima to his youngest brother. Even now the brother shares in her sexual services. Kaobawa recently gave his third wife to another of his brothers because she was beshi: "horny." In fact, this girl had been married to two other men, both of whom discarded her because of her infidelity. Kaobawa had one daughter by her; she is being raised by his brother.

Kaobawa's eldest wife, Bahimi, is about thirty-five years old. She is his first cross-cousin. Bahimi was pregnant when I began my fieldwork, but she killed the new baby, a boy, at birth, explaining tearfully that it would have competed with Ariwari, her nursing son, for milk. Rather than expose Ariwari to the dangers and uncertainty of an early weaning, she killed the new child instead. By Yąnomamö standards, she and Kaobawa have a very tranquil household. He only beats her once in a while, and never very hard. She never has affairs with other men.

Kaobawa is quiet, intense, wise, and unobtrusive. He leads more by example than by threats and coercion. He can afford to be this way as he established his reputation for being fierce long ago, and other men respect him. He also has five mature brothers who support him, and he has given a number of his sisters to other men in the village, thereby putting them under some obligation to him. In short, his "natural" following (kinsmen) is large, and he does not have to constantly display his ferocity. People already respect him and take his suggestions seriously.

Rerebawa is much younger, only about twenty-two years old. He has just one wife by whom he has had three children. He is from Karohi-teri, one of the villages to which Kaobawa is allied. Rerebawa left his village to seek a wife in Kaobawa's group because there were no eligible women there for him to marry.

Rerebawa is perhaps more typical than Kaobawa in the sense that he is concerned about his reputation for ferocity and goes out of his way to act tough. He is, however, much braver than the other men his age and backs up his threats with action. Moreover, he is concerned about politics and knows the details of intervillage relationships over a large area. In this respect he shows all the attributes of a headman, although he is still too young and has too many competent older brothers in his own village to expect to move easily into the position of leadership there.

He does not intend to stay in Kaobawa's group and has not made a garden. He feels that he has adequately discharged his obligations to his wife's parents by providing them with fresh game for three years. They should let him take the wife and return to his own village with her, but they refuse and try to entice him to remain permanently in Bisaasi-teri to provide them with game when they are old. They have even promised to give him their second daughter if he will stay permanently.

Although he has displayed his ferocity in many ways, one incident in particular shows what his character is like. Before he left his own village to seek a wife, he had an affair with the wife of an older brother. When he was discovered, his brother attacked him with a club. Rerebawa was infuriated so he grabbed an axe and drove his brother out of the village after soundly beating him with the flat of the blade. The brother was so afraid that he did not return to the village for several days. I recently visited his village with him. He made a point to introduce me to this brother. Rerebawa dragged him out of his hammock by the arm and told me, "This is the brother whose wife I had an affair with," a deadly insult. His brother did nothing and slunk back into his hammock, shamed, but relieved to have Rerebawa release the vise-grip on his arm.

Despite the fact that he admires Kaobawa, he has a low opinion of the others in Bisaasi-teri. He admitted confidentially that he thought Bisaasi-teri was an abominable group: "This is a terrible neighborhood! All the young men are lazy and cowards and everybody is committing incest! I'll be glad to get back home." He also admired Kaobawa's brother, the headman of Monou-teri. This man was killed by raiders while I was doing my fieldwork. Rerebawa was disgusted that the others did not chase the raiders when they discovered the shooting: "He was the only fierce one in the whole group; he was my close friend. The cowardly Monou-teri hid like women in the jungle and didn't even chase the raiders!"

Even though Rerebawa is fierce and capable of being quite nasty, he has a good side as well. He has a very biting sense of humor and can entertain the group for hours on end with jokes and witty comments. And, he is one of few Yąnomamö that I feel I can trust. When I returned to Bisaasi-teri after having been away for a year, Rerebawa was in his own village visiting his kinsmen. Word reached him that I had returned, and he immediately came to see me. He greeted me with an immense bear hug and exclaimed, "Shaki! Why did you stay away so long? Did you know that my will was so cold while you were gone that at times I could not eat for want of seeing you?" I had to admit that I missed him, too.

Of all the Yąnomamö I know, he is the most genuine and the most devoted to his culture's ways and values. I admire him for that, although I can't say that I subscribe to or endorse these same values. By contrast, Kaobawa is older and wiser. He sees his own culture in a different light and criticizes aspects of it he does not like. While many of his peers accept some of the superstitions and explanatory myths as truth and as the way things ought to be, Kaobawa questions them and privately pokes fun at some of them. Probably, more of the Yąnomamö are like Rerebawa, or at least try to be.

NOTES

1. "Shaki," or, rather, "Shakiwa," is the name they gave me because they could not pronounce "Chagnon." They like to name people for some distinctive feature when possible. Shaki is the name of a species of noisome bees; they accumulate in large numbers around ripening bananas and make pests of themselves by eating into the fruit, showering the people below with the debris. They probably adopted this name for me because I was also a nuisance, continuously prying into their business, taking pictures of them, and, in general, being where they did not want me.

2. This is the closest English translation of his actual statement, the literal translation of which would be nonsensical in our language.

Anybody's Son Will Do

Gwynne Dyer

introduction ■ ■ ■ ■

To understand the term *socialization,* just substitute the word *learning.* Socialization does not refer only to children. All of us are being socialized all the time. Each time we are exposed to something new, we are being socialized. If we learn how to operate a new computer, play a new (or old) video game, watch a movie, read a book, or listen to a college lecture, we are being socialized. Even when we talk to a friend, socialization occurs. And socialization doesn't stop at a certain age. When we are old, we will still have experiences (even watching televised news) that influence the ways we look at ourselves and the world. Socialization, then, is a lifelong process. You could say that in this process we are becoming more and more a part of our culture (or of our subculture).

From the examples just given, you can see that socialization is usually gentle and gradual. But there are remarkable exceptions, and in this reading we look at one of them. Gwynne Dyer analyzes the process by which the U.S. Marine Corps turns young men into killers—and how this organization accomplishes such a drastic change in just a few weeks. As you will see, the Marines' techniques are brutal, swift, and effective.

Thinking Critically

As you read this selection, ask yourself:

1. How do the U.S. Marines socialize their recruits?

2. How do the socialization techniques of the Marines compare with the socialization techniques that have been used to bring you to your current place in life?

3. Why are the socialization techniques of the Marines so effective?

You think about it and you know you're going to have to kill but you don't understand the implications of that, because in the society in which you've lived murder is the most heinous of crimes . . . and you are in a situation in which it's turned the other way round. . . . When you do actually kill someone the experience, my experience, was one of revulsion and disgust. . . .

I was utterly terrified—petrified—but I knew there had to be a Japanese sniper in a small fishing shack near the shore. He was firing in the other direction at Marines in another battalion, but I knew as soon as he picked off the people there—there was a window on our side—that he would start picking us off. And there was nobody else to go . . . and so I ran towards the shack and broke in and found myself in an empty room. . . .

There was a door which meant there was another room and the sniper was in that—and I just broke that down. I was just absolutely gripped by the fear that this man would expect me and would shoot me. But as it turned out he was in a sniper harness and he couldn't turn around fast enough. He was entangled in the harness so I shot him with a .45, and I felt remorse and shame. I can remember whispering foolishly, "I'm sorry" and then just throwing up. . . . I threw up all over myself. It was a betrayal of what I'd been taught since a child.

—William Manchester

Yet he did kill the Japanese soldier, just as he had been trained to—the revulsion only came afterward. And even after Manchester knew what it was like to kill another human being, a young man like himself, he went on trying to kill his "enemies" until the war was over. Like all the other tens of millions of soldiers who had been taught from infancy that killing was wrong, and had then been sent off to kill for their countries, he was almost helpless to disobey, for he had fallen into the hands of an institution so powerful and so subtle that it could quickly reverse the moral training of a lifetime.

The whole vast edifice of the military institution rests on its ability to obtain obedience from its members even unto death—and the killing of others. It has enormous powers of compulsion at its command, of course, but all authority must be based ultimately on consent. The task of extracting that consent from its members has probably grown harder in recent times, for the gulf between the military and the civilian worlds has undoubtedly widened: Civilians no longer perceive the threat of violent death as an everyday hazard of existence, and the categories of people whom it is not morally permissible to kill have broadened to include (in peacetime) the entire human race. Yet the armed forces of every country can still take almost any young male civilian and turn him into a soldier with all the right reflexes and attitudes in only a few weeks. Their recruits usually have no more than twenty years' experience of the world, most of it as children, while the armies have had all of history to practice and perfect their techniques.

Just think of how the soldier is treated. While still a child he is shut up in the barracks. During his training he is always being knocked about. If he makes the least mistake he is beaten, a burning blow on his body, another on his eye, perhaps his head is laid open with a wound. He is battered and bruised with flogging. On the march . . . they hang heavy loads round his neck like that of an ass.

—Egyptian, ca. 1500 B.C.

The moment I talk to the new conscripts about the homeland I strike a land mine. So I kept quiet. Instead, I try to make soldiers of them. I give them hell from morning to sunset. They begin to curse me, curse the army, curse the state.

Then they begin to curse together, and become a truly cohesive group, a unit, a fighting unit.

—Israeli, ca. A.D. 1970

All soldiers belong to the same profession, no matter what country they serve, and it makes them different from everybody else. They have to be different, for their job is ultimately about killing and dying, and those things are not a natural vocation for any human being. Yet all soldiers are born civilians. The method for turning young men into soldiers—people who kill other people and expose themselves to death—is basic training. It's essentially the same all over the world, and it always has been, because young men everywhere are pretty much alike.

Human beings are fairly malleable, especially when they are young, and in every young man there are attitudes for any army to work with: the inherited values and postures, more or less dimly recalled, of the tribal warriors who were once the model for every young boy to emulate. Civilization did not involve a sudden clean break in the way people behave, but merely the progressive distortion and redirection of all the ways in which people in the old tribal societies used to behave, and modern definitions of maleness still contain a great deal of the old warrior ethic. The anarchic machismo of the primitive warrior is not what modern armies really need in their soldiers, but it does provide them with promising raw material for the transformation they must work in their recruits.

Just how this transformation is wrought varies from time to time and from country to country. In totally militarized societies—ancient Sparta, the samurai class of medieval Japan, the areas controlled by organizations like the Eritrean People's Liberation Front today—it begins at puberty or before, when the young boy is immersed in a disciplined society in which only the military values are allowed to penetrate. In more sophisticated modern societies, the process is briefer and more concentrated, and the way it works is much more visible. It is, essentially, a conversion process in an almost religious sense—and as in all conversion phenomena, the emotions are far more important than the specific ideas. . . .

Armies know this. It is their business to get men to fight, and they have had a long time to work out the best way of doing it. All of them pay lip service to the symbols and slogans of their political masters, though the amount of time they must devote to this activity varies from country to country. . . . Nor should it be thought that the armies are hypocritical—most of their members really do believe in their particular national symbols and slogans. But their secret is that they know these are not the things that sustain men in combat.

What really enables men to fight is their own self-respect, and a special kind of love that has nothing to do with sex or idealism. Very few men have died in battle, when the moment actually arrived, for the United States of America or for the sacred cause of Communism, or even for their homes and families; if they had any choice in the matter at all, they chose to die for each other and for their own vision of themselves. . . .

The way armies produce this sense of brotherhood in a peacetime environment is basic training: a feat of psychological manipulation on the grand scale which has been so consistently successful and so universal that we fail to notice it as remarkable. In countries where the army must extract its recruits in their late teens, whether voluntarily or by conscription, from a civilian environment that does not share the military values, basic training involves a brief but intense period of indoctrination whose purpose is not really to teach the recruits basic military skills, but rather to change their values and their loyalties. "I guess you could say we brainwash them a little bit," admitted a U.S. Marine drill instructor, "but you know they're good people."

The duration and intensity of basic training, and even its major emphases, depend on what kind of society the recruits are coming from, and on what sort of military organization they are going to. It is obviously quicker to train men from a martial culture than from one in which the dominant values are civilian and commercial, and easier to deal with volunteers than with reluctant conscripts. Conscripts are not always unwilling, however; there are many instances in which the army is popular for economic reasons. . . .

It's easier if you catch them young. You can train older men to be soldiers; it's done in every major war. But you can never get them to believe that they like it, which is the major reason armies try to get their recruits before they are 20. There are other reasons too, of course, like the physical fitness, lack of dependents, and economic dispensability of teenagers, that make armies prefer them, but the most important qualities teenagers bring to basic training are enthusiasm and naiveté. Many of them actively want the discipline and the closely structured environment that the armed forces will provide, so there is no need for the recruiters to deceive the kids about what will happen to them after they join.

> There is discipline. There is drill. . . . When you are relying on your mates and they are relying on you, there's no room for slackness or sloppiness. If you're not prepared to accept the rules, you're better off where you are.
> —British army recruiting advertisement, 1976

> People are not born soldiers, they become soldiers. . . . And it should not begin at the moment when a new recruit is enlisted into the ranks, but rather much earlier, at the time of the first signs of maturity, during the time of adolescent dreams.
> —Red Star (Soviet army newspaper), 1973

Young civilians who have volunteered and have been accepted by the Marine Corps arrive at Parris Island, the Corps's East Coast facility for basic training, in a state of considerable excitement and apprehension: Most are aware that they are about to undergo an extraordinary and very difficult experience. But they do not make their own way to the base; rather, they trickle in to Charleston airport on various flights throughout the day on which their training platoon is due to form, and are held there, in a state of suppressed but mounting nervous tension, until late in the evening. When the buses finally come to carry them the seventy-six miles to Parris Island, it is often after midnight—and this is not an administrative oversight. The shock treatment they are about to receive will work most efficiently if they are worn out and somewhat disoriented when they arrive.

The basic training organization is a machine, processing several thousand young men every month, and every facet and gear of it has been designed with the sole purpose of turning civilians into Marines as efficiently as possible. Provided it can have total control over their bodies and their environment for approximately three months, it can practically guarantee converts. Parris Island provides that controlled environment, and the recruits do not set foot outside it again until they graduate as Marine privates eleven weeks later.

> They're allowed to call home, so long as it doesn't get out of hand—every three weeks or so they can call home and make sure everything's all right, if they haven't gotten a letter or there's a particular set of circumstances. If it's a case of an emergency call coming in, then they're allowed to accept that call; if not, one of my staff will take the message. . . .
>
> In some cases I'll get calls from parents who haven't quite gotten adjusted to the idea that their son had cut the strings—and in a lot of cases that's what they're doing. The military provides them with an opportunity to leave home but they're still in a rather secure environment.
>
> —Captain Brassington, USMC

For the young recruits, basic training is the closest thing their society can offer to a formal rite of passage, and the institution probably stands in an unbroken line of descent from the lengthy ordeals by which young males in precivilized groups were initiated into the adult community of warriors. But in civilized societies it is a highly functional institution whose product is not anarchic warriors, but trained soldiers.

Basic training is not really about teaching people skills; it's about changing them, so that they can do things they wouldn't have dreamt of otherwise. It works by applying enormous physical and mental pressure to men who have been isolated from their normal civilian environment and placed in one where the only right way to think and behave is the way the Marine Corps wants them to. The key word the men who run the machine use to describe this process is *motivation*.

> I can motivate a recruit and in third phase, if I tell him to jump off the third deck, he'll jump off the third deck. Like I said before, it's a captive audience and I can train that guy; I can get him to do anything I want him to do. . . . They're good kids and they're out to do the right thing. We get some bad kids, but you know, we weed those out. But as far as motivation—here, we can motivate them to do anything you want, in recruit training.
>
> —USMC drill instructor, Parris Island

The first three days the raw recruits spend at Parris Island are actually relatively easy, though they are hustled and shouted at continuously. It is during this time that they are documented and inoculated, receive uniforms, and learn the basic orders of drill that will enable young Americans (who are not very accustomed to this aspect of life) to do everything simultaneously in large groups. But the most important thing that happens in "forming" is the surrender of the recruits' own clothes, their hair—all the physical evidence of their individual civilian identities.

During a period of only 72 hours, in which they are allowed little sleep, the recruits lay aside their former lives in a series of hasty rituals (like being shaven to the scalp) whose symbolic significance is quite clear to them even though they are quite deliberately given absolutely no time for reflection, or any hint that they might have the option of turning back from their commitment. The men in charge of them know how delicate a tightrope they are walking, though, because at this stage the recruits are still newly caught civilians who have not yet made their ultimate inward submission to the discipline of the Corps.

> Forming Day One makes me nervous. You've got a whole new mob of recruits, you know, 60 or 70 depending, and they don't know anything. You don't know what kind of a reaction you're going to get from the stress you're going to lay on them, and it just worries me the first day . . . .
>
> Things could happen, I'm not going to lie to you. Something might happen. A recruit might decide he doesn't want any part of this stuff and maybe take a poke at you or something like that. In a situation like that it's going to be a spur-of-the-moment thing and that worries me.
>
> —USMC drill instructor

But it rarely happens. The frantic bustle of forming is designed to give the recruit no time to think about resisting what is happening to him. And so the recruits emerge from their initiation into the system, stripped of their civilian clothes, shorn of their hair, and deprived of whatever confidence in their own identity they may previously have had as 18-year-olds, like so many blanks ready to have the Marine identity impressed upon them.

The first stage in any conversion process is the destruction of an individual's former beliefs and confidence, and his reduction to a position of helplessness and need. It isn't really as drastic as all that, of course, for three days cannot cancel out 18 years; the inner thoughts and the basic character are not erased. But the recruits have already learned that the only acceptable behavior is to repress any unorthodox thoughts and to mimic the character the Marine Corps wants. Nor are they, on the whole, reluctant to do so, for they *want* to be Marines. From the moment they arrive at Parris Island, the vague notion that has been passed down for a thousand generations that masculinity means being a warrior becomes an explicit article of faith, relentlessly preached: To be a man means to be a Marine.

There are very few 18-year-old boys who do not have highly romanticized ideas of what it means to be a man, so the Marine Corps has plenty of buttons to push. And it starts pushing them on the first day of real training: The officer in charge of the formation appears before them for the first time, in full dress uniform with medals, and tells them how to become men.

> The United States Marine Corps has 205 years of illustrious history to speak for itself. You have made the most important decision in your life . . . by signing your name, your life, pledge to the Government of the United States, and even more importantly, to the United States Marine Corps—a brotherhood, an elite unit. In 10.3 weeks you are going to become a member of that history, those traditions, this organization—if you have what it takes. . . .

All of you want to do that by virtue of your signing your name as a man. The Marine Corps says that we build men. Well, I'll go a little bit further. We develop the tools that you have—and everybody has those tools to a certain extent right now. We're going to give you the blueprints, and we are going to show you how to build a Marine. You've got to build a Marine—you understand?

—Captain Pingree, USMC

The recruits, gazing at him with awe and adoration, shout in unison, "Yes, sir!" just as they have been taught. They do it willingly, because they are volunteers—but even conscripts tend to have the romantic fervor of volunteers if they are only 18 years old. Basic training, whatever its hardships, is a quick way to become a man among men, with an undeniable status, and beyond the initial consent to undergo it, it doesn't even require any decisions.

I had just dropped out of high school and I wasn't doing much on the street except hanging out, as most teenagers would be doing. So they gave me an opportunity—a recruiter picked me up, gave me a good line, and said that I could make it in the Marines, that I have a future ahead of me. And since I was living with my parents, I figured that I could start my own life here and grow up a little.

—USMC recruit

I like the hand-to-hand combat and . . . things like that. It's a little rough going on me, and since I have a small frame I would like to become deadly, as I would put it. I like to have them words, especially the way they've been teaching me here.

—USMC recruit (from Brooklyn), Parris Island

The training, when it starts, seems impossibly demanding physically for most of the recruits—and then it gets harder week by week. There is a constant barrage of abuse and insults aimed at the recruits, with the deliberate purpose of breaking down their pride and so destroying their ability to resist the transformation of values and attitudes that the Corps intends them to undergo. At the same time the demands for constant alertness and for instant obedience are continuously stepped up, and the standards by which the dress and behavior of the recruits are judged become steadily more unforgiving. But it is all carefully calculated by the men who run the machine, who think and talk in terms of the stress they are placing on the recruits: "We take so many c.c.'s of stress and we administer it to each man—they should be a little bit scared and they should be unsure, but they're adjusting." The aim is to keep the training arduous but just within most of the recruits' capability to withstand. One of the most striking achievements of the drill instructors is to create and maintain the illusion that basic training is an extraordinary challenge, one that will set those who graduate apart from others, when in fact almost everyone can succeed.

There has been some preliminary weeding out of potential recruits even before they begin training, to eliminate the obviously unsuitable minority, and some people do "fail" basic training and get sent home, at least in peacetime. The standards of acceptable performance in the U.S. armed forces, for example, tend to rise and fall in inverse proportion to the number and quality of recruits available to fill the forces to the authorized manpower levels. But there are very few young men who cannot be turned into passable soldiers if the forces are willing to invest enough effort in it.

Not even physical violence is necessary to effect the transformation, though it has been used by most armies at most times.

> *It's not what it was 15 years ago down here. The Marine Corps still occupies the position of a tool which the society uses when it feels like that is a resort that they have to fall to. Our society changes as all societies do, and our society felt that through enlightened training methods we could still produce the same product—and when you examine it, they're right. . . . Our 100 c.c.'s of stress is really all we need, not two gallons of it, which is what used to be. . . . In some cases with some of the younger drill instructors it was more an initiation than it was an acute test, and so we introduced extra officers and we select our drill instructors to "fine-tune" it.*
>
> —Captain Brassington, USMC

There is, indeed, a good deal of fine-tuning in the roles that the men in charge of training any specific group of recruits assume. At the simplest level, there is a sort of "good cop–bad cop" manipulation of the recruits' attitudes toward those applying the stress. The three younger drill instructors with a particular serial are quite close to them in age and unremittingly harsh in their demands for ever higher performance, but the senior drill instructor, a man almost old enough to be their father, plays a more benevolent and understanding part and is available for individual counseling. And generally offstage, but always looming in the background, is the company commander, an impossibly austere and almost godlike personage.

At least these are the images conveyed to the recruits, although of course all these men cooperate closely with an identical goal in view. It works: In the end they become not just role models and authority figures, but the focus of the recruits' developing loyalty to the organization.

> *I imagine there's some fear, especially in the beginning, because they don't know what to expect. . . . I think they hate you at first, at least for a week or two, but it turns to respect. . . . They're seeking discipline, they're seeking someone to take charge, 'cause at home they never got it. . . . They're looking to be told what to do and then someone is standing there enforcing what they tell them to do, and it's kind of like the father-and-son game, all the way through. They form a fatherly image of the DI whether they want to or not.*
>
> —Sergeant Carrington, USMC

Just the sheer physical exercise, administered in massive doses, soon has the recruits feeling stronger and more competent than ever before. Inspections, often several times daily, quickly build up their ability to wear the uniform and carry themselves like real Marines, which is a considerable source of pride. The inspections also help to set up the pattern in the recruits of unquestioning submission to military authority: Standing stock-still, staring straight ahead, while somebody else examines you closely for faults is about as extreme a ritual act of submission as you can make with your clothes on.

But they are not submitting themselves merely to the abusive sergeant making unpleasant remarks about the hair in their nostrils. All around them are deliberate reminders—the flags and insignia displayed on parade, the military music, the marching formations and drill instructors' cadenced calls—of the idealized organization, the "brotherhood" to which they will be admitted as full members if they submit and conform. Nowhere in the armed forces are the military courtesies so elaborately observed, the staffs' uniforms so immaculate (some DIs change several times a day), and the ritual aspects of military life so highly visible as on a basic training establishment.

Even the seeming inanity of close-order drill has a practical role in the conversion process. It has been over a century since mass formations of men were of any use on the battlefield, but every army in the world still drills its troops, especially during basic training, because marching in formation, with every man moving his body in the same way at the same moment, is a direct physical way of learning two things a soldier must believe: that orders have to be obeyed automatically and instantly, and that you are no longer an individual, but part of a group.

The recruits' total identification with the other members of their unit is the most important lesson of all, and everything possible is done to foster it. They spend almost every waking moment together—a recruit alone is an anomaly to be looked into at once—and during most of that time they are enduring shared hardships. They also undergo collective punishments, often for the misdeed or omission of a single individual (talking in the ranks, a bed not swept under during barracks inspection), which is a highly effective way of suppressing any tendencies toward individualism. And, of course, the DIs place relentless emphasis on competition with other "serials" in training: there may be something infinitely pathetic to outsiders about a marching group of anonymous recruits chanting, "Lift your heads and hold them high, 3313 is a-passin' by," but it doesn't seem like that to the men in the ranks.

Nothing is quite so effective in building up a group's morale and solidarity, though, as a steady diet of small triumphs. Quite early in basic training, the recruits begin to do things that seem, at first sight, quite dangerous: descend by ropes from fifty-foot towers, cross yawning gaps hand-over-hand on high wires (known as the Slide for Life, of course), and the like. The common denominator is that these activities are daunting but not really dangerous: the ropes will prevent anyone from falling to his death off the rappelling tower, and there is a pond of just the right depth—deep enough to cushion a falling man, but not deep enough that he is likely to drown—under the Slide for Life. The goal is not to kill recruits, but to build up their confidence as individuals and as a group by allowing them to overcome apparently frightening obstacles.

> *You have an enemy here at Parris Island. The enemy that you're going to have at Parris Island is in every one of us. It's in the form of cowardice. The most rewarding experience you're going to have in recruit training is standing on line every evening, and you'll be able to look into each other's eyes, and you'll be able to say to each other with your eyes: "By God, we've made it one more day! We've defeated the coward."*
>
> —Captain Pingree

*Number on deck, sir, 45 . . . highly motivated, truly dedicated, rompin', stompin',
bloodthirsty, kill-crazy United States Marine Corps recruits, SIR!*
—Marine chant, Parris Island

If somebody does fail a particular test, he tends to be alone, for the hurdles
are deliberately set low enough that most recruits can clear them if they try. In any
large group of people there is usually a goat: someone whose intelligence or manner
or lack of physical stamina marks him for failure and contempt. The competent drill
instructor, without deliberately setting up this unfortunate individual for disgrace,
will use his failure to strengthen the solidarity and confidence of the rest. When one
hapless young man fell off the Slide for Life into the pond, for example, his drill instructor shouted the usual invective—"Well, get out of the water. Don't contaminate
it all day"—and then delivered the payoff line: "Go back and change your clothes.
You're useless to your unit now."

"Useless to your unit" is the key phrase, and all the recruits know that what it
means is "useless in *battle*." The Marine drill instructors at Parris Island know exactly
what they are doing to the recruits, and why. They are not rear-echelon people filling
comfortable jobs, but the most dedicated and intelligent NCOs the Marine Corps
can find; even now, many of them have combat experience. The Corps has a clear-
eyed understanding of precisely what it is training its recruits for—combat—and it
ensures that those who do the training keep that objective constantly in sight.

The DIs "stress" the recruits, feed them their daily ration of synthetic triumphs
over apparent obstacles, and bear in mind all the time that the goal is to instill the
foundations for the instinctive, selfless reactions and the fierce group loyalty that is
what the recruits will need if they ever see combat. They are arch-manipulators, fully
conscious of it, and utterly unashamed. These kids have signed up as Marines, and
they could well see combat; this is the way they have to think if they want to live.

*I've seen guys come to Vietnam from all over. They were all sorts of people that
had been scared—some of them had been scared all their life and still scared.
Some of them had been a country boy, city boys—you know, all different kinds
of people—but when they got in combat they all reacted the same—99 percent of
them reacted the same. . . . A lot of it is training here at Parris Island, but the other
part of it is survival. They know if they don't conform—conform I call it, but if
they don't react in the same way other people are reacting, they won't survive.
That's just it. You know, if you don't react together, then nobody survives.*
—USMC drill instructor, Parris Island

*When I went to boot camp and did individual combat training they said if you
walk into an ambush what you want to do is just do a right face—you just turn
right or left, whichever way the fire is coming from, and assault. I said, "Man,
that's crazy. I'd never do anything like that. It's stupid." . . .
   The first time we came under fire, on Hill 1044 in Operation Beauty Canyon
in Laos, we did it automatically. Just like you look at your watch to see what time
it is. We done a right face, assaulted the hill—a fortified position with concrete
bunkers emplaced, machine guns, automatic weapons—and we took it. And we
killed—I'd estimate probably 35 North Vietnamese soldiers in the assault, and*

we only lost three killed. I think it was about two or three, and about eight or ten wounded. . . .

But you know, what they teach you, it doesn't faze you until it comes down to the time to use it, but it's in the back of your head, like, What do you do when you come to a stop sign? It's in the back of your head, and you react automatically.

—USMC sergeant

Combat is the ultimate reality that Marines—or any other soldiers, under any flag—have to deal with. Physical fitness, weapons training, battle drills, are all indispensable elements of basic training, and it is absolutely essential that the recruits learn the attitudes of group loyalty and interdependency which will be their sole hope of survival and success in combat. The training inculcates or fosters all of those things, and even by the halfway point in the 11-week course, the recruits are generally responding with enthusiasm to their tasks . . . .

In basic training establishments, . . . the malleability is all one way: in the direction of submission to military authority and the internalization of military values. What a place like Parris Island produces when it is successful, as it usually is, is a soldier who will kill because that is his job.

Hooking Up
on the Internet

Helene M. Lawson and Kira Leck

introduction ▪ ▪ ▪ ▪ ▪

The meaning of dating changes with geography, from one society to another, and with time, from one historical period to another. In some societies, dating is forbidden. Among traditional people in India and Arab countries, for example, to date would be an explicit violation of norms, a repudiation of the background assumptions that underlie morality. For a woman to see a man alone is taboo. Breaking this taboo brings swift and severe censure upon the transgressor. If something sexual took place—or even the suspicion that it did—the sanction can be death, with the father, brothers, or uncles carrying out the punishment.

In early United States, also a traditional society, dating as we know it was not practiced. Among the middle class, a young man who became interested in a young woman had to make his "intentions," as they were called, known to the girl's parents—and his "intentions" had better be good. Good meant marriage. To seek the girl's and parents' approval for marriage, the suitor, as he was called, would begin formal courtship. He would visit the parents' house, bringing flowers or candy, and sit stiffly in the parlor, the formal living room reserved for visitors. The parents would check out his manners and especially his potential for supporting their daughter. Only after the parents had approved of the young man was the couple allowed to sit in the parlor alone, and that for only limited periods of time with adults hovering in the background.

As society industrialized and traditional relationships changed, so did the custom of courting. The automobile gave young people freedom unknown to previous generations, freedom from the watchful eyes of parents, freedom to be alone in places where they weren't known, and, ultimately, freedom to have sex. We can trace the beginning of the "sexual revolution" to the invention of the automobile, not the invention of the birth control pill. The pill merely speeded things up.

Dating customs, then, like most social behavior, respond to technology, changing as technology bends society. Just as the automobile ushered in fundamental changes in courtship, followed by the pill, so the Internet is having its impact. In this selection, Helene Lawson and Kira Leck examine some of these preliminary changes. You can be certain that the current influence of the Internet on dating is only the beginning of extensive change to come.

Thinking Critically

As you read this selection, ask yourself:

1. How would your life be different if you had been born and reared in one of the traditional societies described in the introduction to this article?

2. Have you done any Internet dating? Would you? Why or why not?

3. Do you think that meeting people online is risky? If so, how can you protect yourself?

The present research focused on the dynamics of Internet dating, a method of courting used by individuals who meet on the Internet and continue online correspondence in hopes of forming a supportive romantic relationship. It sought to determine why people choose to date online, what aspects of face-to-face relations are reproduced, and the rationales and strategies Internet daters use to negotiate and manage problems of risk accompanying the technology.

■ ■ ■ A BRIEF HISTORY OF DATING PRACTICES

Although the practices of courting vary from culture to culture and change over time, technologies of communication have historically shaped courtship, making it freer and expanding possibilities. The timeless love letter notwithstanding, courtship interaction in the United States has been limited to supervised situations or contained within the bounds of engagement for marriage. This was especially true during the puritan, colonial, and Victorian eras (Hunt, 1959). Historians believe that freer dating practices, such as meeting privately and face-to-face for romantic interactions at scheduled times and places, emerged among middle-class teenagers in the 1920s. These practices developed alongside new technologies such as telephones, automobiles, and drive-in theaters, which allowed teenagers to become more independent from their parents. . . .

In the 1990s, the Internet became a major vehicle for social encounters. Through the Internet, people can interact over greater distances in a shorter period and at less expense than in the past. Theorists have debated the positive and negative effects this technology has on social interactions. Initially, theorists such as Zuboff (1991) believed "the Internet reduced face-to-face interaction" and created an "uncomfortable isolation" (pp. 479–482) for people at work. Conversely, Raney (2000) argued that online communication expands social networks. According to Raney, the Pew Internet and American Life Project found supporting evidence for this view in a study

From Helene M. Lawson and Kira Leck, "Dynamics of Internet Dating," *Social Sciences Computer Review* 24(2), pp. 189–208. Copyright © 2006. Reprinted by permission of Sage Publications, Inc.

in which "more than half of Internet users reported that e-mail was strengthening their family ties. And Internet users reported far more offline social contact than non-users" (p. G7). . . . Today Internet video and sound communications are commonplace, and photographs, video, and sound clips can all be altered or fabricated entirely. These new technologies allow Internet daters enormous latitude to prepare their presentations of self.

■ ■ ■ USING THE INTERNET FOR DATING

The Internet is a new social institution that has the ability to connect people who have never met face to face and is thus likely to transform the dating process. Beginning with newsgroups such as Usenet and various bulletin boards that operated under the now-obsolete Gopher system, the Internet facilitated the formation of communities. . . .

We explored the phenomenology of Internet dating, which we defined as the pattern of periodic communication between potential partners using the Internet as a medium. We examined the respondents' concerns over the risk of being deceived, their anxieties about physical appearance, and the hazards of romantic involvement.

■ ■ ■ METHOD

Participants

Because we needed a sample of respondents who could be tracked over time and whose reliability could be verified, we began to investigate the phenomenon of Internet dating by interviewing people who were personally accessible, such as coworkers, acquaintances, and students. Soon the sample expanded because respondents told us about people they knew who dated online, which resulted in a snowball sample. . . . It was composed of 32% students, 24% business and clerical workers, 14% trade workers, and 14% professionals and semiprofessionals. The sample also included unemployed persons, small business owners, and housewives.

Because we were interested in romantic dating relationships that could result in commitment, we did not include people interested only in pornography or online sexual encounters as their primary focus. We defined dating as setting up specific times to mutually disclose personal information with potential romantic partners on an ongoing basis. We did not place any other restrictions on whom we were willing to interview. Consequently, the sample included homosexuals and unhappily married persons. Romance was not necessarily the goal of online dating, but in our sample, three married persons changed partners as a result of Internet interactions.

Interview Questions

Interviews were open-ended and informal. We asked respondents to (a) describe their experiences with Internet dating, (b) state whether these experiences were positive or negative, (c) state how and why they entered the world of online dating, and (d) state whether they used online dating services or met incidentally through chat rooms, online games, or common interest groups. Respondents were eager to relate their experiences, and many interviews lasted an hour or longer.

Interviews were conducted during lunch in restaurants, at respondents' homes, at the home of the first author, in the university cafeteria, and on walks in various neighborhoods. All respondents had ready access to computers in their homes, dorm rooms, or places of work. We watched while they talked back and forth online. In addition, the first author invited three newly paired couples to her home for dinner. Follow-up data were collected in person, on the phone, by e-mail, and by mail. Interviews were later transcribed and coded by keywords according to concepts that emerged through the dialogue, such as trust, time, risk, and need satisfaction.

We limited the number of respondents to 25 men and 25 women because we wanted to compare gender variables in a balanced sample. The men ranged in age from 18 to 58 with a mean age of 32.6. The women ranged in age from 15 to 48 with a mean age of 33. In all, 17 men and 11 women were single (never married), 7 men and 10 women were divorced, and 1 man and 4 women were married. Two men and one woman were gay. Two women and one man were African American. One man was Indian. Six men and seven women were the parents of young children, and as previously stated, five respondents were married when they began to interact romantically online.

■ ■ ■ **RESULTS**

Companionship

Lonely people tend to report being dissatisfied with their relationships and are often cynical, rejecting, bored, and depressed. They also have difficulty making friends, engaging in conversations, getting involved in social activities, and dating (Chelune, Sultan, & Williams, 1980; W. H. Jones, Hobbs, & Hockenbury, 1982). Their tendency to engage in minimal self-disclosure and be unresponsive to conversational partners often results in poor interactions that are unrewarding for both partners, which leads lonely individuals to feel dissatisfied with their relationships (McAdams, 1989). Both relationship dissatisfaction and difficulty with social behavior may lead lonely people to seek online relationships.

Regardless of their marital status, respondents of all ages tended to report being lonely. They all talked about needing more communication, emotional support, and companionship. Fred, a 19-year-old student who had never been married, said, "I hate being alone. You want to know someone out there at least cares."

Greta, a 43-year-old, unhappily married mother of a 9-year-old, worked a night shift. Her husband worked during the day, and they both dated others online through chat rooms. Chat rooms often require only token (username) identification. The face presented is largely cloaked, but marital status is usually not hidden. Rather, it is explained:

> I guess the big problem is that my husband works 6 days a week, is gone all day long, and doesn't spend time with me. It is like we are strangers living in the same house. We haven't actually gone out with anyone.

Kelly, a 48-year-old, unhappily married student also blamed her lack of communication with her husband for why she dated online:

> I think I qualify for this interview because I date someone online. In our house there is no communication. That is no way to be. It's two people living in the same house like roommates that have totally different lives. We never talk. That is how my life was before I met George [online]. . . .

Regardless of their marital status, . . . individuals seemed to perceive their social lives as incomplete. This may be a reflection of the separation of family and friends because of current societal structure. Thus, it is not surprising that they were highly motivated to become involved in online relationships with people who were willing to talk, listen, and serve a supportive function. . . .

Comfort After a Life Crisis

. . . [S]everal respondents in the present sample reported seeking comfort after a life crisis, such as the loss of a job, a divorce, or a death in the family. Robin, a 32-year-old, never married woman, said,

> I had suffered such a great loss when my grandpa died. We were very close and he raised me. I guess at that particular point in time in my life I needed someone in my life. One night I was searching for someone to talk with. There is a button you can hit to find a random chat partner. I must have gone through about 10 to 15 different people until his name popped up. I read his details that he provided about himself, and I sent him a message. The first night we talked for about 5 to 6 hours straight, nonstop.

Anna, a 39-year-old, divorced woman, also got online because of her recent divorce: "After my divorce, I cried all the time. My friends were tired of listening to me. I wanted a support group so I went into this chat room.". . .

Our society's lack of support structure for individuals who experience life crises may lead them to seek out comfort from online sources. . . . The online setting allows them to select which aspects of themselves to reveal to their online companions, which lessens the probability of unfavorable judgment that may be leveled by real-life friends and family members.

Control Over Presentation and Environment

The Internet provides a medium for people to present themselves in a way that they think is flattering. Clark (1998) reports that girls describe themselves as "thinner and taller" and otherwise prettier in Internet communications than they actually are. Because contact is mediated, individuals do not have to expose themselves directly on the Internet. In general, "the surest way for a person to prevent threats to his face is to avoid contacts in which these threats are likely to occur" (Goffman, 1967, p. 15).

Jean, a 35-year-old, never married woman, said if you were heavy, you could get to know someone who might like you instead of having to attract people with your looks before they wanted to know you:

> Many of the women I met from my chat room were way overweight. It's easy to sit at home and talk online, say things, and be appealing. I mean it's safe. It's totally safe if you don't ever plan on ever meeting anyone [face to face]. Later on, you do meet them, maybe they will like you anyway. By that time it's worth the risk. . . .

Reid, a 37-year-old, divorced father with two children, said,

> The Internet is a place where people can take risks without consequences. You can experiment with people you wouldn't normally meet or get involved with. You can grocery shop. There are more people to meet. You can play games for a long time. You can look at so many pictures; it's fun like a candy store.

. . . For people who are shy, anxious, and deficient in social skills, use of the Internet may facilitate social interaction because it requires different skills that are necessary for initiating heterosocial interaction in a face-to-face setting. In one study, college students reported using the Internet to meet people because they found it reduced their anxiety about social interaction (Knox, Daniels, Sturdivant, & Zusman, 2001).

Some respondents of both sexes claimed they found it difficult to talk to strangers in social situations such as parties or even in places such as the school cafeteria or a classroom. Rick, a 32-year-old, never married man, said he liked using the Internet because "I'm shy. That is why I went into a chat room. I can say things online that I can't say in person. I am so quiet. But, I can talk on the telephone too."

Pete, a 22-year-old, never married man, did not trust dating in general, but he liked the Internet better than bars:

> Bars are a meat market, and I feel that everybody there is putting on more of a show than actuality. I mean when you meet them [women] in a bar, it's like they are a different person than in real life. And it's the same thing with the Internet, you know, with a lot of women. So many haven't returned messages, or they just leave you hanging, or they pretend to be someone they are not. I'm too shy, too afraid of getting turned down. It's easier, less painful getting turned down on type than it is in person.

Men and women respondents complained that bars were not a good place to get to know prospective partner. Many argued that he did not trust the character of bar pickups:

> One thing I found with the bar is that most ladies who go there will say yes and say yes to about anybody given the time of night. Some ladies have propositioned me! Let's just say I don't like being in that situation.

Anna also said, "I don't want to go to bars to meet people. This is a lot safer."

Societal expectations for appearance and behavior can result in individuals who do not fit the norm and perceive themselves as deviants who will not be accepted. Furthermore, they may fear negative reprisals from more mainstream members of society and thus may retreat into an online setting where they feel safer and have control.

Freedom from Commitment and Stereotypes

Clark (1998) found that Internet dating is particularly appealing to teenage girls because it allows them to be aggressive while remaining sheltered. Clark argued that "Internet dating affords teenage girls in particular the opportunity to experiment with and claim power within heterosexual relationships," but she questioned whether the resulting relationships were any more emancipative than those found in the real-life experiences of teenagers. She suggested that "power afforded through self-construction on the Internet does not translate into changed gender roles and expectations in the social world beyond cyberspace." The teenage girls in Clark's study were "not interested in meeting the boys with whom they conversed as they might undermine (their) attractive and aggressive online persona" (pp. 160–169).

. . . Traditional gender norms that dictate that women wait for men to ask them out and men be assertive leaders are still common today (Mongeau, Hale, Johnson, & Hillis, 1993; Simmel, 1911). However, some research (e.g., Cooper & Sportolan, 1997) and responses from the interviewees suggest that these norms may not operate online.

Cathryn, a 15-year-old girl, stated.

> I like to play but not really be there. I met this boy and we talked about school and movies, but we didn't meet. We live in different states. I don't know much about him really. He's just fun to talk to. I tease him a lot. Sometimes my friends pretend they are older or even guys instead of girls.

This online interaction is free from commitment.

Five of the respondents, both men and women, talked about freedom from commitment and stereotypic sex roles. Anna said,

> We agreed that there would be no expectations and if we didn't like each other, we'd have a few laughs, go to a baseball game or two, have a few beers, who cares. Since I like to travel, I also felt if the guy was a jerk, I had a credit card and would go to a different hotel and stay in San Diego and have a nice vacation. . . .

Ross, a 40-year-old, divorced father who had custody of his 10-year-old son, said,

> There is such a difference between actually talking to somebody and putting things in print. You can make yourself sound like I could be Joe Big Stud or whatever on the Internet. Then when we met, we'd see if we got along.

Greg, a 21-year-old, never married student, said,

Every few weeks we'd say "Hey, how's it going?" I told her from day one we'd never know each other's real names, where we lived, or anything about it. She didn't know how old I was or if I was married or single or anything. But we loved talking, and we talked about meeting.

Although many respondents initially wanted freedom from commitment, they liked spending a lot of time online getting to know each other. Often after a period of months, they decided to meet face to face. Some changed their minds about having no commitment and increased their involvement, whereas others concluded that they had too little in common to justify continuing the relationship. Thus, as with traditional dating, online daters seemed to want to get to know their partners better before committing. . . .

Trust, Risk, and Lying Online

Trust may not be important in an interaction when compared to that of opening an opportunity for taking a gamble. Goffman (1967) believed, "Chance lies in the attitude of the individual himself—his creative capacity to redefine the world around him into its decisional potentialities" (p. 201). Goffman saw all forms of action as gambling. Similarly, Simmel (1911) argued that when a person is offered a token of trust, the recipient is expected to respond in kind. When people place online personals ads, those who respond may be perceived as offering a gift; the implication is made that "I trust you enough to treat me well.". . .

The Internet has been described as a "revolutionary social space" (Hardey, 2002, p. 577) in which old rules for social interaction are discarded in favor of new ones that may be better suited to the technology. However, Hardey (2002) found that Internet daters' interactions are often guided by "rituals and norms that protect the self" (p. 577), which was originally suggested by Goffman (1967). The technology of the Internet may present new challenges to building intimacy and avoiding rejection, but the basic motivations for protecting the self remain. New risks inspire new coping strategies to maintain an environment of trust. Such an environment is necessary to maintain the solidarity of society, according to Simmel (1978). Giddens (1990) emphasized a need to establish trust among individuals and observed that the alternative to trust is inaction, which in itself may be risky because if we do not take the risk of interacting, we will not develop a supportive friendship network. He saw relationships as "ties based upon trust, where trust is not pre-given but worked upon, and where the work involved means a mutual process of self-disclosure" (p. 121).

To establish close relationships within the constraints of the Internet, people use creative methods to identify themselves as cool and trustworthy. Emoticons, abbreviations, unconventional spellings, and specialized grammar are used to weed out people who do not share others' realities or ways of being (Waskul, 2003).[1] Turkle (1995) observed that through photographs, profiles, and narratives, "people create and cycle through a sometimes surprising range of online identities" (p. 10). . . .

Online, people commonly misrepresent their appearance, making it more flattering (Clark, 1998). One sample of college students reported lying about their age, weight, and marital status (Knox et al., 2001). They may also misrepresent their gender (Danet, 1998; Knox et al., 2001). Misrepresentation in online social interactions seems so natural that few seem to give much thought to what usually could be dismissed as a makeover of one's persona. Given the limited amount of information available to respondents about each other in Internet interactions and their transitory nature, deception is common.

Most respondents said they had been lied to more than once, and some reported surprise when this happened. Robin, the 32-year-old, single woman, wanted to trust people:

> I was raised to believe and trust in people when they tell you things. So it was very hard for me to believe that someone could play on another person's feelings the way he did with me [a previous Internet relationship had not worked, and Robin believes he had not told her the truth about being truly interested in meeting her and being there for her]. But I have accepted the fact that it happened, and I have moved on with my life and met [also online] someone better. The only advice I have for people who are thinking of Internet dating is just be careful. There is a Web site out there where you can have someone's background checked out to see if they are telling you the truth. In the back of my mind I had a feeling he [her previous online date] was lying, but for some reason I didn't want to face the reality of it. . . .

Most men and women in this study took physical and emotional risks to gain risks and were willing to continue seeking online relationships even after others had lied to them. A few teenagers and adults who did not want committed relationships took fewer risks by taking on unrealistic roles, not being open, and postponing face-to-face meetings. Others developed symbolic trust indicators to lessen the consequential risks of interacting.

Indicators of Trust

Berger and Luckmann (1967) believed people decide to trust based on intuitive impressions that we refer to as "trust indicators." This research uncovered the presence of early and late trust indicators as part of early and late negotiating strategies that serve to minimize harm to the self.

The development of trust in an online dating relationship requires not only the assurance that the other means no physical harm but also that the other will treat the online persona with ritual deference. A remark such as, "I did not know you were so large; do you use Photoshop?" would be a devastating blow.[2] This is one of the reasons some Internet daters postpone or evade face-to-face meetings. . . .

Younger respondents were concerned with the hermeneutics of keystrokes and codes. Arlene, a 17-year-old interviewed by the first author, used *LOL* (laughing out loud), *BRB* (be right back), and other abbreviations when chatting. We found younger people used this coded language more frequently than did older individuals. Respondents who were not adept in the use of such codes exposed their lack of grace in social interaction and were weeded out. Participants selected for interactions of usually only a few minutes duration were chosen many times based on one word or the speed of their typing. More mature respondents had different early indicators. Lisa, a 41-year-old, divorced woman, said,

> I don't use chat rooms much anymore. They are filled with a vast bastion of people looking for absolutely nothing. They are "players." They are talking to you while having cybersex with someone else and talking with a third person in another room at the same time. If you get serious, they don't like it. They use romance and dating rooms, sex cams, interest and game rooms, and they chat on the side at the same time. . . .

Chet, a 28-year-old, divorced man, said chat rooms were for mindless, immature people. He used dating services also:

> I look for women who are funny, sarcastic, you know, intellectual, sharp-witted. I can't start a conversation with someone who says she wants to come over and have sex the next day. Or the stereotypic interaction with emphasis on age, hobbies. . . . It's mindless, immature.

Janet, an 18-year-old, female student, said she could tell right away if it was going to work:

> You talk to them. If they answer with one-word sentences. . . . if the [online] conversation is really unbalanced, I look and see how much I have said and how much they have said. If I tell them what my field of study is and they don't understand anything at all about it. . . . Most people in chat rooms are uneducated, working class, and just plain dumb. You need to weed them out.

Respondents used indicators contained in e-mailed or posted pictures to help evaluate their potential mates and attempted to determine their age and degree of affluence. Clothing, hairstyle, and projected lifestyle were augured from photographs. Jessie, a 24-year-old woman, focused on economic status:

> I met this man online in a church chat room. He was from South Africa, and he sent me e-mail pictures where he was standing in front of a very expensive car. His clothes were expensive-looking, too, and his house was like a mansion. He said he was a professional businessman with lots of money. He said he wanted to come over here to meet me and my family. He had never been in the States before. I told my mother about him.

Other indicators deal with time. Through face-to-face relating, we have come to expect a certain pattern of flow through which a relationship develops. This pattern is reflected through the timing of conversation and self-disclosure. Often on the Internet there is a pressure to disclose much in a short time to establish trust and kinship quickly. Some respondents dislike this pressure. Julian, 25-year-old salesman, observed,

> Internet people are more desperate; things move fast in weird ways. People put pictures up for everyone to see, but you don't know their personal mannerisms. Do they smell bad? Have a funny laugh? Do they bite their nails? The beginning is different. It [meeting online] sets you off on a weird path. You get way too intense too soon. There's like a speed to get to know each other. All you have is conversation that becomes exaggerated and magnified. It becomes drama. People attach deep meaning and feeling prematurely.

Feelings get hurt. Self-revelation leads to distortion of the picture. One woman I met online said, "I think I am ready for a relationship now." This scared me. I wanted to just maybe have at least one date in person and get to know her better before committing to a relationship.

Although this respondent felt it was not a good practice to discuss personal matters too soon, we observed him doing just that in his second e-mail to a woman he had just recently met online.

To develop intimacy to create a bond with an online partner, Internet daters felt pressed to self-disclose as much information as they could in the shortest possible time, though letting people know one's shortcomings begs rejection. Furthermore, disclosing too much too fast violates social conventions and norms. The woman who told Julian, "I think I am ready for a relationship now," scared her potential partner away. . . .

Once Internet daters find each other compatible, they move on to the next step of relationship building. This involves spending more time getting to know one another to build trust. Basic interpersonal trust is either contractual trust based on social contracts as in family relationships or trust based on time in relations (Govier, 1992). Most respondents liked the time they spent getting to know each other. They said this time helped develop trust and intimacy. Robin said it seemed safer to get to know people over time:

> I guess I chose the Internet over meeting someone in a bar or on a blind date because to me it felt a little safer. In a bar you are meeting someone and you get the impression that they want just a one-night stand and that is it. That is not how I was raised. On the Internet you could talk to this person for as long as you wanted to before you went ahead and met that person.

Josh, a 56-year-old, never married man, also felt he had developed trust during time spent online:

> I felt I knew her even though we had not met yet. She was not a stranger. We had spoken over the phone and e-mailed over a period of 11 months. I was not afraid at all. It didn't even enter my mind. I didn't have any reason to believe she would be any different in person than she appeared to be. . . .

■ ■ ■ DISCUSSION

The Internet has opened a new avenue for romantic interaction. In the present study, Internet daters reported being able to reach a larger pool of potential partners and experiencing increased freedom of choice among partners. The Internet also raises new issues of negotiating risk and establishing trust. Respondents said they were willing to take risks to take advantage of the new courting opportunities offered by this new technology. Some risks involved physical danger, and others involved loss of face and possible rejection, though interviewees developed rationales and strategies to deal with these risks to trust that they would have positive experiences.

Dating online modified gendered interactions by allowing women to behave more assertively and men to be more open. It also necessitated the development of new strategies based on keystrokes, codes interpreting online photographs, and reading user profiles to develop trust and confirm compatibility. In Internet interactions, gains and losses are only symbolic, and rejection by an online entity identified only as "suv4" can represent no great material loss. It is this very abstraction that motivates people to use the Internet for dating to avoid stereotyped gender roles and the pain of rejection.

The interrelating of Internet daters also reflects old patterns and problems common to all forms of courtship. Even if they do not find objectification and harassment online, meeting offline often brings objectification or harassment into a formerly nonjudgmental relationship. There is irony in seeking a way out of loneliness through a medium that ensures the insularity of participants and perpetuates gender stereotyping once participants meet.

Several old problems remain in Internet dating. It is easy for people to lie to each other, and appearance issues and shyness do not completely disappear when dating online. Rejection and its emotional pain are ultimately a part of Internet dating as much as of dating that is entirely face to face from the start. The fundamental issues of trust, self-presentation, and compatibility carry over from conventional courtship into its Internet variant.

The need to obtain companionship motivates people to seek out romantic relationships in a variety of ways, and the Internet is merely the latest technological development used by people to assist their romantic goals. Participants in the current study reported reducing their loneliness, obtaining comfort, and finding fun and excitement. These benefits appeared to outweigh the risks.

NOTES

1. Emoticons are small icons bearing emotive faces. These can be inserted into text messages.

2. Adobe Photoshop is a very popular photograph manipulation program that allows users to drastically alter photographs and cinematographic video.

REFERENCES

Berger, P. L., & Luckmann, T. (1967). *The social construction of reality: A treatise in the sociology of knowledge.* New York: Anchor.

Chelune, G. J., Sultan, F. E., & Williams, C. L. (1980). Loneliness, self-disclosure, and interpersonal effectiveness. *Journal of Counseling Psychology, 27,* 462–468.

Clark, L. S. (1998). Dating on the Net: Teens and the rise of "pure" relationships. In S. Jones (Ed.), *Cybersociety 2.0: Revisiting computer-mediated communication and community* (pp. 159–181). Thousand Oaks, CA: Sage.

Cooper, A., & Sportolari, L. (1997). Romance in cyberspace: Understanding online attraction. *Journal of Sex Education and Therapy, 22,* 7–14.

Danet, B. (1998). Text as mask: Gender, play, and performance on the Internet. In S. Jones (Ed.), *Cybersociety 2.0: Revisiting computer-mediated communication and community* (pp. 129–157). Thousand Oaks, CA: Sage.

Giddens, A. (1990). *The consequences of modernity.* Stanford, CA: Stanford University Press.

Goffman, E. (1959). *The presentation of self in everyday life.* New York: Doubleday.

Goffman, E. (1967). *Interaction ritual: Essays on face-to-face behavior.* Doubleday.

Govier, T. (1992). Trust, distrust, and feminist theory. *Hypatia, 7,* NI.

Hardey, M. (2002). Life beyond the screen: Embodiment and identify through the Internet. *Sociological Review, 50,* 570–585.

Hunt, M. M. (1959). *The natural history of love.* New York: Knopf.

Jones, W. H., Hobbs, S. A., & Hockenbury, D. (1982). Loneliness and social skills deficits. *Journal of Personality and Social Psychology, 42,* 682–689.

Knox, D., Daniels, V., Sturdivant, L., & Zusman, M. (2001). College student use of the Internet for mate rejection. *College Student Journal, 35,* 158–160.

Mongeau, P. A., Hale, J. L., Johnson, K. L., & Hillis, J. D. (1993). Who's wooing whom? An investigation of female initiated dating. In P. J. Kalbfleisch (Ed.), *Interpersonal communication: Evolving interpersonal relationships* (pp. 51–68). Hillsdale, NJ: Lawrence Erlbaum.

Raney, R. F. (2000, May 11). Study finds Internet of social benefit to users. *New York Times.* p. G7.

Simmel, G. (1911). *Philosophische kultur: Gesammelte essays* [Philosophical culture: Collected essays] (2nd ed.). Leipzig, Germany: Alfred Kroner.

Turkle, S. (1995). *Life on the screen: Identity in the age of the Internet.* New York: Simon & Schuster.

Waskul, D. (2003). *Self-games and body-play: Personhood in online chat and cybersex.* New York: Peter Lang.

Zuboff, S. (1991). New worlds of computer-mediated work. In J. M. Hepslin (Ed.), *Down to earth sociology: Introductory readings* (6th ed., pp. 476–485). New York: Free Press.

Social Groups and Social Control

It is easy to lose sight of the significance that our birth ushers us into a world that already exists. For the most part, we yawn at such a statement. It seems to be an "Of-course-we-all-know-that" type of thing, and we ordinarily fail to grasp its profound implications. That we are entering a world that is already constructed means that we are joining a human group that has established ways of "doing social life."

Social life is like a game already in progress when we enter it, leaving us little choice but to play it the way it is set out. From birth, we are immersed in its sea of expectations, the arbitrary norms that our group has adopted and expects us to follow. They may pinch, but it matters little for we are only individuals. The group has already made the rules, and it dictates the way we are to live our lives.

Like a game, for social life to exist, rules are necessary. If you can't depend on people to do things, everything falls apart. For social groups to function, then, to do whatever they have set out to do, they must be able to depend on their members. This applies to all social groups, whether as small as our family or as large as a multinational corporation.

Deviance, however, is as inevitable as rules are necessary.

Where there are rules, there will be rule breakers. *All* of us violate some of our group's many rules; that is, we all fail to meet some of the expectations that others have of us. When we do this, we become deviants. In sociology, *deviant* simply means someone who has deviated from the rules, someone who has wandered from the path that they were expected to follow. Deviant does *not* mean a horrible person—although horrible people are included in this term.

It has been said that the first rule of sociology is that nothing is as it appears, that behind the scenes lies a different reality. If so, then a goal of sociology is to penetrate the façade that groups so carefully put forward for public consumption. As sociologists analyze this hidden reality, it is inevitable that they will encounter resistance, for sociological research often exposes what groups want to keep hidden.

Sociologists have found that participant observation (reviewed in Chapter 1 of the text) is a good way to peer behind the scenes, helping us explore the reality that is usually open only to insiders. In the first article in this part, Daniel Chambliss does just this. He goes behind the scenes of the hospital

51

to tell us what really goes on there. Sociologists also use in-depth interviews to probe behind the scenes. In the second and final selection of this part, in the only research by a sociologist on this topic, Ken Levi explores the experiences of a hit man, focusing on the ways by which he neutralizes his extreme deviance.

Just Another Routine Emergency

Daniel F. Chambliss

introduction ■ ■ ■ ■ ■

Just as buildings have façades—attractive, carefully manicured front exteriors that are designed to give a good impression of what might be inside—so social groups and organizations have façades. Some organizations hire public relations firms to put out favorable messages. Others contribute to charitable causes to cultivate images of caring. Even oil companies that exploit the environment publish expensive, full-page glossy ads in national magazines to convince the public that they care more about the environment than does *Greenpeace* or *The Sea Shepherds*.

Behind the social façade put out for public consumption lies a different reality. As in the case of some oil companies, the reality may conflict greatly with the cultivated public image. But in the typical case, the hidden reality has more to do with dissension among the group's members, or with less dedication to the group's goals, than the organization wants to reveal. At times, the façade may have more to do with maintaining an appearance of competence and order, whereas the reality is a looming incompetence and disorder. This selection by Daniel Chambliss takes a look behind the social façade of the hospital, revealing a reality that few of us are familiar with.

Thinking Critically

As you read this selection, ask yourself:

1. How do the personnel of hospitals keep outsiders from seeing past their social façade?

2. What did this participant observation study reveal about hospitals that we otherwise would not have known?

3. Use this reading to prove or disprove this statement: From their callous and inappropriate humor, we can see that doctors and nurses don't really care about their patients.

Every unit in the hospital . . . has its own normality, its own typical patients, number of deaths, and crises to be faced. But just as predictably, every unit has its emergencies that threaten the routine and challenge the staff's ability to maintain workaday attitudes and practices. Emergencies threaten the staff's ability to carry on as usual, to maintain their own distance from the patient's suffering, and to hold at bay their awe at the enormity of events. Occasionally breakdowns occur in unit discipline or the ability to do the required work.

Staff follow several strategies when trying to manage the threat of breakdowns: they will keep outsiders outside, follow routinization rituals, or use humor to distance themselves. Finally, even when all efforts fail, they will keep going, no matter what. Consider in turn each of these implicit maxims:

■ ■ ■ 1. KEEP OUTSIDERS OUTSIDE

Every hospital has policies about visiting hours, designed not only to "let patients rest" but also to protect staff from outsiders' interference in their work. Visitors are limited to certain hours, perhaps two to a patient room for fifteen-minute visits; they may have to be announced before entering the unit or may be kept waiting in a room down the hall. No doubt many such policies are good for the patient. No doubt, too, they keep visitors out of the nurse's way, prevent too many obtrusive questions or requests for small services, and prevent curious laypersons from seeing the messier, less presentable sides of nursing care.

When visitors cannot be physically excluded, they can still be cognitively controlled, that is, prevented from knowing that something untoward is happening. Typically, the staff behave in such episodes as if everything were OK, even when it is not. This is similar to what Erving Goffman observed in conversations: when the shared flow of interaction is threatened by an accidental insult or a body failure such as a sneeze or flatulence, people simply try to ignore the break in reality and carry on as if nothing has happened. Such "reality maintenance" is often well-orchestrated, requiring cooperation on the part of several parties. For Goffman, normal people in normal interactions accept at face value each other's presentation of who they are:

> A state where everyone temporarily accepts everyone else's line is established. This kind of mutual acceptance seems to be a basic structural feature of interaction, especially the interaction of face-to-face talk. It is typically a "working" acceptance, not a "real" one.[1]

And when this routine breaks down, the immediate strategy is simple denial:

> When a person fails to prevent an incident, he can still attempt to maintain the fiction that no threat to face has occurred. The most blatant example of this is found where the person acts as if an event that contains a threatening expression has not occurred at all.[2]

In the hospital, the unexpected entrance of outsiders into a delicate situation can disrupt the staff's routine activities and create unmanageable chaos. To avoid this, the staff may pretend to outsiders that nothing special is happening; this pretense itself can be part of the routine. During a code (resuscitation) effort I witnessed, there were three such potential disruptions by outsiders: another patient calling for help, a new incoming patient being wheeled in, and the new patient's family members entering the unit. All three challenges were handled by the staff diverting the outsiders from the code with a show, as if nothing were happening:

> Code in CCU [Cardiac Care Unit] . . . woman patient, asystole [abnormal ventricle contractions]. Doc (res[ident]) pumping chest—*deep* pumps, I'm struck by how far down they push. Serious stuff. Matter of factness of process is striking. This was a surprise code, not expected. Patient was in Vtak [ventricular fibrillation], pulse started slowing, then asystole. N[urse]s pumping for a while, RT [Respiratory Therapist] ambu-bagging [pumping air into lungs]. Maybe 7–8 people in patient's room working. Calm, but busy. Occasionally a laugh.
>
> Pt in next room (no more than 10 feet away) called for nurse—a doc went in, real loose and casual, strolled in, pt said something; doc said, "There's something going on next door that's taking people's time; we'll get to you"—real easy, like nothing at all happening. Then strolls back to code room. Very calm . . .
>
> Two N[urse]s came into unit wheeling a new patient. One said, "Uh, oh, bad time," very quietly as she realized, going in the door, that a code was on. Somebody said, "Close the door"—the outside door to the unit, which the Ns with the new pt were holding open . . .
>
> When the new pt was brought in and rolled into his room, the family with him was stopped at unit door, told to stay in waiting room and "we'll call you" with a casual wave of hand, as if this is routine. [No one said a code was on. Patient lying on gurney was wheeled in, went right by the code room and never knew a thing.] [Field Notes]

This is a simple example of protecting the routine from the chaos of a panicking patient or a horrified family; the outsiders never knew that a resuscitation was occurring fifteen feet away. The staff's work was, in their own eyes, routine; their challenge was protecting that routine from outside disruption.

■ ■ ■ 2. FOLLOW ROUTINIZATION RITUALS

The staff's sense of routine is maintained by the protective rituals of hospital life. Under stress, one may use them more and more compulsively, falling back on the old forms to reconvince oneself that order is still present. Frantic prayers in the foxhole are the prototype cases.

Most prominent of such rituals in hospitals are "rounds," the standard ritual for the routine handling of patient disasters in the hospital. "Rounds" is the generic term for almost any organized staff group discussion of patients' conditions. "Walking rounds" refers to a physician walking through the hospital, usually trailed by various residents and interns, going from patient to patient and reviewing their condition. "Grand rounds" are large meetings of the medical staff featuring the presentation of an interesting case, with elaborate discussion and questions, for the purpose of education and review of standard practices. Nursing rounds usually consist of a meeting between the staff for one (outgoing) shift reporting to the staff of the next (incoming) shift on the condition of all patients on the floor. Here the staff collectively explains what has happened and why, bringing every case into the staff's framework of thinking, and systematically enforcing the system's capability for handling medical problems without falling to pieces. In rounds, the staff confirm to each other that things are under control. Once a week, for instance, the Burn Unit at one hospital holds rounds in their conference room with a group of residents, one or two attending, several nurses, the social workers, dieticians, and physical therapists. The patients here are in terrible shape; one can sometimes hear moans in the hallway outside as patients are taken for walks by the nurses. But rounds continue:

> Macho style of the docs very evident. . . . Resident will present a case, then the attendings take rapid-fire shots at what he [the resident] had done: wrong dressing, wrong feeding schedule, failure to note some abnormality in the lab results. Much of the talk was a flurry of physiological jargon, many numbers and abbreviations. The intensity of the presentation, the mercilessness of the grilling, is surprising. . . . Focus is on no errors made in situation of extreme pressure—i.e., both in patient treatment and then here in rounds presenting the case. Goal here is to be predictable, *controlled,* nothing left out. [Field Notes]

■ ■ ■ 3. USE HUMOR TO DISTANCE YOURSELF

Keeping outsiders away and following the standard rituals for maintaining normality can help, but sometimes the pathos of hospital life becomes psychologically threatening to staff members. One response is to break down, cry, and run out, but this is what they are trying to avoid; the more common reaction is the sort of black humor that notoriously characterizes hospitals and armies everywhere. Humor provides an outlet; when physical space is not available, humor is a way to separate oneself psychologically from what is happening. It says both that I am not involved and that this really isn't so important. (In brain surgery, when parts of that organ are, essentially, vacuumed away, one may hear comments like "There goes 2d grade, there go the piano lessons," etc.) With laughter, things seem less consequential, less of a burden. What has been ghastly can perhaps be made funny:

> Today they got a 600-gram baby in the Newborn Unit. When Ns heard [the baby] was in Delivery, they were praying, "Please God let it be under 500 grams"—because that's the definite cutoff under which they won't try to save it—but the doc said admit it anyway. Ns unhappy.
> I came in the unit tonight; N came up to me and said brightly, with a big smile, "Have you seen our fetus?" Ns on the Newborn Unit have nicknames for some. There's "Fetus," the 600-gram one; "Munchkin"; and "Thrasher," in the corner, the one with constant seizures. Grim humor, but common. ["Fetus" was born at 24 weeks, "Munchkin" at 28.] [Field Notes]

The functions of such humor for medical workers have been described in a number of classic works of medical sociology. Renée Fox, writing in her book *Experiment Perilous* about physicians on a metabolic research unit, says, "The members of the group were especially inclined to make jokes about events that disturbed them a good deal," and she summarizes that

> by freeing them from some of the tension to which they were subject, enabling them to achieve greater detachment and equipoise, and strengthening their resolve to do something about the problems with which they were faced, the grim medical humor of the Metabolic Group helped them to come to terms with their situation in a useful and professionally acceptable way.[3]

Fox and other students of hospital culture (notably Rose Coser)[4] have emphasized that humor fills a functional purpose of "tension release," allowing medical workers to get on with the job in the face of trauma; their analyses usually focus on jokes explicitly told in medical settings. This analysis is correct as far as it goes, but in a sense I think it almost "explains away" hospital humor—as if to say that "these people are under a lot of strain, so it's understandable that they tell these gruesome jokes." It suggests, in a functionalist fallacy, that jokes are made because of the strain and that things somehow aren't "really" funny.

But they are. An appreciation of hospital life must recognize that funny things—genuinely funny, even if sometimes simultaneously horrible—do happen. Hospitals are scenes of irony, where good and bad are inseparably blended, where funny things happen, where to analytically excuse laughter as a defense mechanism is simultaneously to deny the human reality, the experience, that even to a nonstressed outsider *this is funny.*[5] The humor isn't found only in contrived jokes but in the scenes one witnesses; laughter can be spontaneous, and it's not always nervous. True, one must usually have a fairly normalized sense of the hospital to laugh here, but laugh one does.

Certainly, the staff make jokes:

> In the OR [operating room]:
>   "This is his [pt's] 6th time [for a hernia repair]."
>   "After two, I hear you're officially disabled."
>   "Oh good, does that mean he gets a special parking place?"
>   [Field Notes]
> In the ICU [Intensive Care Unit], two Ns—one male, one female—working on pt.
>   Nurse 1 (male): "This guy has bowel sounds in his scrotum."
>   Nurse 2 (female): "In his scrotum?"
>   Nurse 1: "Yeah, didn't you pick that up?"
>   Nurse 2: "I didn't put my stethoscope there!" (Big laughs.) [Field Notes]

Sometimes jokes are more elaborate and are obviously derived from the tragedy of the situation:

> In another ICU, staff member taped a stick to the door of the unit, symbolizing (for them) "The Stake," a sign of some form of euthanasia [perhaps the expression sometimes used, "to stake" a patient, derives from the myth that vampires can only be killed by driving a stake through the heart]. Periodically word went around that a resident had just won the "Green Stake Award," meaning that he or she had, for the first time, allowed or helped a patient to die. [Field Notes]
>   Some colorful balloons with "Get Well Soon" were delivered to a patient's room. The patient died the following night. Someone on the staff moved the balloons to the

door of another patient's room; that patient died! Now the staff has put the balloons at the door of the patient they believe is "most likely to die next." [Field Notes]

But jokes have to be contrived; they are deliberate efforts at humor and so make a good example of efforts to distance oneself, or to make the tragic funny. But the inherent irony of the hospital is better seen in situations that spontaneously provoke laughter. These things are funny in themselves; even an outsider can laugh at them:

Nurse preparing to wheel a patient into the OR tells him, "Take out your false teeth, take off your glasses . . . ," and continuing, trying to make a joke, "Take off your leg, take out your eyes." The patient said, "Oh, I almost forgot—" and pulled out his [false] eye! [Interview]

Or:

Lady patient [Geriatric floor] is upset because she called home, there's no answer; she's afraid her husband has died. Sylvia [a nurse] told her he probably just went somewhere for lunch, but patient said he would have called. She's afraid.
[Later] Sylvia went back in lady's room—she's crying. Husband called! Sylvia happy, smiling, "You should be happy!" "But," says the old lady, "he called to say he was out burying the dog!"
Sylvia had to leave the room because she was starting to laugh; she and Janie laughing at this at the N's station, saying it's really sad but funny at the same time. [Field Notes]

Or:

In looking at X-rays of a patient's colon, the resident explains to the team a shadow on the film: "Radiology says it could be a tumor, or it might just be stool." Jokes all around about how "helpful" Rays [Radiology] is. [Field Notes]

One needn't be under pressure to find such things funny. People do laugh to ease pressure or to distance oneself. But sometimes the distance comes first: laughter is made possible by the routinization that has gone before.

■ ■ ■ 4. WHEN THINGS FALL APART, KEEP GOING

Sometimes routinization fails: outsiders come into the room and, seeing their dead mother, break down, screaming and wailing; or a longtime, cared-for patient begins irretrievably to "decompensate" and lose blood pressure, sliding quickly to death; or emergency surgery goes bad, the trauma shakes the staff, and there are other patients coming in from the ambulances. Any of these can destroy the staff's sense of "work as usual." In such cases, the typical practice seems to be, remarkably: just keep going. Trauma teams specialize in the psychological strength (or cold-bloodedness, perhaps) to continue working when the world seems to be falling apart. Finally, nurses and physicians are notable for continuing to work even, in the final case, after the patient is for almost all purposes dead, or will be soon.

> A resident said to the attending [physician] on one floor, discussing a terminal patient: "If we transfuse him, he might get hepatitis."
> Another resident: "By the time he gets hepatitis he'll be dead."
> Attending: "OK, so let's transfuse." [Field Notes]

Perseverance is a habit; it's also a moral imperative, a way of managing disaster as if it were routine.

In every unit there are nurses known for being good under pressure. These are people who, whatever their other skills (and, typically, their other skills are quite good), are able to maintain their presence of mind in any crisis. Whereas "being organized" is a key quality for nurses in routine situations, staying calm is crucial in emergency situations. Compare two nurses known for remaining calm (Mavis and Anna) to two others who are prone to alarm (Linda and Julie):

> Mavis [in Neonatal ICU] is cited as a good nurse (great starting IVs, e.g.) who doesn't get shook, even in a code, even if her pt is dying, she still keeps doing what you're supposed to do. Linda, by contrast, is real smart, very good technically, but can freak out, start yelling, etc., if things are going badly. [Field Notes]
> Julie [in Medical ICU], hurrying around, looks just one step ahead of disaster, can't keep up, etc. Doc says something about the patient in room 1. Julie says, walking past, "He's not mine," keeps going. But Anna, calm, walks in pt's room—pt with oxygen mask, wants something. Anna goes out, calmly, comes back in a minute w/cup of crushed ice, gives pt a spoonful to ease thirst. She *always* seems to be doing that little thing that others "don't have time for"—never flustered and yet seems to get more done than anyone else. [Field Notes, Interview]

But to "keep going" depends not so much on the individual fortitude of nurses such [as] Mavis and Anna, but on the professional and institutional habits of the nursing staff and the hospital. The continuance of care even in the face of obvious failure of efforts is itself a norm. Whatever one's personal disposition, one keeps working; the staff keep working, often when the patient is all but dead, or "dead" but not officially recognized as such:

> Dr. K., walking rounds with four residents, discussing a 30-year-old male patient, HIV-positive, gone totally septic [has bloodstream infection, a deadly problem], no hope at all of recovery—Dr. K. says this is a "100 percent mortality" case; so they decide how to proceed with minimal treatment, at the end of which Dr. K. says brightly, "And if he codes—code him!" [Field Notes]

Coding such a patient is an exercise in technique; there is no hope entailed, no optimism, no idea that he might be saved. There is only the institutional habit which substitutes for hope, which in many cases obviates the staff's pessimism or lack of interest. When standard procedure is followed, courage is unnecessary. It is one thing to be routinely busy, caring for vegetative patients; it happens every day. It is quite another to handle emergency surgery with no time and a life at stake. Sometimes such a case will challenge all the staff's resources—their personal fortitude, their habitualization of procedures, the self-protection offered by an indefatigable sense of humor. To maintain one's composure while under tremendous pressures of time and fatefulness requires all the courage a staff can muster.

One such case was that of emergency surgery on a thirty-five-year-old woman who came to Southwestern Regional hospital in severe abdominal pain; she was diagnosed with a ruptured ectopic [tubal] pregnancy estimated at sixteen weeks. The case provides us with a dramatic example of the pressure placed on the staff to retain their composure in the face of disaster.

The long description which follows is graphic. The scene was more than bloody; it was grotesque. More than one staff member—including one member of the surgical team itself—left the room during the operation, sickened. Other nurses, even very experienced ones, told me they have never witnessed such a scene and hope never to witness one. I include it here, in some detail, to exemplify both what health professionals face in their work and how, incredibly, some of them can carry on. The description is reconstructed from Field Notes (some written at the time on the inside of a surgical mask, some on sheets of paper carried in a pocket), and from interviews afterward with participants:

> Saturday night OR suite; hasn't been busy. Only one case so far, a guy who got beat up with a tire iron (drug deal), finished about 8:30 P.M. It's about 10:00. 2 Ns—the Saturday night staff—sitting around in the conference room, just chatting and waiting for anything that happens.
>
> Call comes over intercom: ruptured tubal (pregnancy) just came in OR, bringing to the crash room. 35-year-old black woman, very heavy—250 pounds maybe—apparently pregnant for 16 weeks, which means she's been in pain for 10 weeks or more without coming in. Friends brought her to ER screaming in pain. Blood pressure is at "60 over palpable," i.e., the diastolic doesn't even register on the manometer. She's obviously bleeding bad internally, will die fast if not opened up. Ns run to OR and set up fast. I've never seen people work so quickly here, no wasted motion at all. This is full speed *emergency*.
>
> When patient is rolled in, fully conscious, there are more than a dozen staff people in the room, including three gynecological surgery residents, who will operate; all three are women. The surgeons are scrubbed and gowned and stand in a line, back from the table, watching without moving, the one in charge periodically giving orders to the nurses who are setting up. At one point there are twelve separate people working on the patient—IVs going into both arms, anesthesiologist putting mask on pt to gas, nurse inserting a Foley [bladder] catheter, others tying pt's arms to the straightout arms of the table, others scrubbing the huge belly, an incredible scene. The patient is shaking terribly, in pain and fear. Her eyes are bugging out, looking around terribly fast. She's whimpering, groaning as needles go in, crying out softly. No one has time even to speak to her; one nurse briefly leans over and speaks into her ear something like "try not to worry, we're going to take care of you," but there is no time for this. I've never seen anyone so afraid, sweating and crying and the violent shaking.
>
> As soon as they have prepped her—the belly cleansed and covered with Opsite, in a matter of minutes, very, very fast, the anesthesiologist says, "All set?" And someone says "yes," and they gas her. I'm standing right by her head, looking to the head side of the drape which separates her head from her body; the instant that her eyes close, I look to the other side—and the surgeon has already slit her belly open. No hesitation at all, maybe before the patient was out.

What happened next, more extraordinary than the very fast prep, was the opening. Usually in surgery the scalpel makes the skin cut, then slowly scissors are used, snipping piece by piece at muscle, the Bovie cauterizing each blood vessel on the way, very methodical and painstaking. This was nothing like that. It was an entirely different style. They cut fast and deep, sliced her open deep, just chopped through everything, in a—not a panic, but something like a "blitzkrieg," maybe—to get down into the Fallopian tube that had burst and was shooting blood into the abdomen.

When they first got into the abdominal cavity, usually there would be some oozing blood; here as they opened blood splattered out all over the draping on the belly. It was a godawful mess, blood everywhere. They had one surgeon mopping up with gauze sponges, another using a suction pump, a little plastic hose, trying to clean the way. Unbelievable. They got down to the tubes, reaching down and digging around with their hands. And then they found it—suddenly out of this bloody mess down in the abdomen, with the surgeons groping around trying to feel where things were, out of this popped up, right out of the patient and, literally, onto the sheet covering her, the 16-week fetus itself. Immediately one surgeon said mock-cheerfully, "It's a boy!" "God, don't do that," said the scrub tech, turning her head away.

The scrub tech then began to lose it, tears running down her cheeks. Two other people on the team—there were maybe six around the table—said about the same time, nearly together, "Damien!" and "Alien!" recalling recent horror movies, "children of the devil" themes. The fetus lay on the sheet just below the open abdomen for a few moments. The head surgery resident, working, just kept working. The scrub tech should have put the fetus into a specimen tray, but she was falling to pieces fast, crying, and starting to have trouble handing the proper tools to the surgeon, who said something like, "What are you doing?" At this point the circulating nurse, a man, said, "If nobody else will do it," picked up the fetus and put it in a specimen tray, which he then covered with a towel and put aside. He then told another nurse to help him into a gown—he wasn't scrubbed. This violates sterile technique badly, for him to start handling tools, but the scrub tech was becoming a problem. The circulating nurse then quickly gowned and gloved, gently pulled the scrub tech aside and said, "I'll do it." The scrub tech ran out of the room in tears. And the circulating nurse began passing tools to the surgeons himself. It is the circulating nurse's responsibility to handle problems this way, and he did. Another nurse had gone out to scrub properly, and when she came back, maybe ten minutes later, she gowned and gloved and relieved him; so he (the circulating nurse) went back to his regular job of charting the procedure, answering the phone, etc.

By this time, things were under control; the bleeding was stopped, the tube tied off. The other tube was OK and left alone so the pt can get pregnant again. The blood in the abdomen was cleaned up—over 1500 cc's were lost, that's just under a half-gallon of blood. The pt would have died fast if they hadn't gotten in there.

Within two hours after the patient had first rolled in, the room was quiet, only three staff members left, two surgeons and the scrub nurse closing up and talking quietly. Most of the mess—the bloody sponges, the used tools, and all—was gone, cleared away, and all the other staff people, including the chief surgeon, had left. Very calm. The patient, who two hours ago was on the end of a fast terrible death, will be out of the hospital in two days with no permanent damage beyond the loss of one Fallopian tube. [Field Notes, Interviews]

In this situation, we can see two somewhat distinct problems in maintaining the routine order of things: first, the challenge simply in getting the work done; and second, the challenge of upholding the moral order of the hospital.[6] The first issue was resolved by replacing the scrub tech so the operation could continue. The second issue is trickier. The scrub tech's response appeared to be set off not by the horror of what she saw—the bloody fetus—but by the reaction of the assisting surgeon—"It's a boy!" I can only guess that the joke was too much for her. In continuing to work without her, and continuing without noticeable change of demeanor, the surgical team was asserting not only the imperative to protect the operational routine but also, I think, to protect the moral order of emergency surgery as well. That order includes:

1. The job comes first, before personal reactions of fear or disgust.
2. Cynicism is an acceptable form of expression if it helps to maintain composure and distance.
3. The medical team is rightfully in charge and above what may be happening in the OR [operating room].
4. Preserving life is the central value; others (such as niceties of language or etiquette) fall far behind.

There is clearly a morality here. Just as clearly, it is not the morality of everyday life.

NOTES

1. Erving Goffman, "On Face-Work," in *Interaction Ritual: Essays on Face-to-Face Behavior* (New York: Pantheon Books, 1967), p. 11.

2. Ibid., pp. 17–18.

3. Renée C. Fox, *Experiment Perilous* (New York: Free Press, 1959; reprint ed., Philadelphia: University of Pennsylvania Press, 1974), pp. 80–82.

4. Rose Laub Coser, "Some Social Functions of Laughter," in Lewis Coser, *The Pleasures of Sociology,* edited and with an introduction and notes by Lewis Coser (New York: New American Library, 1980), pp. 81–97.

5. The genius of Shem's *House of God* is that it accepts this fact and presents it honestly.

6. I am indebted to Robert Zussman, who suggested these in his review of the manuscript.

Becoming a Hit Man

Ken Levi

introduction

There is no doubt that we all have deviant desires. We all feel hedged in at times, and we want to break loose, throwing aside some of the rules that constrain us. But there is more to our deviant desires than this. If we probe our deeper recesses, we might even find a cesspool of feelings and impulses that we don't want to reveal to others or, at times, even to ourselves. If we were to give in to them, at a minimum we would be unwelcome in most places—or we might see our name and photo on some wanted poster. To get along in society, for the most part we accede to social norms and ignore or suppress our desires for deviance. Ignored or suppressed, however, these desires remain, sometimes hidden, sometimes cautiously entertained. Yet we—or I should say, some of us—are aware of our capacity for deviance. Even highly conforming people, those whose deviant desires are under tight control, can do appalling things when the conditions are right.

But killing people in cold blood? Shooting men and women because someone offers money for their deaths? Who would do such a thing? And those who do, how do they think of themselves—as monsters, the way we might think of them? On the contrary, as Levi shows, just as we have ways of neutralizing our deviances (telling a "white" lie or using the Internet to do a "little" cheating on a class paper), so hit men have ways of neutralizing what they do. They, after all, just like us, have to live with themselves.

Thinking Critically

As you read this selection, ask yourself:

1. Under what conditions could I become a hit man or a hit woman?

2. How do hit men neutralize their murders?

3. How do you use neutralization techniques to neutralize your own deviances?

*O*ur knowledge about deviance management is based primarily on behavior that is easily mitigated. The literature dwells on unwed fathers (Pfuhl, 1978), and childless mothers (Veevers, 1975), pilfering bread salesmen (Ditton, 1977), and conniving shoe salesmen (Freidman, 1974), bridge pros (Holtz, 1975), and poker pros

(Hayano, 1977), marijuana smokers (Langer, 1976), massage parlor prostitutes (Verlarde, 1975), and other minor offenders (see, for example, Berk, 1977; Farrell and Nelson, 1976; Gross, 1977). There is a dearth of deviance management articles on serious offenders, and no scholarly articles at all about one of the (legally) most serious offenders of all, the professional murderer. Drift may be possible for the minor offender exploiting society's *ambivalence* toward his relatively unserious behavior (Sykes and Matza, 1957). However, excuses for the more inexcusable forms of deviant behavior are, by definition, less easily come by, and the very serious offender may enter his career with few of the usual defenses.

This article will focus on ways that one type of serious offender, the professional hit man, neutralizes stigma in the early stages of his career. As we shall see, the social organization of the "profession" provides "neutralizers" which distance its members from the shameful aspects of their careers. But for the novice, without professional insulation, the problem is more acute. With very little outside help, he must negate his feelings, neutralize them, and adopt a "framework" (Goffman, 1974) appropriate to his chosen career. This process, called "reframing," is the main focus of the present article. Cognitively, the novice must *reframe his experience* in order to enter his profession.

▪ ▪ ▪ THE SOCIAL ORGANIZATION OF MURDER

Murder, the unlawful killing of a person, is considered a serious criminal offense in the United States, and it is punished by extreme penalties. In addition, most Americans do not feel that the penalties are extreme enough (Reid, 1976:482). In overcoming the intense stigma associated with murder, the hit man lacks the supports available to more ordinary types of killers.

Some cultures allow special circumstances or sanction special organizations wherein people who kill are insulated from the taint of murder. Soldiers at war, or police in the line of duty, or citizens protecting their property operate under what are considered justifiable or excusable conditions. They receive so much informal support from the general public and from members of their own group that it may protect even a sadistic member from blame (Westley, 1966).

Subcultures (Wolfgang and Ferracuti, 1967), organizations (Maas, 1968), and gangs (Yablonsky, 1962) that unlawfully promote killing can at least provide their members with an "appeal to higher loyalties" (Sykes and Matza, 1957), if not a fully developed set of deviance justifying norms.

Individuals acting on their own, who kill in a spontaneous "irrational" outburst of violence can also mitigate the stigma of their behavior.

> I mean, people will go ape for one minute and shoot, but there are very few people who are capable of thinking about, planning, and then doing it [Joey, 1974:56].

Individuals who kill in a hot-blooded burst of passion can retrospectively draw comfort from the law which provides a lighter ban against killings performed without premeditation or malice or intent (Lester and Lester, 1975:35). At one extreme, the spontaneous killing may seem the result of a mental disease (Lester and Lester, 1975:39) or dissociative reaction (Tanay, 1972), and excused entirely as insanity.

But when an individual who generally shares society's ban against murder, is fully aware that his act of homicide is (1) unlawful, (2) self-serving, and (3) intentional, he does not have the usual defenses to fall back on. How does such an individual manage *to overcome his inhibitions and avoid serious damage to his self-image* (assuming that he does share society's ban)? This is the special dilemma of the professional hit man who hires himself out for murder.

■ ■ ■ **RESEARCH METHODS**

Information for this article comes primarily from a series of intensive interviews with one self-styled "hit man." The interviews were spread over seven, tape-recorded sessions during a four-month period. The respondent was one of fifty prison inmates randomly sampled from a population of people convicted of murder in Metropolitan Detroit. The respondent told about an "accidental" killing, involving a drunken bar patron who badgered the respondent and finally forced his hand by pulling a knife on him. In court he claimed self-defense, but the witnesses at the bar claimed otherwise, so they sent him to prison. During the first two interview sessions, the respondent acted progressively ashamed of this particular killing, not on moral ground, but because of its "sloppiness" or "amateurishness." Finally, he indicated there was more he would like to say. So, I stopped the tape recorder. I asked him if he was a hit man. He said he was.

He had already been given certain guarantees, including no names in the interview, a private conference room, and a signed contract promising his anonymity. Now, as a further guarantee, we agreed to talk about him in the third person, as a fictitious character named "Pete," so that none of his statements would sound like a personal confession. With these assurances, future interviews were devoted to his career as a professional murderer, with particular emphasis on his entry into the career and his orientation toward his victims.

Was he reliable? Since we did not use names, I had no way of checking the veracity of the individual cases he reported. Nevertheless, I was able to compare his account of the hit man's career with information from other convicted murderers, with police experts, and with accounts from the available literature (Gage, 1972; Joey, 1974; Maas, 1968). Pete's information was generally supported by these other sources. As to his motive for submitting to the interview, it is hard to gauge. He apparently was ashamed of the one "accidental" killing that had landed him in prison, and he desired to set the record straight concerning what he deemed an illustrious career, now that he had arrived, as he said, at the end of it. Hit men pride themselves on not "falling" (going to jail) for murder, and Pete's incarceration hastened a decision to retire—that he had already been contemplating, anyway.

A question might arise about the ethics of researching self-confessed "hit men" and granting them anonymity. Legally, since Pete never mentioned specific names or specific dates or possible future crimes, there does not seem to be a problem. Morally, if confidentiality is a necessary condition to obtaining information about serious offenders, then we have to ask: Is it worth it? Pete insisted that he had retired from the profession. Therefore, there seems to be no "clear and imminent danger" that would justify the violation of confidentiality, in the terms set forth by the American Psychological Association (1978:40). On the other hand, the *possibility* of danger does exist, and future researchers will have to exercise their judgment.

Finally, hit men are hard to come by. Unlike more lawful killers, such as judges or night watchmen, and unlike run-of-the-mill murderers, the hit man (usually) takes infinite care to conceal his identity. Therefore, while it is regrettable that this paper has only one case to report on, and while it would be ideal to perform a comparative analysis on a number of hit men, it would be very difficult to obtain such a sample. Instead, Pete's responses will be compared to similar accounts from the available literature. While such a method can never produce verified findings, it can point to suggestive hypotheses.

■ ■ ■ THE SOCIAL ORGANIZATION OF PROFESSIONAL MURDER

There are two types of professional murderers: the organized and the independent. The killer who belongs to an organized syndicate does not usually get paid on a contract basis, and performs his job out of loyalty and obedience to the organization (Maas, 1968:81). The independent professional killer is a freelance agent who hires himself out for a fee (Pete). It is the career organization of the second type of killer that will be discussed.

The organized killer can mitigate his behavior through an "appeal to higher loyalties" (Sykes and Matza, 1957). He also can view his victim as an enemy of the group and then choose from a variety of techniques available for neutralizing an offense against an enemy (see, for example, Hirschi, 1969; Rogers and Buffalo, 1974). But the independent professional murderer lacks most of these defenses. Nevertheless, built into his role are certain structural features that help him avoid deviance ascription. These features include:

(1) *Contract.* A contract is an unwritten agreement to provide a sum of money to a second party who agrees, in return, to commit a designated murder (Joey, 1974:9). It is most often arranged over the phone, between people who have never had personal contact. And the victim, or "hit," is usually unknown to the killer (Gage, 1972:57; Joey, 1974:61–62). This arrangement is meant to protect both parties from the law. But it also helps the killer "deny the victim" (Sykes and Matza, 1957) by keeping him relatively anonymous.

In arranging the contract, the hired killer will try to find out the difficulty of the hit and how much the customer wants the killing done. According to Pete, these considerations determine his price. He does not ask about the motive for the killing, treating it as none of his concern. Not knowing the motive may hamper the killer from morally justifying his behavior, but it also enables him to further deny the victim by maintaining his distance and reserve. Finally, the contract is backed up by a further understanding.

> Like this guy who left here (prison) last summer, he was out two months before he got killed. Made a mistake somewhere. The way I heard it, he didn't finish filling a contract [Pete].

If the killer fails to live up to his part of the bargain, the penalties could be extreme (Gage, 1972:53; Joey, 1974:9). This has the ironic effect that after the contract is arranged, the killer can somewhat "deny responsibility" (Sykes and Matza, 1957), by pleading self-defense.

(2) *Reputation and Money.* Reputation is especially important in an area where killers are unknown to their customers, and where the less written, the better (Joey, 1974:58). Reputation, in turn, reflects how much money the hit man has commanded in the past,

> And that was the first time that I ever got 30 grand . . . it's based on his reputation. . . . Yeah, how good he really is. To be so-so, you get so-so money. If you're good, you get good money [Pete].

Pete, who could not recall the exact number of people he had killed, did, like other hit men, keep an accounting of his highest fees (Joey, 1974:58, 62). To him big money meant not only a way to earn a living, but also a way to maintain his professional reputation.

People who accept low fees can also find work as hired killers. Heroin addicts are the usual example. But, as Pete says, they often receive a bullet for their pains. It is believed that people who would kill for so little would also require little persuasion to make them talk to the police (Joey, 1974:63). This further reinforces the single-minded emphasis on making big money. As a result, killing is conceptualized as a "business" or as "just a job." Framing the hit in a normal businesslike context enables the hit man to deny wrongfulness, or "deny injury" (Sykes and Matza, 1957).

In addition to the economic motive, Pete and hit men discussed by other authors, refer to excitement, fun, game-playing, power, and impressing women as incentives for murder (Joey, 1974:81–82). However, none of these motives are mentioned by all sources. None are as necessary to the career as money. And, after a while, these other motives diminish and killing becomes only "just a job" (Joey, 1974:20). The primacy of the economic motive has been aptly expressed in the case of another deviant profession.

> Women who enjoy sex with their customers do not make good prostitutes, according to those who are acquainted with this institution first hand. Instead of thinking about the most effective way of making money at the job, they would be doing things for their own pleasure and enjoyment [Goode, 1974:342].

(3) *Skill.* Most of the hit man's training focuses on acquiring skill in the use of weapons.

> Then, he met these two guys, these two white guys . . . them two, them two was the best. And but they stayed around over there and they got together, and Pete told [them] that he really wanted to be good. He said, if [I] got to do something, I want to be good at it. So, they got together, showed him, showed him *how to shoot.* . . . And gradually, he became good. . . . Like he told me, like when he shoots somebody, he always goes for the head; he said, that's about the best shot. I mean, if you want him dead then and there. . . . And these two guys showed him, and to him, I mean, hey, I mean, he don't believe nobody could really outshoot these two guys, you know what I mean. *They know everything you want to know about guns, knives, and stuff like that* [Pete].

The hit man's reputation, and the amount of money he makes depends on his skill, his effective ability to serve as a means to someone else's ends. The result is a focus on technique.

> Like in anything you do, when you do it, you want to do it just right. . . . On your target and you hit it, how you feel: I hit it! I hit it! [Pete].

This focus on technique, on means, helps the hit man to "deny responsibility" and intent (Sykes and Matza, 1957). In frame-analytic terms, the hit man separates his morally responsible, or "principal" self from the rest of himself, and performs the killing mainly as a "strategist" (Goffman, 1974:523). In other words, he sees himself as a "hired gun." The saying, "If I didn't do it, they'd find someone else who would," reflects this narrowly technical orientation.

To sum up thus far, the contract, based as it is on the hit man's reputation for profit and skill, provides the hit man with opportunities for denying the victim, denying injury, and denying responsibility. But this is not enough. To point out the defenses of the professional hit man is one thing, but it is unlikely that the *novice* hit man would have a totally professional attitude so early in his career. The novice is at a point where he both lacks the conventional defense against the stigma of murder, *and* he has not yet fully acquired the exceptional defenses of the professional. How, then, does he cope?

■ ■ ■ THE FIRST TIME: NEGATIVE EXPERIENCE

Goffman defines "negative experience" as a feeling of disorientation.

> Expecting to take up a position in a well-framed realm, he finds that no particular frame is immediately applicable, or the frame that he thought was applicable no longer seems to be, or he cannot bind himself within the frame that does apparently apply. He loses command over the formulation of viable response. He flounders. Experience, the meld of what the current scene brings to him and what be brings to it—meant to settle into a form even while it is beginning, finds no form and is therefore no experience. Reality anomically flutters. He has a "negative experience"—negative in the sense that it takes its character from what it is not, and what it is not is an organized and organizationally affirmed response [1974:378–379].

Negative experience can occur when a person finds himself lapsing into an old understanding of the situation, only to suddenly awaken to the fact that it no longer applies. In this regard, we should expect negative experience to be a special problem for the novice. For example, the first time he killed a man for money, Pete supposedly became violently ill:

> When he [Pete], you know, hit the guy, when he shot the guy, the guy said, "You killed me"... something like that, cause he struck him all up here. And what he said, it was just, I mean, *the look right in the guy's eye,* you know. I mean he looked like: *why me?* Yeah? And he [Pete] couldn't shake that. Cause he remembered a time or two when he got cut, and all he wanted to do was get back and cut this guy that cut him. And this here.... No, he just could not shake it. And then he said that at night-time he'll start thinking about the guy: like he shouldn't have looked at him like that.... I mean actually [Pete] was sick.... He couldn't keep his food down, I mean, or nothing like that.... [It lasted] I'd say about two months.... Like he said that he had feelings ... that he never did kill nobody before [Pete].

Pete's account conforms to the definition of negative experience. He had never killed anyone for money before. It started when a member of the Detroit drug world had spotted Pete in a knife fight outside an inner city bar, was apparently impressed with the young man's style, and offered him fifty dollars to do a "job." Pete accepted. He wanted the money. But when the first hit came about, Pete of course knew that he was doing it for money, but yet his orientation was revenge. Thus, he stared his victim in the *face,* a characteristic gesture of people who kill enemies for revenge (Levi, 1975:190). Expecting to see defiance turn into a look of defeat, they attempt to gain "face" at the loser's expense.

But when Pete stared his victim in the face, he saw not an enemy, but an innocent man. He saw a look of: "Why me?" And this *discordant* image is what remained in his mind during the weeks and months to follow and made him sick. As Pete says, "He shouldn't have looked at him like that." The victim's look of innocence brought about what Goffman (1974:347) refers to as a "frame break":

> Given that the frame applied to an activity is expected to enable us to come to terms with all events in that activity (informing and regulating many of them), it is understandable that the unmanageable might occur, an occurrence which cannot be effectively ignored and to which the frame cannot be applied, with resulting bewilderment and chagrin on the part of the participants. In brief, a break can occur in the applicability of the frame, a break in its governance.

When such a frame break occurs, it produces negative experience. Pete's extremely uncomfortable disorientation may reflect the extreme dissonance between the revenge frame, that he expected to apply, and the unexpected look of innocence that he encountered and continued to recall.

■ ■ ■ SUBSEQUENT TIME: REFRAMING THE HIT

According to Goffman (1974:319), a structural feature of frames of experience is that they are divided into different "tracks" or types of information. These include, "a main track or story line and ancillary tracks of various kinds." The ancillary tracks are the directional track, the overlay track, the concealment tracks, and the disattend track. The disattend track contains the information that is perceived but supposed to be *ignored*. For example, the prostitute manages the distasteful necessity of having sex with "tricks" by remaining "absolutely . . . detached. Removed. Miles and miles away" (1974:344). The existence of different tracks allows an individual to define and redefine his experience by the strategic placement of information.

Sometimes, the individual receives outside help. For example, when Milgram in 1963 placed a barrier between people administering electric shocks, and the bogus "subjects" who were supposedly receiving the shocks, he made it easier for the shockers to "disattend" signs of human distress from their hapless victims. Surgeons provide another example. Having their patients completely covered, except for the part to be operated on, helps them work in a more impersonal manner. In both examples, certain crucial information is stored away in the "concealment track" (Goffman, 1974:218).

In other cases help can come from guides who direct the novice on what to experience and what to block out. Beginning marijuana smokers are cautioned to ignore feelings of nausea (Becker, 1953:240). On the other hand, novice hit men like Pete are reluctant to share their "experience" with anyone else. It would be a sign of weakness.

In still other cases, however, it is possible that the subject can do the reframing *on his own*. And this is what appears to have happened to Pete.

> And when the second one [the second hit] came up, [Pete] was still thinking about the first one. . . . Yeah, when he got ready to go, he was thinking about it. *Something changed. I don't know how to put it right.* Up to the moment that he killed the second guy now, he waited, you know. Going through his mind was the first guy he killed. He still seeing him, still see *the expression on his face.* Soon, the second guy walked up; I mean, it was like his mind just *blanked out* for a minute, everything just blanked out. . . . Next thing he know, he had killed the second guy. . . . *He knew what he was doing, but* what I mean, he just didn't have nothing on his mind. Everything was wiped out [Pete].

When the second victim approached, Pete says that he noticed the victim's approach, he was aware of the man's presence. But he noticed none of the victim's personal features. He did not see the victim's face or its expression. Thus, he did not see the very thing that gave him so much trouble the first time. It is as if Pete had *negatively conditioned* himself to avoid certain cues. Since he shot the victim in the head, it is probable that Pete saw him in one sense; this is not the same kind of experience as a "dissociative reaction," which has been likened to sleepwalking (Tanay, 1972). Pete says that, "he knew what he was doing." But he either did not pay attention to his victim's personal features at the time of the killing, or he blocked them out immediately afterward, so that now the only aspect of his victim he recalls is the victim's approach (if we are to believe him).

After that, Pete says that killing became *routine*. He learned to view his victims as "targets," rather than as people. Thus, he believes that the second experience is the crucial one, and that the disattendance of the victim's personal features made it so.

Support from other accounts of hit men is scant, due to a lack of data. Furthermore, not everything in Pete's account supports the "reframing" hypothesis. In talking about later killings, it is clear that he not only attends to his victims' personal features, on occasion, but he also derives a certain grim pleasure in doing so.

> [the victim was] a nice looking woman. . . . She started weeping, and [she cried], "I ain't did this, I ain't did that . . . and [Pete] said that he shot her. Like it wasn't nothing . . . he didn't feel nothing. It was just money [Pete].

In a parallel story, Joey, the narrator of the *Killer,* also observes his victim in personal terms.

> [The victim] began to beg. He even went so far as to tell us where he had stashed his money. Finally, he realized there was absolutely nothing he could do. He sat there quietly. Then, he started crying. I didn't feel a thing for him [1974:56].

It may be that this evidence contradicts what I have said about reframing; but perhaps another interpretation is possible. Reframing may play a more crucial role in the original redefinition of an experience than in the continued maintenance of that redefinition. Once Pete has accustomed himself to viewing his victims as merely targets, as "just money," then it may be less threatening to look upon them as persons, once again. Once the "main story line" has been established, discordant information can be presented in the "overlay track" (Goffman, 1974:215), without doing too much damage. Indeed, this seems to be the point that both hit men are trying to make in the above excerpts.

■ ■ ■ THE HEART OF THE HIT MAN

For what I have been referring to as "disattendance" Pete used the term "heart," which he defined as a "coldness." When asked what he would look for in an aspiring hit man, Peter replied,

> See if he's got a whole lot of heart . . . you got to be cold . . . you got to build a coldness in yourself. It's not something that comes automatically. Cause, see, I don't care who he is, first, you've got feelings [Pete].

In contrast to this view, Joey (1974:56) said,

> There are three things you need to kill a man: the gun, the bullets, and the balls. A lot of people will point a gun at you, but they haven't got the courage to pull the trigger. It's as simple as that.

It may be that some are born with "heart," while others acquire it in the way I have described.

However, the "made rather than born" thesis does explain one perplexing feature of hit men and other "evil" men whose banality has sometimes seemed discordant. In other aspects of their lives they all seem perfectly capable of feeling ordinary human emotions. Their inhumanity, their coldness, seems narrowly restricted to their jobs. Pete, for example, talked about his "love" for little children. Eddie "The Hawk" Ruppolo meekly allowed his mistress to openly insult him in a public bar (Gage, 1972). And Joey (1974:55) has this to say about himself:

> Believe it or not, I'm a human being. I laugh at funny jokes. I love children around the house, and I can spend hours playing with my mutt.

All of these examples of human warmth indicate that the cold heart of the hit man may be less a characteristic of the killer's individual personality, than a feature of the professional framework of experience which the hit man has learned to adapt himself to, when he is on the job.

■ ■ ■ DISCUSSION

This article is meant as a contribution to the study of deviance neutralization. The freelance hit man is an example of an individual who, relatively alone, must deal with a profound and unambiguous stigma in order to enter his career. Both Pete and Joey emphasize "heart" as a determining factor in becoming a professional. And Pete's experience, after the first hit, further indicates that the inhibitions against murder-for-money are real.

In this article "heart"—or the ability to adapt to a rationalized framework for killing—has been portrayed as the outcome of an initial process of reframing, in addition to other neutralization techniques established during the further stages of professionalization. As several theorists (see, for example, Becker, 1953; Douglas et al., 1977; Matza, 1969) have noted, people often enter into deviant acts first, and then develop rationales for their behavior later on. This was also the case with Pete, who began his career by first, (1) "being willing" (Matza, 1969), (2) encountering a frame break, (3) undergoing negative experience, (4) being willing to try again (also known as "getting back on the horse"), (5) reframing the experience, and (6) having future, routine experiences wherein his professionalization increasingly enabled him to "deny the victim," "deny injury," and "deny responsibility." Through the process of reframing, the experience of victim-as-target emerged as the "main story line," and the experience of victim-as-person was downgraded from the main track to the disattend track to the overlay track. Ironically, the intensity of the negative experience seemed to make the process all the more successful. Thus, it may be possible for a person with "ordinary human feelings" to both pass through the novice stage, and to continue "normal relations" thereafter. The reframing hypothesis has implications for other people who knowingly perform stigmatized behaviors. It may be particularly useful in explaining a personal conversion experience that occurs despite the relative absence of deviant peer groups, deviant norms, extenuating circumstances, and neutralization rationales.

▪ ▪ ▪ REFERENCES

American Psychological Association (1978) Directory of the American Psychological Association, Washington, DC: Author.

Becker, H. (1953) "Becoming a marijuana user." Amer. J. of Sociology 59: 235–243.

Berk, B. (1977) "Face-saving at the singles dance." Social Problems 24, 5: 530–544.

Ditton, J. (1977) "Alibis and aliases: some notes on motives of fiddling bread salesmen." Sociology 11, 2: 233–255.

Douglas, J., P. Rasmussen, and C. Flanagan (1977) The Nude Beach. Beverly Hills: Sage.

Farrell, R. and J. Nelson (1976) "A causal model of secondary deviance; the case of homosexuality," Soc. Q 17: 109–120.

Friedman, N. L. (1974) "Cookies and contests: notes on ordinary occupational deviance and its neutralization." Soc. Symposium (Spring): 1–9.

Gage, N. (1972) Mafia, U.S.A. New York: Dell.

Goffman, E. (1974) Frame Analysis. Cambridge, MA: Harvard Univ. Press.

Goode, E. (1978) Deviant Behavior: An Interactionist Approach. Englewood Cliffs, NJ: Prentice-Hall.

Gross, H. (1977) "Micro and macro level implications for a sociology of virtue—case of draft protesters to Vietnam War." Soc. Q. 18, 3: 319–339.

Hayano, D. (1977) "The professional poker player: career identification and the problem of respectability." Social Problems 24 (June): 556–564.

Hirschi, T. (1969) Causes of Delinquency. Berkeley: Univ. of California Press.

Holtz, J. (1975) "The professional duplicate bridge player: conflict management in a free, legal, quasi-deviant occupation." Urban Life 4, 2: 131–160.

Joey (1974) Killer: Autobiography of a Mafia Hit Man. New York: Pocket Books.

Langer, J. (1976) "Drug entrepreneurs and the dealing culture." Australian and New Zealand J. of Sociology 12. 2: 82–90.

Lester, D. and G. Lester (1975) Crime of Passion: Murder and the Murderer. Chicago: Nelson-Hall.

Levi, K. (1975) Icemen. Ann Arbor, MI: University Microfilms.

Maas, P. (1968) The Valachi Papers. New York: G. P. Putnam.

Matza, D. (1969) Becoming Deviant. Englewood Cliffs, NJ: Prentice-Hall.

Pfuhl, E. (1978) "The unwed father: a non-deviant rule breaker." Soc. Q. 19: 113–128.

Reid, S. (1976) Crime and Criminology. Hinsdale, IL: Dryden Press.

Rogers, J. and M. Buffalo (1974) "Neutralization techniques: toward a simplified measurement scale." Pacific Soc. Rev. 17, 3: 313.

Sykes, G. and D. Matza (1957) "Techniques of neutralization: a theory of delinquency." Amer. Soc. Rev. 22: 664–670.

Tanay, E. (1972) "Psychiatric aspects of homicide prevention." Amer. J. of Psychology 128: 814–817.

Veevers, J. (1975) "The moral careers of voluntarily childless wives: notes on the defense of a variant world view." Family Coordinator 24, 4: 473–487.

Verlarde, A. (1975) "Becoming prostituted: the decline of the massage parlor profession and the masseuse." British J. of Criminology 15, 3: 251–263.

Westley, W. (1966) "The escalation of violence through legitimation." Annals of the American Association of Political and Social Science 364 (March) 120–126.

Wolfgang, M. and F. Ferracuti (1967) The Subculture of Violence. London: Tavistock.

Yablosnky, L. (1962) The Violent Gang. New York: Macmillan.

III Social Inequality

It is impossible to have a society of equals. Despite laudable desires to build an egalitarian society, every society will have inequality. Always there will be what sociologists call *social stratification*. Why?

Each social group has a value system. That is, it values certain things above others. In a tribal group, this could be running, shooting arrows, throwing spears, or showing bravery in the face of danger. Some members of the tribe will have greater abilities or exert greater effort to do the particular things that their group values—no matter what those things may be. Their abilities and accomplishments will mark them as distinctive. These people will be looked up to, and they will likely be treated differently.

By considering abilities and accomplishments, as in a tribal group, we can see why social distinctions are inevitable. Social stratification, however, is based on much more than ability and accomplishment. In fact, ability and achievement are seldom the bases of social stratification. Much more common are inherited factors.

Every society stratifies its members according to the particular values and characteristics it cherishes. That is, every human group divides its people into layers, treating each layer differently. Once a society is stratified, birth ushers children into different positions. By virtue of where their parents are located in this structure, children inherit some of the social distinctions of their parents. These can be their religion (Christian, Jew, Muslim), social class (upper, middle, lower), caste (Brahmin, Shudra, Dalit), or any other distinction that their group makes.

Because their group has already set up the rules, children also inherit *statuses* (positions) based on their birth. With these come wide-ranging expectations of behaviors and attitudes. The behaviors, attitudes, and other orientations associated with sex are called *gender*. In some human groups, such distinctions and statuses also apply to race–ethnicity. In addition, the globalization of capitalism, resulting in our current geopolitical arrangements, ushers children onto a world stage. At birth, they inherit their country's position in *global stratification*. Their nation may be rich and powerful or poor and weak, or somewhere in between. A nation's location on this world continuum of power and wealth also has fundamental consequences for people's lives.

In this part of the book, we look at some of the major aspects of social inequality. We begin with the broad view of global stratification. William

Adler's opening article makes it evident that where your nation is located in the global scheme of things makes a fundamental difference for what happens to you in life. Herbert Gans follows with a provocative analysis of poverty. Using a functionalist perspective, he suggests that poverty is inevitable because poor people perform valuable services for society. In his report on the social inequality of race, Lawrence Graham, a lawyer-turned-bus-boy, gives us a fascinating account of his experiences at an exclusive country club. With Robert Edgerton's controversial suggestion that some societies may be "sick," we close this part with a focus on the social inequality of gender.

Job on the Line

William M. Adler

introduction ▪ ▪ ▪ ▪ ▪

One of history's most significant changes is the *globalization of capitalism*. Because capitalism is based on competition and the pursuit of profits, capitalists are constantly trying to lower their production costs and find ways to expand their markets. The globalization of capitalism is helping them reach both of these goals. Not only do the workers in the Least Industrialized Nations work cheaply, but also, as their incomes increase, they become consumers. By lowering the costs of the goods we buy, this process increases our own standard of living. Almost all of us, for example, buy clothing produced in the Least Industrialized Nations, spending only a fraction of what such clothing would have cost years ago.

One of the downsides of the globalization of capitalism is *downsizing*, a fancy way of saying that a company is firing workers. In their frenetic pursuit of profits, U.S. firms, followed more reluctantly by the Europeans and the Japanese, have laid off millions of workers. Awaiting their jobs are deprived people in the Least Industrialized Nations, who eagerly take any crumbs offered by the Most Industrialized Nations. This situation is a capitalist's dream—docile workers who are willing to accept peanuts for wages, and glad to get them.

We don't have to go to Thailand or Indonesia to follow this process. We have an example much closer to home. Just south of the U.S. border are countries where millions of unemployed men and women are eager to take any kind of work, and to work for almost any wages in any conditions. Adler compares the experiences of two workers to explore implications of this aspect of the globalization of capitalism.

Thinking Critically

As you read this selection, ask yourself:

1. Is the employment of young workers in U.S. factories that have been relocated to Mexico an example of exploitation by capitalists or opportunity for the workers?

2. Besides a paycheck that doesn't bounce, what do you think employers owe workers?

3. What solutions do you see to the problems described in this selection?

At 3 o'clock on a warm June afternoon, the second of two wash-up bells rings for the final time. Mollie James stands hunched over the sink as she rinses her hands with industrial soap alongside her co-workers. She first came to work here, on the assembly line at Universal Manufacturing Company in Paterson, New Jersey, a few years after the factory opened in 1951. She was the first woman at the factory to run a stamping machine, the first to laminate steel. She was among the first female union stewards and among the first African American stewards; hers was a self-assured presence any grievant would want on their side. And now, after 34 years on the line—nearly two-thirds of her life—she is the last to go.

At the end of every other shift for more than three decades, Mollie and her fellow employees beat a quick path to the plant parking lot. On this day there is less sense of hurry. There are still children to feed, clothes to wash, bills to pay, errands to run, other jobs to race to. But as she and the others leave the washroom, no one seems pressed to leave. All about the plant entrance, and out in the lot, people stand in small clusters, like mourners at their own wake, talking, laughing, hugging, crying. Almost always Mollie James is outgoing and outspoken, her voice loud and assertive, her smile nicely lighted. At 59 she is a strong woman, her strength forged from a life of hard work and sacrifice, and faith in God. She is not one to betray her emotions, but this day is different. Her bearing has turned to reserve, her normally quick eyes dull and watery. Her working life is over, and that is the only life she has ever known.

Universal had always turned a tidy profit. Its signature product, ballasts that regulate the current in fluorescent lights, attracted attention only when the ballast failed—causing the light fixture to hum or flicker. In the mid-1980s, however, the locally owned company was twice swept up in the gale of winds of Wall Street's merger mania. Twice within eight months Universal was sold, both times to firms headed by disciples of Michael Milken, the Street's reigning evil genius. Not long after the second sale, to a Los Angeles-based electrical components conglomerate called MagneTek, Inc., movers began pulling up the plant's massive machinery, much of which had been bolted to the floor when the factory opened.

Mollie had sensed what was happening in January 1989, the morning she came to work and noticed a hole in the floor. It wasn't a hole, really, in the sense an opening; it was more of a void: a great yawning space of discolored concrete where just the afternoon before had sat a steel-stamping machine, a hulking piece of American industrial might. Before long, more holes appeared, each tracing the outline of the base of another machine, like chalk around a sidewalk corpse.

Now, on the last day, when there is no one left to say goodbye to, Mollie slumps behind the wheel of her rusting 1977 Dodge Charger and follows the procession out of the lot. It is not far, three miles or so from the plant in Paterson's industrial Bunker Hill neighborhood to the three-story, three-family house she owns on the near East Side. Upon pulling into her customary space in the driveway, Mollie sits in the car a good long while, letting the heat of the summer afternoon settle her. By the time she fits the key into the back-door lock and begins climbing the three flights of stairs to her bedroom, she has stopped crying.

The machine that Mollie used to stamp steel for three decades makes its way south, past factories that Universal opened in Mississippi and Arkansas during the 1960s and 1970s to take advantage of cheaper labor and taxes, before arriving in Matamoros, Mexico, a booming border city just across the Rio Grande from Browns-ville, Texas. On a blindingly blue morning, MagneTek executives from "corporate" in L.A. arrive for the gala ribbon cutting of the first MagneTek plant here. Plant man-ager Chuck Peeples, an affable Arkansas expatriate, leads the officials on a tour of the gleaming factory. Outfitted in natty going-native panama hats emblazoned with the company's royal-blue capital-M "power" logo, the MagneTek honchos parade past equipment ripped from the shopworn floor in Paterson, machinery now oper-ated by a young, almost entirely female workforce. These women, primarily in their teens and 20s, have come north to Matamoros in search of work and a better future than the bleakness promised in the jobless farming towns of the interior.

Balbina Duque Granados found a job at MagneTek in 1993, after leaving her family's home in a picturesque but poor mountain village of central Mexico. Just out of her teens, she has an easy, dimpled smile and long black hair worn in a ponytail. With its comparatively low wages, endless supply of labor, lack of regulation, and proximity to the United States, Matamoros is a magnet for *ma-quiladoras,* the foreign-owned assembly plants that wed First World engineering with Third World working conditions. Balbina's probationary pay is slightly less than $26 a week, or about 65 cents an hour. It is difficult work, winding coils, repetitive and tiring and mind numbing, but it is a job she is thrilled to have—her "answered prayer." And although Balbina doesn't know it, it is not just any job. It is Mollie's job. . . .

At a few minutes before 2 o'clock on a cold, pitch-black morning in November 1950, Mollie and her father, Lorenzo Brown, waited anxiously on the platform of the or-nate World War I–era train station in Richmond, Virginia. The Browns were from Cartersville, 45 miles west, in the rolling farmland of central Virginia. Mollie was headed to Penn Station in Newark, New Jersey, to meet her fiance, Sam James, who would take her home, to Paterson, to her new life. She was dressed in her finest: a new navy-blue suit, new shoes, new hairdo. She carried nearly everything she owned in a half-dozen sky-blue suitcases her father had given her for the trip.

Mollie was traveling alone, but the "colored" train cars of the Silver Meteor, and indeed those of the other great northbound coaches—the Champion, the Florida Sunbeam, the Silver Comet—were full of Mollie Browns: black southerners crossing the Mason-Dixon Line, heading for the promised land. Mollie's intended was wait-ing at the station in his new, yellow, two-door Ford to take her to Paterson, a city of 140,000 residents some 15 miles west of New York City. Sam drove her home to the one-room apartment he rented for $20 a week above the flat where his sister and brother-in-law lived. Although the accommodations were far from luxurious— Mollie and Sam shared a kitchen and bath with other upstairs tenants—her new life seemed as bright as Sam's shiny car.

Paterson at precisely the middle of the 20th century was absolutely humming, filled with vibrant neighborhoods, a bustling downtown retail and cultural district, and above all, factories small and large, producing everything from textiles to machine tools to electrical components. "There were so many places to work, I could have five jobs in the same day," Mollie recalled years later. "And if I didn't like one, I could leave and get another, sure."

Mollie's new hometown was born of entrepreneurial dreamers and schemers. The city had been founded on the 16th anniversary of the Declaration of Independence, July 4, 1792, not as a municipality but as a business: the home of the country's first industrial corporation, the Society for Useful Manufactures. The grand plans of the society and its guiding light, Alexander Hamilton, ultimately failed, but Paterson established itself as a cradle of American industry. The city became renowned for its textile mills—silk especially—and later for the union-busting tactics of its mill owners. During the 19th century, textile manufacturers in Paterson were responsible for what were probably the nation's first runaway shops, opening "annexes" in rural Pennsylvania to take advantage of workers who could be subjected to longer hours for half the wages paid in New Jersey. In 1913, the Industrial Workers of the World mobilized Paterson's 25,000 employees to walk away from their looms, effectively nailing shut the nation's silk-manufacturing center. Able to rely on their nonunion factories, mill owners refused to negotiate; starved into submission, the strikers were forced to return to work with neither gains in wages nor improved working conditions.

By the time the 19-year-old Mollie Brown arrived in Paterson, the economy was booming. Unemployment was low, wages high. In her first few years in town, Mollie ran through several jobs. "You'd just catch the bus and go from factory to factory and see who was hiring." Among her stops was a low-slung cement building in northeast Paterson. The sign out front said UNIVERSAL MANUFACTURING CO. The owner himself, a gregarious man named Archie Sergy, showed her through the plant, explaining that the company made a part for fluorescent lights called a ballast. "They showed me how it was made, the whole assembly line. I learned there's a lot to it, a *very* lot." The starting salary was 90 cents an hour, but the company was about to implement a second shift, from 3 P.M. to midnight, that would pay an extra dime an hour. Those hours were ideal for Mollie. She and Sam had three children under the age of five and another on the way, and if she were to work nights and he days, the couple could care for the children without hiring a sitter. She accepted the job. "I hope you'll be here a long time," Sergy told her. "I hope we'll all be here a long time!"

By the early 1960s, Universal employed a workforce of some 1,200. Archie Sergy and his top managers continued to demonstrate a sincere interest in the welfare of their employees. "They never treated you as inferior, regardless of whether you cleaned the toilets or whatever your job was," Mollie says. "They'd walk up and down the line and talk to us, joke with us, sometimes have their sandwiches with us right there on the line. . . . If you needed a home loan, they'd give it to you, and you could make arrangements to pay it back."

Sergy saw the world as an industrialist, not a financier, and he maintained a steely eyed focus on quality and customer service to the degree that it probably hurt profit margins. But his company was no social service agency; it venerated the bottom line as much as any self-respecting capitalist enterprise. Mollie and her co-workers enjoyed good wages and job security in large part because they belonged to Teamsters Local 945, which bargained for higher pay and better benefits. In 1963, determined to insulate Universal from threats of work stoppage, Sergy followed the tradition established by the early Paterson silk makers: He opened an annex, a Universal factory in the Deep South. The new plant was located in rural Mississippi, providing Sergy with a low-wage workforce as well as an ever-present threat of plant closing to quiet employees in Paterson.

That same year, strapped for operating capital and lacking a successor, Sergy also succumbed to the lure of Wall Street: He sold Universal to a New York-based conglomerate. Sergy remained as titular head of Universal, but outsiders controlled the economic destiny of the women and men who toiled there. This was most evidently revealed when Sergy announced to the employees in April 1968, seven months before his death, that the parent company itself had been swallowed whole by *another* conglomerate. "We're all working for a company out of Chicago," he said. "Who they are I have no idea."

Whether those who held the purse strings were faceless financiers from New York or Chicago or Los Angeles didn't matter much to Mollie James. Owners came and went, and the principal visible sign of each transition was a new company name on the payroll checks. So when word spread in early 1986 that an outfit called MagneTek was the new owner, Mollie took the news calmly. Surely some things would change—managers in, managers out, maybe—but she had no reason to question her job security. Although the company had added a second Southern plant, in Arkansas, Paterson was still the flagship. Mollie came to work for Universal—and stayed—because of the peace of mind that came from a secure job: a job she could raise a family on, buy a house, a car, borrow money against, count on for the future.

But right away Mollie could tell the future was darkening. Like the earlier owners, MagneTek was a faraway, far-flung holding company, but the previous management's hands-off, don't fix-it-if-it-ain't-broke page was missing from its corporate manual. "It started the day our name disappeared from the building," she says. "Poof, no more Universal."

By the end of 1988, not only had Universal's name vanished from the plant; its machines, too, were disappearing, torn from the floor like trees from their roots. "The movers came at night, like thieves, sometimes just taking one piece at a time," Mollie recalls. "We'd come in in the mornings and there'd be another hole in the floor."

The machinery had been used to make a large specialty ballast known as the HID, or High Intensity Discharge, the kind used in thousand-watt fixtures installed in outdoor stadiums. Paterson was the lone Universal plant manufacturing the HID; making its precision-wound coils required different training and equipment than the garden-variety 40-watt fluorescent ballast the two Southern plants pumped out by the tens of thousands daily.

If Paterson's workers were more sophisticated, they were also more costly; Mollie earned $7.91 an hour, 75 cents more than she would have earned in Mississippi and almost a dollar more than in Arkansas. But if the wages down South were low, they were not low enough. They were not the cheapest possible wages. They weren't as low as workers earned in Mexico, where the prevailing pay at the maquiladoras was less than $8 a day. And so, in the early months of 1988, the machines began disappearing, bound ultimately for Matamoros. "All we kept hearing was how good a job we were doing." Mollie says, "that we had nothing to worry about, that we'd always have work in Paterson."

The nightly bus to Matamoros would not roll through the depot nearest Balbina Duque's village until 9:15. It was only mid-morning, just a couple of hours since she'd said her goodbyes to the family, since she'd pressed her lips for the last time to her baby son's cheek and handed him to her mother. It was only mid-morning, and already Balbina could feel the tropical sun on her face, could feel her funds dwindling fast. She had started with 200 pesos, the equivalent of about $65, and now that she'd paid a man nearly $20 to taxi her the hour from Monte Bello, her mountain village—a place of clean and clear air, brilliant high-desert flowers, and almost surrealistically bright light—to the bus station in town, and now that she'd bought a couple of tamales from a sidewalk vendor and a one-way ticket to the border for $30, Balbina was down to less than $15.

Balbina had turned 20 only weeks earlier. She was leaving for Matamoros, 400 miles north, to look for work in the maquiladoras. She was torn about going, especially about having to leave behind her 18-month-old son, Iban. "If there were work here," Balbina said in Spanish during a visit home some years later, "everyone would stay."

There was nothing to keep them at home. Balbina's village comprised maybe 1,000 people living in a couple of hundred pastel-colored homes with thatched roofs. There was neither running water nor electricity. Much of Balbina's day was spent filling and refilling a water bucket from a central well down a hill and carrying it back on her head to use for bathing, laundry, washing dishes, cooking, and drinking. A typical day might require 24 trips to the well, a chore that claimed three to four hours beginning at first light.

The interminable, grueling days were not for Balbina. Monte Bello felt like a sentence from which she needed to escape. It was a place for "people too old to work or too young to work," she said. "For me there was nothing. If you do not work in the fields there is nothing else to do." She decided she would celebrate her 20th birthday with her family, and then, as soon as she had saved enough for the bus fare, would take off for the border, where the maquiladoras favor young women for their nimble fingers and compliant minds, and where a job in a *maquila* trumps any other employment options.

It was dark when Balbina finally boarded the bus. Heading north, through a vast valley of corn, Highway 85 was flat as a tortilla. With two seats to herself, Balbina was able to curl into a comfortable enough position, and sleep came at once. When the bus pulled into Matamoros at dawn, she had to rouse herself from a dream about her son. Meeting her at the central station on Canales Avenue was a distant aunt, who escorted her to a small dwelling in the liltingly named *Colonia Vista Hermosa*—Beautiful View. But there was little beauty in the *colonia;* it was wedged between a pungent, milky-white irrigation canal and the Finsa park, the massive industrial park where MagneTek and other foreign-owned maquiladoras employed most of the working-age residents of Vista Hermosa.

One morning, the second Friday of 1993, Balbina and her younger sister, Elsa, caught a ride downtown to the headquarters of the big maquiladora workers' union, the SJOI—the Spanish acronym for the Union of Industrial Workers and Day Laborers. Four times weekly, waves of several thousand applicants washed up at dawn at the SJOI offices, the de facto employment agency for the maquilas. All nonsalaried workers applied through its central hiring hall, women on Mondays and Fridays, men on Tuesdays and Thursdays.

It was not yet 7 o'clock, and Balbina and Elsa had already been in line for an hour, a line that snaked through the three-story building, past the armed guard at the door, and stretched outside for more than a block. By eight, they had squeezed and elbowed and prodded their way inside the assembly hall, a room roughly the size and ambience of a drafty old high-school gymnasium. Mounted fans whirred overhead, efficiently distributing the rank air and grime into all corners.

At 8:30, with no conspicuous signal that the cattle call was on the verge of starting, there was a near stampede toward the makeshift elevated stage at the front quadrant of the room. The entire room seemed like an aquarium, one rear corner of which had suddenly been tipped, causing its entire contents to flow into its diagonal. For the next few hours, Balbina, Elsa, and 1,600 other hopefuls would be crammed nose to shoulder, as close to the stage as possible, like groupies at a rock concert.

At 8:40, three union officials emerged from the anteroom beside the stage. Through a two-way mirror, they had been keeping an eye on the surging crowd while their clerks matched the day's maquila employment needs with the application forms on file. All morning long, the fax machines and phones in the union headquarters had been ringing with the day's specifications from the companies. One maquila, for instance, asked for 91 applicants, all of whom should be 16 (the legal minimum age) or older, with a secondary-school education and without "scheduling problems"— code for childless. All the maquilas favor youth, and some, MagneTek for one, insist on it. *"No mayores de 27 años"*—None older than 27—the company's director of industrial relations instructed in a faxed letter to the union. Women in their late teens and early 20s are considered in the prime of their working lives; a 31-year-old is unlikely to be hired, and a 35-year-old is considered a relic.

When the tally of the day's employment needs was deemed complete, the officials stepped onto the stage, and into the bedlam. Between them and the spirited throng were three steps cordoned by a thin chain, a flimsy plywood railing, and a bouncer the size of an offensive lineman, whose sartorial taste ran to late Elvis: a white shirt unbuttoned nearly the length of his heroic torso, a gold medallion dangling to his midsection, and a formidable, gleaming pompadour crowning a Frigidaire face and muttonchop sideburns.

Following a call to order on a tinny public-address system, a woman unceremoniously announced the day's available jobs. "We're calling workers for Deltronicos," she said, referring to the GM car-radio subsidiary, and then read a list of 50 names. The "lucky ones," as one disappointed applicant called them, made their way through a pair of swinging doors, where a fleet of old Loadstar school buses waited to transport them to the Finsa park for a job interview and medical screening with their prospective employer. If their luck held, they would then be hired for a 30-day probationary period at lower, "training" wages before attaining full-employee status.

The drill was repeated for each maquila until the day's hiring needs were met. Neither Balbina nor Elsa were among the lucky ones, but they knew that few are chosen on the first go-round; some they met had endured several months of twice-weekly trips to the hall. Each Monday and Friday over the next few weeks the Duques returned faithfully. In March, Balbina's prayers were finally answered. She was assigned to a third-shift coil-winding job at MagneTek. All she knew about the job was that her sister-in-law once worked in the same plant, a low-lying white building no more than 75 yards from her tiny house. What she did not know was that Mollie James once held that very job.

Balbina started work at MagneTek the same year President Clinton signed the North American Free Trade Agreement, designed in large part to hasten the spread of maquiladoras. The trade deal enables companies to take advantage of 700,000 workers at 1,800 plants all along the border in ways that would not be tolerated in the United States. When MagneTek first set up shop in Matamoros, employees worked six-day weeks in a stifling, poorly ventilated plant; speaking on the line or going to the bathroom was grounds for suspension.

Although the company has improved working conditions in the last few years, sexual harassment and discrimination remain a constant of factory life. Many female employees at MagneTek have firsthand stories to tell about sexism on the job. "When new girls come in," says a 31-year-old MagneTek retiree who asked not to be identified, "a supervisor gives them the eye and asks them to go for a walk." Balbina says she received similar propositions when she started work at Plant 1. "My supervisor asked if I wanted to work more overtime. I told him I did, but that I wouldn't go to a hotel with him to get it."

The other constant of factory life is low wages. Even when she works an eight-hour overtime shift, as she usually does two or three times a week, Balbina finds it impossible to make ends meet on a MagneTek salary. "No alcance," she says. It doesn't reach. For years she surmounted her weekly shortfall by pooling her income and expenses with Elsa. The sisters lived, like nearly all of their co-workers, "en montón"—in a heap: two adults and five children in two small rooms, the kitchen in front, the bedroom in the rear. Their shared three-family flat was a cement structure

45 feet by 15 feet by 10 feet high. Its corrugated metal roof doubled as the ceiling. There were cinder-block walls between the three units that stopped about a foot short of the ceiling, making for a pungent stew of sound and aroma when all three families were home.

The shadeless yard—of mud or dust, depending on the season—was fenced by chicken wire and a rickety gate, and served as an extension of the kitchen. The residents shared a clothesline, an outhouse, and a single spigot—the lone source of water. Balbina believes the water flowed from an open canal running near plants in the industrial park that manufacture pesticides or use toxic solvents. The water had to be boiled, of course; sometimes there was propane to do so, sometimes not.

The neighborhood, Vista Hermosa, exists in a commercial and municipal twilight zone. It sprang up to serve the maquiladoras, not the residents. There are several high-priced convenience stores in the colonia, but no full-fledged grocers, no place to buy meat. Nor is there a pharmacy or medical clinic. There is no police presence, and vandalism and petty theft are rampant. There is one school, an overcrowded kindergarten. Older students catch the same bus to school that drops off first-shift workers at the industrial park. "You have to adapt to the maquilas' routine," says a neighbor with school-age children, "because they're not going to adapt to ours.". . .

Vista Hermosa breeds disease like it does mosquitoes. The lack of septic and sewage lines, potable water, and sanitation services puts the neighborhood at great risk for all manner of illnesses, from intestinal parasites to tuberculosis. But the gravest, most frightening threat comes not from the neighborhood, but from beyond the chain-link fence around the Finsa park. The fence, less than a football field away from Balbina's house, may divide the First and Third worlds, but it also unites them under a single toxic cloud. When the maquilas illegally dump toxic waste into irrigation canals, when a hot north wind blows the acrid smell of *chapapote*—pitch—from the MagneTek plant over its workers' homes, when runoff from a pesticide plant spills into a ditch, when chemical spills or leaks or explosions or fires erupt in the air, it doesn't take a Sierra Club member to understand the environmental wasteland the maquilas have created.

Nor does it take an epidemiologist to question the cause of an outbreak of anencephaly—babies born with either incomplete or missing brains and skulls. In one 36-hour period in the spring of 1991, three babies were born without brains at a single hospital across the river in Brownsville. Doctors soon learned of dozens of other anencephalic births in Brownsville and Matamoros. From 1989 to 1991, the rate of such defects for Brownsville was 10 times the U.S. average, or about 30 anencephalic births per 10,000 births. During the same years, there were 68 cases in Matamoros and 81 in Reynosa, a maquila site upriver.

Many who have studied the outbreak suspect it was due to industrial pollution unchecked by regulatory agencies in both countries. "These were atrocities committed by two uncaring governments," says Dr. Margaret Diaz, the occupational health specialist in Brownsville who detected the anencephaly cluster. "They are the product of years of neglect."

In a lawsuit filed in 1993, families of 28 children born with anencephaly or spina bifida—an incomplete closure of the spinal cord—blamed the outbreak on contamination from the Matamoros maquilas. The families sued 40 maquilas, including MagneTek, charging that the companies negligently handled "toxic compounds" and that the birth defects occurred after "exposure to toxins present in the local environment." The companies steadfastly denied wrongdoing, but internal memoranda documented that some plants released toxic emissions into the air in quantities impermissible in the United States. And trash sifted from the Matamoros city dump established that the maquilas were burning their industrial waste there, rather than disposing of it in the United States, as required by law. One videotape made by an investigator for the families portrays the charred but clearly visible remains of a MagneTek rapid-start ballast. The companies eventually paid a total of $17 million to the stricken families and cleaned up their worst excesses.

Although MagneTek and other companies insist they are improving conditions both inside and outside their plants, wages remain at poverty levels. Rolando Gonzalez Barron, a maquila owner and former president of the Matamoros Maquila Association, points to an advertising supplement in the *Brownsville Herald* lauding companies for their financial contributions to Matamoros schools. "Take 'Adopt-a-School,'" he says. "We put sewerage and bathrooms in schools where little girls had to do their necessities outside."

What about paying a living wage so that the parents of those little girls could afford indoor plumbing themselves? "Yes," Gonzalez replies, "housing needs to be developed, but our main goal is to create value for our customers."

What about your employees? What is your obligation to them? "If a worker is not eating," Gonzalez says, sounding every bit the farmer discussing a plow horse, "he's not going to work for you. We need to meet at least the basic needs."

But the basic needs—"eating, housing, clothing," as Gonzalez puts it—are unmet, and the evidence is as obvious and irrefutable as the colonia in MagneTek's backyard, where Balbina and her neighbors wrestle every single day with ferociously difficult decisions: Should I work overtime or huddle with my children to keep them warm? Buy meat or medicine? Pay the light bill or the gas bill? She makes those decisions based on a daily salary of 58 pesos, the equivalent of $7.43. That's an hourly wage of 92 cents—roughly the same starting wage Mollie James earned nearly half a century before. And Balbina often makes those decisions after working a grueling double shift—from 3:30 in the afternoon until six the following morning, after which she arrives home in time to fix breakfast for her children, accompany her oldest to school, and squeeze in a few hours of sleep before heading back to the plant in the afternoon.

No alcance. It doesn't reach. Over and over one hears this. No alcance, but we make it reach. They make it reach by taking odd jobs, or by scavenging for recyclables at the Matamoros city dump—an otherworldly metropolis of its own covering 50 acres—or peddling wares in the plant during breaks and shift changes. "It's prohibited," Balbina says, "but the company looks the other way and almost everybody does it." There are the ubiquitous Avon ladies, as well as sellers of homemade candy, tamales and gorditas, clothes, marijuana. And some sell their bodies, living la doble vida—the double life of coil-winder by day and prostitute by night.

Balbina has yet to resort to a second job. Instead, she works overtime as often as possible and recently moved into a government-subsized house; it is more comfortable than the one she shared with her sister, but it is hers only as long as she keeps her job. She is 29, an advanced age for a maquiladora worker. She lives with her boyfriend, a fellow MagneTek employee, and they stagger their shifts so that one provides child care while the other is working. Still, even the small necessities remain out of reach. "I need a lock for the door," Balbina says one afternoon. "I don't need it now, but soon I will."

Why not now?

"There is nothing worth locking now," she replies.

Mollie James never again found full-time work. She received a severance payment, after taxes, of $3,171.66—about $93 for each of the 34 years she worked. She collected unemployment benefits for six months and then enrolled in a computer-repair school, receiving a certificate of completion and numerous don't-call-us responses to job inquiries. Late last year, at the age of 68, she took a part-time job as an attendant at a nursing home. For the remainder of her income, she depends on Social Security and the rent she collects from the three-family house she owns, as well as a monthly pension of $71.23 from her Teamsters local. "That's nothing," she says. "That doesn't even pay your telephone bill. It's gone before you know it."

Although Paterson is a tenacious city, it seems defined by what is gone. Its last heyday was during and after World War II, when entrepreneurs like Archie Sergy and migrants like Mollie James helped sustain the city as a proud symbol of industrial might. But the old factory district near the Great Falls has been in ruins for decades, and although a number of the ancient brick mills have been splendidly restored—as a museum, a hospital clinic, and housing for artists—Paterson today is thought of as one of those discarded American places, a city so squalid, so defeated, that few people who do not live or work in Paterson venture there.

Mollie James has spent a half-century in Paterson. She married and divorced there, raised four children, bought a house. She sunk deep roots, and would like nothing better than to see the seeds of renewal take sprout, but she is fed up with high taxes, crime, the unstable economy. Like many "up-South" blacks of retirement age, she thinks often about going home, to rural central Virginia, to the land she left as a teenager. She still owns her childhood home amid three wooded acres.

During a trip back home not long ago, Mollie visited the cemetery where her parents are buried. It is where she wishes to be buried as well. "They better not put me in no dirt up there in New Jersey," she says. "Bring me back home, brother."

Balbina, too, dreams of returning to her ancestral home, to the quiet and clear air of Monte Bello, where she could raise her children in a calm, safe place. But there is no work around Monte Bello for her, no future there for her children. She is more concerned with the immediate future of her job. In the last couple of years, MagneTek closed the two old Universal plants in Arkansas and Mississippi and transferred the bulk of those operations not to Matamoros, but 60 miles upriver to Reynosa, where the union is even weaker, the wages lower still. Now the talk in Matamoros is that the company will once again use the threat of a move, as it did first in Paterson and then in the Southern plants, as a lever for lower wages.

Balbina scoffs at the notion of transferring to Reynosa if the company relocates her job there. "What if they were to move again?" she asks. "Maybe to Juárez or Tijuana? What then? Do I chase my job all over the world?"

The Uses of Poverty:
The Poor Pay All

Herbert J. Gans

introduction ▪ ▪ ▪ ▪

Of the several social classes in the United States, sociologists have concentrated their studies on the poor. The super-rich and, for the most part, the ordinarily wealthy are beyond the reach of researchers. Sociologists are not members of the wealthy classes or of the power elite, and members of these groups have the means to insulate themselves from the prying eyes (and questionnaires and tape recorders) of sociologists. When it comes to the middle classes, sociologists are likely to take their members for granted. The middle classes are part of their everyday life, and, like others, sociologists often overlook the things closest to them. The characteristics and situations of the poor, however, are different enough to strike the interests of sociologists. And the poor are accessible. People in poverty are generally willing to be interviewed. They are even a bit flattered that sociologists, for the most part members of the upper middle class, will take the time to talk to them. Hardly anyone else takes them seriously.

A couple of thousand years ago, Jesus said, "The poor you'll always have with you." In this selection, as Herbert Gans places the sociological lens yet again on people in poverty, he uses a functionalist perspective to explain why we always will have people in poverty. Simply put, from a functionalist perspective, we *need* the poor.

Thinking Critically

As you read this selection, ask yourself:

1. What functions (or uses) of poverty does Gans identify?

2. Of the functions of poverty that Gans identifies, which two do you think are the most important? Which two the least important? Why?

3. Do you think that Gans has gone overboard with his analysis? That he has stretched the functionalist perspective beyond reason? Or do you agree with him? Why or why not?

Some years ago Robert K. Merton applied the notion of functional analysis to explain the continuing though maligned existence of the urban political machine: If it continued to exist, perhaps it fulfilled latent—unintended or unrecognized—positive functions. Clearly it did. Merton pointed out how the political machine provided central authority to get things done when a decentralized local government could not act, humanized the services of the impersonal bureaucracy for fearful citizens, offered concrete help (rather than abstract law or justice) to the poor, and otherwise performed services needed or demanded by many people but considered unconventional or even illegal by formal public agencies.

Today, poverty is more maligned than the political machine ever was; yet it, too, is a persistent social phenomenon. Consequently, there may be some merit in applying functional analysis to poverty, in asking whether it also has positive functions that explain its persistence.

Merton defined functions as "those observed consequences [of a phenomenon] which make for the adaptation or adjustment of a given [social] system." I shall use a slightly different definition; instead of identifying functions for an entire social system, I shall identify them for the interest groups, socioeconomic classes, and other population aggregates with shared values that "inhabit" a social system. I suspect that in a modern heterogeneous society, few phenomena are functional or dysfunctional for the society as a whole, and that most result in benefits to some groups and costs to others. Nor are any phenomena indispensable; in most instances, one can suggest what Merton calls "functional alternatives" or equivalents for them, i.e., other social patterns or policies that achieve the same positive functions but avoid the dysfunction. (In the following discussion, positive functions will be abbreviated as functions and negative functions as dysfunctions. Functions and dysfunctions, in the planner's terminology, will be described as benefits and costs.)

Associating poverty with positive functions seems at first glance to be unimaginable. Of course, the slumlord and the loan shark are commonly known to profit from the existence of poverty, but they are viewed as evil men, so their activities are classified among the dysfunctions of poverty. However, what is less often recognized, at least by the conventional wisdom, is that poverty also makes possible the existence or expansion of respectable professions and occupations, for example, penology, criminology, social work, and public health. More recently, the poor have provided jobs for professional and para-professional "poverty warriors," and for journalists and social scientists, this author included, who have supplied the information demanded by the revival of public interest in poverty.

Clearly, then, poverty and the poor may well satisfy a number of positive functions for many nonpoor groups in American society. I shall describe 13 such functions—economic, social and political—that seem to me most significant.

From "The Uses of Poverty: The Poor Pay All," by Herbert J. Gans, *Social Policy*, July/August 1971. Copyright © 1971 by Social Policy Magazine. Reprinted by permission of the publisher.

■ ■ ■ THE FUNCTIONS OF POVERTY

First, the existence of poverty ensures that society's "dirty work" will be done. Every society has such work: physically dirty or dangerous, temporary, dead-end and underpaid, undignified, and menial jobs. Society can fill these jobs by paying higher wages than for "clean" work, or it can force people who have no other choice to do the dirty work—and at low wages. In America, poverty functions to provide a low-wage labor pool that is willing—or rather, unable to be *un*willing—to perform dirty work at low cost. Indeed, this function of the poor is so important that in some Southern states, welfare payments have been cut off during the summer months when the poor are needed to work in the fields. Moreover, much of the debate about the Negative Income Tax and the Family Assistance Plan [welfare programs] has concerned their impact on the work incentive, by which is actually meant the incentive of the poor to do the needed dirty work if the wages therefrom are no larger than the income grant. Many economic activities that involve dirty work depend on the poor for their existence: restaurants, hospitals, parts of the garment industry, and "truck farming," among others, could not persist in their present form without the poor.

Second, because the poor are required to work at low wages, they subsidize a variety of economic activities that benefit the affluent. For example, domestics subsidize the upper-middle and upper classes, making life easier for their employers and freeing affluent women for a variety of professional, cultural, civic, and partying activities. Similarly, because the poor pay a higher proportion of their income in property and sales taxes, among others, they subsidize many state and local governmental services that benefit more affluent groups. In addition, the poor support innovation in medical practice as patients in teaching and research hospitals and as guinea pigs in medical experiments.

Third, poverty creates jobs for a number of occupations and professions that serve or "service" the poor, or protect the rest of society from them. As already noted, penology would be minuscule without the poor, as would the police. Other activities and groups that flourish because of the existence of poverty are the numbers game, the sale of heroin and cheap wines and liquors, Pentecostal ministers, faith healers, prostitutes, pawn shops, and the peacetime army, which recruits its enlisted men mainly from among the poor.

Fourth, the poor buy goods others do not want and thus prolong the economic usefulness of such goods—day-old bread, fruit and vegetables that otherwise would have to be thrown out, secondhand clothes, and deteriorating automobiles and buildings. They also provide incomes for doctors, lawyers, teachers, and others who are too old, poorly trained or incompetent to attract more affluent clients.

In addition to economic functions, the poor perform a number of social functions.

Fifth, the poor can be identified and punished as alleged or real deviants in order to uphold the legitimacy of conventional norms. To justify the desirability of hard work, thrift, honesty, and monogamy, for example, the defenders of these norms must be able to find people who can be accused of being lazy, spendthrift, dishonest, and promiscuous. Although there is some evidence that the poor are about as moral and law-abiding as anyone else, they are more likely than middle-class transgressors to be caught and punished when they participate in deviant acts. Moreover, they lack the political and cultural power to correct the stereotypes that other people hold of them and thus continue to be thought of as lazy, spendthrift, etc., by those who need living proof that moral deviance does not pay.

Sixth, and conversely, the poor offer vicarious participation to the rest of the population in the uninhibited sexual, alcoholic, and narcotic behavior in which they are alleged to participate and which, being freed from the constraints of affluence, they are often thought to enjoy more than the middle classes. Thus many people, some social scientists included, believe that the poor not only are more given to uninhibited behavior (which may be true, although it is often motivated by despair more than by lack of inhibition) but derive more pleasure from it than affluent people (which research by Lee Rainwater, Walter Miller and others shows to be patently untrue). However, whether the poor actually have more sex and enjoy it more is irrelevant; so long as middle-class people believe this to be true, they can participate in it vicariously when instances are reported in factual or fictional form.

Seventh, the poor also serve a direct cultural function when culture created by or for them is adopted by the more affluent. The rich often collect artifacts from extinct folk cultures of poor people; and almost all Americans listen to the blues, Negro spirituals, and country music, which originated among the Southern poor. Recently they have enjoyed the rock styles that were born, like the Beatles, in the slums, and in the last year, poetry written by ghetto children has become popular in literary circles. The poor also serve as culture heroes, particularly, of course, to the left; but the hobo, the cowboy, the hipster, and the mythical prostitute with a heart of gold have performed this function for a variety of groups.

Eighth, poverty helps to guarantee the status of those who are not poor. In every hierarchical society, someone has to be at the bottom; but in American society, in which social mobility is an important goal for many and people need to know where they stand, the poor function as a reliable and relatively permanent measuring rod for status comparisons. This is particularly true for the working class, whose politics is influenced by the need to maintain status distinctions between themselves and the poor, much as the aristocracy must find ways of distinguishing itself from the *nouveaux riches.*

Ninth, the poor also aid the upward mobility of groups just above them in the class hierarchy. Thus a goodly number of Americans have entered the middle class through the profits earned from the provision of goods and services in the slums, including illegal or nonrespectable ones that upper-class and upper-middle-class businessmen shun because of their low prestige. As a result, members of almost every immigrant group have financed their upward mobility by providing slum housing, entertainment, gambling, narcotics, etc., to later arrivals—most recently to blacks and Puerto Ricans.

Tenth, the poor help to keep the aristocracy busy, thus justifying its continued existence. "Society" uses the poor as clients of settlement houses and beneficiaries of charity affairs; indeed, the aristocracy must have the poor to demonstrate its superiority over other elites who devote themselves to earning money.

Eleventh, the poor, being powerless, can be made to absorb the costs of change and growth in American society. During the nineteenth century, they did the back-breaking work that built the cities; today, they are pushed out of their neighborhoods to make room for "progress." Urban renewal projects to hold middle-class taxpayers in the city and expressways to enable suburbanites to commute downtown have typically been located in poor neighborhoods, since no other group will allow itself to be displaced. For the same reason, universities, hospitals, and civic centers also expand into land occupied by the poor. The major costs of the industrialization of agriculture have been borne by the poor, who are pushed off the land without recompense; and they have paid a large share of the human cost of the growth of American power overseas, for they have provided many of the foot soldiers for Vietnam and other wars.

Twelfth, the poor facilitate and stabilize the American political process. Because they vote and participate in politics less than other groups, the political system is often free to ignore them. Moreover, since they can rarely support Republicans, they often provide the Democrats with a captive constituency that has no other place to go. As a result, the Democrats can count on their votes, and be more responsive to voters—for example, the white working class—who might otherwise switch to the Republicans.

Thirteenth, the role of the poor in upholding conventional norms (see the *fifth* point, above) also has a significant political function. An economy based on the ideology of laissez-faire requires a deprived population that is allegedly unwilling to work or that can be considered inferior because it must accept charity or welfare in order to survive. Not only does the alleged moral deviancy of the poor reduce the moral pressure on the present political economy to eliminate poverty but socialist alternatives can be made to look quite unattractive if those who will benefit most from them can be described as lazy, spendthrift, dishonest and promiscuous.

■ ■ ■ THE ALTERNATIVES

I have described 13 of the more important functions poverty and the poor satisfy in American society, enough to support the functionalist thesis that poverty, like any other social phenomenon, survives in part because it is useful to society or some of its parts. This analysis is not intended to suggest that because it is often functional, poverty *should* exist, or that it *must* exist. For one thing, poverty has many more dysfunctions than functions; for another, it is possible to suggest functional alternatives.

For example, society's dirty work could be done without poverty, either by automation or by paying "dirty workers" decent wages. Nor is it necessary for the poor to subsidize the many activities they support through their low-wage jobs. This would, however, drive up the costs of these activities, which would result in higher prices to their customers and clients. Similarly, many of the professionals who flourish because of the poor could be given other roles. Social workers could provide counseling to the affluent, as they prefer to do anyway; and the police could devote themselves to traffic and organized crime. Other roles would have to be found for badly trained or incompetent professionals now relegated to serving the poor, and someone else would have to pay their salaries. Fewer penologists would be employable, however. And Pentecostal religion could probably not survive without the poor—nor would parts of the second- and third-hand-goods market. And in many cities, "used" housing that no one else wants would then have to be torn down at public expense.

Alternatives for the cultural functions of the poor could be found more easily and cheaply. Indeed, entertainers and adolescents are already serving as the deviants needed to uphold traditional morality and as devotees of orgies to "staff" the fantasies of vicarious participation.

The status functions of the poor are another matter. In a hierarchical society, some people must be defined as inferior to everyone else with respect to a variety of attributes, but they need not be poor in the absolute sense. One could conceive of a society in which the "lower class," though last in the pecking order, received 75 percent of the median income, rather than 15–40 percent, as is now the case. Needless to say, this would require considerable income redistribution.

The contribution the poor make to the upward mobility of the groups that provide them with goods and services could also be maintained without the poor's having such low incomes. However, it is true that if the poor were more affluent, they would have access to enough capital to take over the provider role, thus competing with, and perhaps rejecting, the "outsiders.". . . Similarly, if the poor were more affluent, they would make less willing clients for upper-class philanthropy, although some would still use settlement houses to achieve upward mobility, as they do now. Thus "Society" could continue to run its philanthropic activities.

The political functions of the poor would be more difficult to replace. With increased affluence the poor would probably obtain more political power and be more active politically. With higher incomes and more political power, the poor would be likely to resist paying the costs of growth and change. Of course, it is possible to imagine urban renewal and highway projects that properly reimbursed the displaced people, but such projects would then become considerably more expensive, and many might never be built. This, in turn, would reduce the comfort and convenience of those who now benefit from urban renewal and expressways.

In sum, then, many of the functions served by the poor could be replaced if poverty were eliminated, but almost always at higher costs to others, particularly more affluent others. Consequently, a functional analysis must conclude that poverty persists not only because it fulfills a number of positive functions but also because many of the functional alternatives to poverty would be quite dysfunctional for the affluent members of society. A functional analysis thus ultimately arrives at much the same conclusion as radical sociology, except that radical thinkers treat as manifest what I describe as latent: that social phenomena that are functional for affluent or powerful groups and dysfunctional for poor or powerless ones persist; that when the elimination of such phenomena through functional alternatives would generate dysfunctions for the affluent or powerful, they will continue to persist; and that phenomena like poverty can be eliminated only when they become dysfunctional for the affluent or powerful, or when the powerless can obtain enough power to change society.

■ ■ ■ POSTSCRIPT

[Note from the editor: When I wrote Gans, asking why he had written this article or if it had any covert meaning, he said:]

Over the years, this article has been interpreted as either a direct attack on functionalism or a tongue-in-cheek satirical comment on it. Neither interpretation is true. I wrote the article for two reasons. First and foremost, I wanted to point out that there are, unfortunately, positive functions of poverty which have to be dealt with by antipoverty policy. Second, I was trying to show that functionalism is not the inherently conservative approach for which it has often been criticized, but that it can be employed in liberal and radical analyses.

Invisible Man

Lawrence Otis Graham

introduction ■ ■■ ■ ■

As you know, the circumstances we inherit at birth have serious consequences for what happens to us in life. Some of us are born poor, others rich, most of us in between. Each of us is born into a racial–ethnic group. Some of us are born to single mothers, others to married parents; some to parents who are college graduates, others to parents who have not finished high school. Even our geography (South, West, rural, urban) sets up background factors that play a significant role in our orientations to life. Sociologists use the term *life chances* to refer to how the background factors that surround our birth affect our fate in life.

A major issue in the sociology of race–ethnic relations is the relative significance of race-ethnicity and social class in determining people's life chances. Is the color of our skin more important than social class for setting us on a course in life? On a narrower level, does social class or race-ethnicity play a greater role in our everyday lives? Although not providing *the* answer to these provocative questions, this selection sheds light on some of the intricate interconnections between race-ethnicity and social class. As Lawrence Graham found, racism is far from dead, and race-ethnicity continues to play a pivotal role in what happens to us in life.

Thinking Critically

As you read this selection, ask yourself:

1. Since Graham is an African American, he should know about racism. Why, then, do you think he did this research?

2. What do you think Graham's most eye-opening experiences were?

3. What situation do you think embarrassed Graham the most? Why?

I drive up the winding lane past a long stone wall and beneath an archway of sixty-foot maples. At one bend of the drive, a freshly clipped lawn and a trail of yellow daffodils slope gently up to the four-pillared portico of a white Georgian colonial.

The building's six huge chimneys, the two wings with slate gray shutters, and the white-brick facade loom over a luxuriant golf course. Before me stands the one-hundred-year-old Greenwich Country Club—*the* country club—in the affluent, patrician, and very white town of Greenwich, Connecticut, where there are eight clubs for fifty-nine thousand people.

I'm a thirty-year-old corporate lawyer at a Midtown Manhattan firm, and I make $105,000 a year. I'm a graduate of Princeton University (1983) and Harvard Law School (1988), and I've written ten nonfiction books. Although these may seem like impressive credentials, they're not the ones that brought me here. Quite frankly, I got into this country club the only way that a black man like me could—as a $7-an-hour busboy.

After seeing dozens of news stories about Dan Quayle, Billy Graham, Ross Perot, and others who either belonged to or frequented white country clubs, I decided to find out what things were really like at a club where I heard there were no black members.

I remember stepping up to the pool at the country club when I was ten and setting off a chain reaction: Several irate parents dragged their children out of the water and fled. When the other kids ran out of the pool, so did I—foolishly thinking that there was something in the water that was going to harm all of us. Back then, in 1972, I saw these clubs only as places where families socialized. I grew up in an affluent white neighborhood in Westchester, and all my playmates and neighbors belonged to one or more of these private institutions. Across the street, my best friend introduced me to the Westchester Country Club before he left for Groton and Yale. My teenage tennis partner from Scarsdale introduced me to the Beach Point Club on weekends before he left for Harvard. The family next door belonged to the Scarsdale Golf Club. In my crowd, the question wasn't "Do you belong?" It was "Where?"

My grandparents owned a Memphis trucking firm, and as far back as I can remember, our family was well off and we had little trouble fitting in even though I was the only black kid on the high school tennis team, the only one in the orchestra, the only one in my Roman Catholic confirmation class.

Today, I'm back where I started—on a street of five- and six-bedroom colonials with expensive cars and neighbors who all belong somewhere. Through my experience as a young lawyer, I have come to realize that these clubs are where business people network, where lawyers and investment bankers meet potential clients and arrange deals. How many clients and deals am I going to line up on the asphalt parking lot of my local public tennis courts?

I am not ashamed to admit that I one day want to be a partner and a part of this network. When I talk to my black lawyer or investment-banker friends or my wife, a brilliant black woman who has degrees from Harvard College, Harvard Law School, and Harvard Business School, I learn that our white counterparts are being accepted by dozens of these elite institutions. So why shouldn't we—especially when we have the same credentials, salaries, social graces, and ambitions?

My black Ivy League friends and I know of black company vice presidents who have to ask white subordinates to invite them out for golf or tennis. We talk about the club in Westchester that rejected black Scarsdale resident and millionaire magazine publisher Earl Graves, who sits on *Fortune* 500 boards, owns a Pepsi distribution franchise, raised three bright Ivy League children, and holds prestigious honorary degrees. We talk about all the clubs that face a scandal and then run out to sign up one quiet, deferential black man who will accept a special "limited-status" membership, remove the taint, and deflect further scrutiny.

I wanted some answers. I knew I could never be treated as an equal at this Greenwich oasis—a place so insular that the word *Negro* is still used in conversation. But I figured I could get close enough to understand what these people were thinking and why country clubs were so set on excluding people like me.

■ ■ ■ MARCH 28 TO APRIL 7, 1992

I invented a completely new résumé for myself. I erased Harvard, Princeton, and my upper-middle-class suburban childhood from my life. So that I'd have to account for fewer years, I made myself seven years younger—an innocent twenty-three. I used my real name and made myself a graduate of the actual high school I attended. Since it would be difficult to pretend that I was from "the street," I decided to become a sophomore-year dropout from Tufts University, a midsize college in suburban Boston. My years at nearby Harvard and the fact that my brother had gone there had given me enough knowledge about the school to pull it off. I contacted some older friends who owned large companies and restaurants in the Boston and New York areas and asked them to serve as references. I was already on a short leave of absence from my law firm to work on a book.

I pieced together a wardrobe that consisted of a blue polyester blazer, white oxford shirt, ironed blue slacks, black loafers, and a horrendous pink, black, and silver tie, and I set up interviews at clubs. Over the telephone, five of the eight said that I sounded as if I would make a great waiter. During each of my phone conversations, I made sure that I spoke to the person who would make the hiring decision. I also confirmed exactly how many waiter positions were available, and I arranged a personal interview within forty minutes to an hour of the conversation, just to be sure that they could not tell me that no such job was available.

"We don't have any job openings—and if you don't leave the building, I will have to call security," the receptionist said at the first club I visited in Greenwich.

I was astounded by the speed with which she made this remark, particularly when I saw that she had just handed an application to a young-looking Hispanic man wearing jeans, sneakers, a T-shirt, and sunglasses. "I'm here to see Donna, your maître d'," I added defensively as I forced a smile at the pasty-looking woman who sat behind a window.

"There's no Donna here."

"But I just spoke to her thirty minutes ago and she said to come by to discuss the waiter job."

"Sorry, but there are no jobs and no one here named Donna."

After convincing the woman to give me an application, I completed it and then walked back into the dining room, which was visible from the foyer.

I came upon a white male waiter and asked him, "Is there a Donna here?"

"The maître d'?" he asked. "Yeah, she's in the kitchen."

When I found Donna and explained that I was the one she had talked to on the phone forty minutes earlier, she crossed her arms and shook her head. "You're the 'Larry' I talked to on the phone?"

"Yes," I answered.

"No way."

"I beg your pardon," I said.

"No. No way," she said while refusing to take the application I waved in front of her.

"We just talked on the phone less than an hour ago. You said I sounded perfect. And I've waited in three different restaurants—I've had two years of college—You said you have five waiter jobs open—I filled out the application—I can start right away—"

She still shook her head. And held her hands behind her back—unwilling to even touch my application. "No," she said. "Can't do it."

My talking did no good. It was 1992. This was the Northeast. If I hadn't been involved, I would never have believed it. I suddenly thought about all the times I quietly disbelieved certain poor blacks who said they had tried to get jobs but no one would hire them. I wanted to say then and there, "Not even as a waiter?"

Only an hour earlier, this woman had enthusiastically urged me to come right over for an interview. Now, as two white kitchen workers looked on, she would only hold her hands tightly behind her back and shake her head emphatically. So I left.

There were three other clubs to go to. When I met them, the club managers told me I "would probably make a much better busboy."

"Busboy? Over the phone, you said you needed a waiter," I argued.

"Yes, I know I said that, but you seem very alert, and I think you'd make an excellent busboy instead."

In his heavy Irish brogue, the club manager said he needed to give me a "perception test." He explained it this way: "This ten-question test will give us an idea of your perception, intellectual strength, and conscious ability to perform the duties assigned to you as a busboy."

I had no idea how much intellectual strength and conscious ability (whatever that meant) could be required of a busboy, but here are some of the questions he asked me:

1. If there are three apples and you take two away, how many do you have?
2. How many of each species of animal did Moses put on his new ark?

3. It's 1963 and you set your digital clock to ring at 9:00 A.M. when you go to bed at 8:00 P.M. How many hours will you sleep?
4. If a house gets southern exposure on all four sides, what color is the bear that walks by the house?

And the responses . . .

1. I answered "one apple" because I thought this was a simple math question, as in "three minus two equals one," but the correct answer was "two" because, as the manager said, "You've got to think, Larry—if you take away two apples and put them in your pocket, you've got two apples, not one."
2. Fortunately, I answered this question as it was presumably designed to smoke out any applicants who hadn't been raised in a Judeo-Christian culture. It was Noah, not Moses, who built an ark.
3. I scored major credibility points here by lying and saying, "Wow, I wasn't even born yet in 1963. . . ." The "right" answer was that there were no digital clocks in 1963. I took his word for it.
4. Although I believed that a house could get southern exposure on all four sides only at the South Pole—and thus the bear had to be a white polar bear—I was told that I was "trying to act too smart" and that all bears are, of course, brown.

■ ■ ■ APRIL 8 TO 11

After interviewing for advertised waiter jobs at five clubs, I had gotten only two offers—both for non-waiter jobs. One offer was to split my time as a towel boy in the locker room and a busboy in the dining room. The second offer—which followed a callback interview—was to work as a busboy. When I told the club manager that I had only wanted a waiter job, he responded, "Well, we've discussed it here and everyone would feel more comfortable if you took a busboy job instead."

"But I've never worked as a busboy," I reminded him.

He nodded sympathetically. "People here have decided that it's busboy or nothing."

Given these choices I made my final job selection in much the way I had decided on a college and a law school: I went for prestige. Not only was the Greenwich Country Club celebrating its hundredth anniversary but its roster boasted former president Gerald Ford, baseball star Tom Seaver, former Securities and Exchange Commission chairman and U.S. ambassador to the Netherlands John Shad, as well as former Timex spokesman John Cameron Swayze. Add to that a few dozen *Fortune* 500 executives, bankers, Wall Street lawyers, European entrepreneurs, a Presbyterian minister, and cartoonist Mort Walker, who does *Beetle Bailey*. (The Greenwich Country Club did not respond to any questions about the club and its members.)

For three days, I worked on my upper-arm muscles by walking around the house with a sterling-silver tray stacked high with heavy dictionaries. I allowed a mustache to grow in, then added a pair of arrestingly ugly Coke-bottle reading glasses.

■ ■ ■ ■ APRIL 12 (SUNDAY)

Today was my first day at work. My shift didn't start until 10:30 A.M., so I laid out my clothes at home: a white button-down shirt, freshly ironed cotton khaki pants, white socks, and white leather sneakers. I'd get my official club uniform in two days. Looking in my wallet, I removed my American Express Gold Card, my Harvard club membership ID, and all of my business cards.

When I arrived at the club, I entered under the large portico, stepping through the heavy doors and onto the black-and-white checkerboard tiles of the entry hall.

A distracted receptionist pointed me toward Mr. Ryan's office. (*All names of club members and personnel have been changed.*) I walked past glistening silver trophies and a guest book on a pedestal to a windowless office with three desks. My new boss waved me in and abruptly hung up the phone.

"Good morning, Larry," he said with a sufficiently warm smile. The tight knot in his green tie made him look more fastidious than I had remembered from the interview.

"Hi, Mr. Ryan. How's it going?"

Glancing at his watch to check my punctuality, he shook my hand and handed me some papers. "Oh, and by the way, where'd you park?"

"In front, near the tennis courts."

Already shaking his head, he tossed his pencil onto the desk. "That's off-limits to you. You should always park in the back, enter in the back, and leave from the back. No exceptions."

"I'll do the forms right now," I said. "And then I'll be an official busboy."

Mr. Ryan threw me an ominous nod. "And Larry, let me stop you now. We don't like that term busboy. We find it demeaning. We prefer to call you busmen."

Leading me down the center stairwell to the basement, he added, "And in the future, you will always use the back stairway by the back entrance." He continued to talk as we trotted through a maze of hallways. "I think I'll have you trail with Carlos or Hector—no, Carlos. Unless you speak Spanish?"

"No." I ran to keep up with Mr. Ryan.

"That's the dishwasher room, where Juan works. And over here is where you'll be working." I looked at the brass sign. MEN'S GRILL.

It was a dark room with a mahogany finish, and it looked like a library in a large Victorian home. Dark walls, dark wood-beamed ceilings. Deep-green wool carpeting. Along one side of the room stood a long, highly polished mahogany bar with liquor bottles, wineglasses, and a two-and-a-half-foot-high silver trophy. Fifteen heavy round wooden tables, each encircled with four to six broad wooden armchairs padded with green leather on the backs and seats, broke up the room. A big-screen TV was set into the wall along with two shelves of books.

"This is the Men's Grill," Mr. Ryan said. "Ladies are not allowed except on Friday evenings."

Next was the brightly lit connecting kitchen. "Our kitchen serves hot and cold foods. You'll work six days a week here. The club is closed on Mondays. The kitchen serves the Men's Grill and an adjoining room called the Mixed Grill. That's where the ladies and kids can eat."

"And what about men? Can they eat in there, too?"

This elicited a laugh. "Of course they can. Time and place restrictions apply only to women and kids."

He showed me the Mixed Grill, a well-lit pastel-blue room with glass French doors and white wood trim.

"Guys, say hello to Larry. He's a new busman at the club."

I waved.

"And this is Rick, Stephen, Drew, Buddy, and Lee." Five white waiters dressed in white polo shirts with blue "1892" club insignias nodded while busily slicing lemons.

"And this is Hector, and Carlos, the other two busmen." Hector, Carlos, and I were the only nonwhites on the serving staff. They greeted me in a mix of English and Spanish.

"Nice to meet all of you," I responded.

"Thank God," one of the taller waiters cried out. "Finally—somebody who can speak English."

Mr. Ryan took me and Carlos through a hall lined with old black-and-white portraits of former presidents of the club. "This is our one hundredth year, so you're joining the club at an important time," Mr. Ryan added before walking off. "Carlos, I'm going to leave Larry to trail with you—and no funny stuff."

Standing outside the ice room, Carlos and I talked about our pasts. He was twenty-five, originally from Colombia, and hadn't finished school. I said I had dropped out, too.

As I stood there talking, Carlos suddenly gestured for me to move out of the hallway. I looked behind me and noticed something staring at us. "A video camera?"

"They're around," Carlos remarked quietly while scooping ice into large white tubs. "Now watch me scoop ice."

After we carried the heavy tubs back to the grill, I saw another video camera point down at us. I dropped my head.

"You gonna live in the Monkey House?" Carlos asked.

"What's that?"

We climbed the stairs to take our ten-minute lunch break before work began. "Monkey House is where workers live here," Carlos said.

I followed him through a rather filthy utility room and into a huge white kitchen. We got in line behind about twenty Hispanic men and women—all dressed in varying uniforms. At the head of the line were the white waiters I'd met earlier.

I was soon handed a hot plate with two red lumps of rice and some kind of sausage-shaped meat. There were two string beans, several pieces of zucchini, and a thin, broken slice of dried meat loaf that looked as if it had been cooked, burned, frozen, and then reheated. Lurking at the very edge of my dish was an ice-cream-scoop-sized helping of yellowish mashed potatoes.

I followed Carlos, plate in hand, out of the kitchen. To my surprise, we walked back into the dank and dingy utility room, which turned out to be the workers' dining area.

The white waiters huddled together at one end of the table, while the Hispanic workers ate quietly at the other end. Before I could decide which end to integrate, Carlos directed me to sit with him on the Hispanic end.

I was soon back downstairs working in the grill. At my first few tables, I tried to avoid making eye contact with members as I removed dirty plates and wiped down tables and chairs. Having known so many people who belonged to these clubs, I was sure I'd be recognized by someone from childhood, college, or work.

At around 1:15, four men who looked to be in their mid- to late fifties sat down at a six-chair table. They pulled off their cotton windbreakers and golf sweaters.

"It's these damned newspeople that cause all the problems," said golfer number one, shoving his hand deep into a popcorn bowl. "These Negroes wouldn't even be thinking about golf. They can't afford to join a club, anyway."

Golfer number two squirmed out of his navy blue sweater and nodded in agreement. "My big problem with this Clinton fellow is that he apologized." As I stood watching from the corner of the bar, I realized the men were talking about then-governor Bill Clinton's recent apology for playing at an all-white golf club in Little Rock, Arkansas.

"Holt, I couldn't agree with you more," added golfer number three, a hefty man who was biting off the end of a cigar.

"You got any iced tea?" golfer number one asked as I put the silverware and menus around the table. Popcorn flew out of his mouth as he attempted to speak and chew at the same time.

"Yes, we certainly do."

Golfer number three removed a beat-up Rolex from his wrist. "It just sets a bad precedent. Instead of apologizing, he should try to discredit them—undercut them somehow. What's to apologize for?" I cleared my throat and backed away from the table.

Suddenly, golfer number one waved me back to his side. "Should we get four iced teas or just a pitcher and four glasses?"

"I'd be happy to bring whatever you'd like, sir."

Throughout the day, I carried "bus buckets" filled with dirty dishes from the grill to the dishwasher room. And each time I returned to the grill, I scanned the room for recognizable faces. Fortunately, I saw none. After almost four hours of running back and forth, clearing dishes, wiping down tables, and thanking departing members who left spilled coffee, dirty napkins, and unwanted business cards in their wake, I helped out in the coed Mixed Grill.

"Oh, busboy," a voice called out as I made the rounds with two pots of coffee. "Here, busboy. Here, busboy," the woman called out. "Busboy, my coffee is cold. Give me a refill."

"Certainly, I would be happy to." I reached over for her cup.

The fiftyish woman pushed her hand through her straw blond hair and turned to look me in the face. "Decaf, thank you."

"You are quite welcome."

Before I turned toward the kitchen, the woman leaned over to her companion. "My goodness. Did you hear that? That busboy has diction like an educated white person."

A curly-haired waiter walked up to me in the kitchen. "Larry, are you living in the Monkey House?"

"No, but why do they call it that?"

"Well, no offense against you, but it got that name since it's the house where the workers have lived at the club. And since the workers used to be Negroes—blacks—it was nicknamed the Monkey House. And the name just stuck—even though Negroes have been replaced by Hispanics."

■ ■ ■ APRIL 13 (MONDAY)

I woke up and felt a pain shooting up my calves. As I turned to the clock, I realized I'd slept for eleven hours. I was thankful the club was closed on Mondays.

■ ■ ■ APRIL 14 (TUESDAY)

Rosa, the club seamstress, measured me for a uniform in the basement laundry room while her barking gray poodle jumped up on my feet and pants. "Down, Margarita, down," Rosa cried with pins in her mouth and marking chalk in her hand. But Margarita ignored her and continued to bark and do tiny pirouettes until I left with all of my new country-club polo shirts and pants.

Today, I worked exclusively with the "veterans," including sixty-five-year-old Sam, the Polish bartender in the Men's Grill. Hazel, an older waitress at the club, is quick, charming, and smart—the kind of waitress who makes any restaurant a success. She has worked for the club nearly twenty years and has become quite territorial with certain older male members. Whenever I was on my way to hand out menus or clear dishes at a table, Hazel would either outrun me or grab me by the arm when she saw that the table contained important male members. Inevitably, Hazel would say, "Oh, Larry, let me take care of Dr. Collingsworth. You go fill this salt shaker," or "Larry, I'll take Judge Wilson's dirty dish. You go slice some lemons in the kitchen," or "Larry, I'll clean up Reverend Gundersen's cracker crumbs. You go find some peanut oil."

During a lull, Sam, who I swear reminded me of a Norman Lear creation circa 1972, asked me to run out and get some supplies from a Mr. Chang.

"Who is Mr. Chang?" I asked.

"You know, the Chinaman. Mr. Chang."

I had recalled seeing an elderly Asian man with a gray uniform in the halls, but we had not been introduced.

"And where would I find him?"

"He's down at the other end of the hall beyond the stairs." Sam handed me a list of items on a printed form. "He's the Chinaman and it's easy to remember 'cause he's right next to the laundry room."

Hector came along and warned me not to lose the signed form because I could be accused of stealing food and supplies if the signed list wasn't given to Mr. Chang.

Down a dark, shadowy hall, we found Mr. Chang, who, in Spanish, shouted phrases at me while swinging his arms in the air.

"Do you understand him?" I asked Hector.

"He said to follow him and bring a cart."

We followed the methodical Mr. Chang from storage room to storage room, where he pulled out various items like a magician. Lemons were stored with paper goods, cans of ketchup were stored with pretzels and simultaneously served as shelves for large sacks of onions. Bottles of soda were stored with old boxes that had "Monkey House" written on them. Combustible popcorn oil and boxes of matches were stored with Styrofoam cups in the furnace room. It was all in a disorder that seemed to make complete sense to Mr. Chang.

Back in the Mixed Grill, members were talking about hotel queen and Greenwich resident Leona Helmsley, who was on the clubhouse TV because of her upcoming prison term for tax evasion.

"I'd like to see them haul her off to jail," one irate woman said to the rest of her table. "She's nothing but a garish you-know-what."

"In every sense of the word," nodded her companion as she adjusted a pink headband in her blondish white hair. "She makes the whole town look bad. The TV keeps showing those aerial shots of Greenwich and that dreadful house of hers."

A third woman shrugged her shoulders and looked into her bowl of salad. "Well, it is a beautiful piece of property."

"Yes, it is, except for those dreadful lampposts all over the lawn," said the first woman. "But why here? She should be in those other places like Beverly Hills or Scarsdale or Long Island, with the rest of them. What's she doing here?"

Woman number three looked up. "Well, you know, *he's* not Jewish."

"Really?"

"So that explains it," said the first woman with an understanding expression on her tanned forehead. "Because, you know, the name didn't sound Jewish."

The second woman agreed: "I can usually tell."

■ ■ ■ **APRIL 15 (WEDNESDAY)**

Today, we introduced a new, extended menu in the two grill rooms. We added shrimp quesadillas ($6) to the appetizer list—and neither the members nor Hazel could pronounce the name of the dish or fathom what it was. One man pounded on the table and demanded to know which country the dish had come from. He told Hazel how much he hated "changes like this. I like to know that some things are going to stay the same."

Another addition was the "New Dog in Town" ($3.50). It was billed as knock-wurst, but one woman of German descent sent the dish back: "This is not knock-wurst—this is just a big hot dog."

As I wiped down the length of the men's bar, I noticed a tall stack of postcards with color photos of nude busty women waving hello from sunny faraway beaches. I saw they had been sent from vacationing members with fond regards to Sam or Hazel. Several had come from married couples. One glossy photo boasted a detailed frontal shot of a red-haired beauty who was naked except for a shoestring around her waist. On the back, the message said, *Dear Sam, Pull string in an emergency. Love always, The Atkinson Family.*

■ ■ ■ APRIL 16 (THURSDAY)

This afternoon, I realized I was learning the routine. I was fairly comfortable with my few "serving" responsibilities and the rules that related to them:

- When a member is seated, bring out the silverware, cloth napkin, and a menu.
- Never take an order for food, but always bring water or iced tea if it is requested by a member or waiter.
- When a waiter takes a chili or salad order, bring out a basket of warm rolls and crackers along with a scoop of butter.
- When getting iced tea, fill a tall glass with ice and serve it with a long spoon, a napkin on the bottom, and a lemon on the rim.
- When a member wants his alcoholic drink refilled, politely respond, "Certainly, I will have your waiter come right over."
- Remember that the member is always right.
- Never make offensive eye contact with a member or his guest.
- When serving a member fresh popcorn, serve to the left.
- When a member is finished with a dish or a glass, clear it from the right.
- Never tell a member that the kitchen is out of something.

But there were also some "informal" rules that I discovered (but did not follow) while watching the more experienced waiters and kitchen staff in action:

- If you drop a hot roll on the floor in front of a member, apologize and throw it out. If you drop a hot roll on the floor in the kitchen, pick it up and put it back in the bread warmer.
- If you have cleared a table and are 75 percent sure that the member did not use the fork, put it back in the bin with the other clean forks.
- If, after pouring one glass of Coke and one of diet Coke, you get distracted and can't remember which is which, stick your finger in one of them to taste it.
- If a member asks for decaffeinated coffee and you have no time to make it, use regular coffee and add water to cut the flavor.

- When members complain that the chili is too hot and spicy, instead of making a new batch, take the sting out by adding some chocolate syrup.
- If you're making tuna on toasted wheat and you accidentally burn one side of the bread, don't throw it out. Instead, put the tuna on the burnt side and lather on some extra mayo.

▪ ▪ ▪ APRIL 17 (FRIDAY)

Today, I heard the word "nigger" four times. And it came from someone on the staff.

In the grill, several members were discussing Arthur Ashe, who had recently announced that he had contracted AIDS through a blood transfusion.

"It's a shame that poor man has to be humiliated like this," one woman golfer remarked to a friend over pasta-and-vegetable salad. "He's been such a good example for his people."

"Well, quite frankly," added a woman in a white sunvisor, "I always knew he was gay. There was something about him that just seemed too perfect."

"No, Anne, he's not gay. It came from a blood transfusion."

"Ohh," said the woman. "I suppose that's a good reason to stay out of all those big-city hospitals. All that bad blood moving around."

Later that afternoon, one of the waiters, who had worked in the Mixed Grill for two years, told me that Tom Seaver and Gerald Ford were members. Of his brush with greatness, he added, "You know, Tom's real first name is George."

"That's something."

"And I've seen O. J. Simpson here, too."

"O. J. belongs here too?" I asked.

"Oh, no, there aren't any black members here. No way. I actually don't even think there are any Jews here either."

"Really? Why is that?" I asked.

"I don't know. I guess it's just that the members probably want to have a place where they can go and not have to think about Jews, blacks, and other minorities. It's not really hurting anyone. It's really a WASP club. . . . But now that I think of it, there's a guy here who some people think is Jewish, but I can't really tell. Upstairs, there's a Jewish secretary too."

"And what about O. J.?"

"Oh, yeah, it was so funny to see him out there playing golf on the eighteenth hole." The waiter paused and pointed outside the window. "It never occurred to me before, but it seemed so odd to see a black man with a golf club here on this course."

▪ ▪ ▪ APRIL 18 (SATURDAY)

When I arrived, Stephen, one of the waiters, was hanging a poster and sign-up sheet for a soccer league whose main purpose was to "bridge the ethnic and language gap" between white and Hispanic workers at the country clubs in the Greenwich area. I congratulated Stephen on his idea. He said he was tired of seeing the whites and Hispanics split up during meals, breaks, and evening activities. "We even go to separate bars and diners," he explained. "I think a weekly soccer game might bring us all closer together."

Later, while I was wiping down a table, I heard a member snap his fingers in my direction. I turned to see a group of young men smoking cigars. They seemed to be my age or a couple of years younger. "Hey, do I know you?" the voice asked.

As I turned slowly toward the voice, I could hear my own heartbeat. I was sure it was someone I knew.

"No," I said, approaching the blond cigar smoker. He had on light green khaki pants and a light yellow V-neck cotton sweater adorned with a tiny green alligator. As I looked at the other men seated around the table, I noticed that all but one had alligators on their sweaters or shirts. Each one of them was a stranger to me.

"I didn't think so. You must be new—what's your name?"

"My name is Larry. I just started a few days ago."

The cigar-smoking host grabbed me by the wrist while looking at his guests. "Well, Larry, welcome to the club. I'm Mr. Billings. And this is Mr. Dennis, a friend and new member."

"Hello, Mr. Dennis," I heard myself saying to a freckle-faced young man who puffed uncomfortably on his fat roll of tobacco.

The first cigar smoker gestured for me to bend over as if he were about to share some important confidence. "Now, Larry, here's what I want you to do. Go get us some of those peanuts and then give my guests and me a fresh ashtray. Can you manage that?"

My workday ended at 4:20.

■ ■ ■ EVENING OF APRIL 18 (SATURDAY)

After changing back into my street clothes at around 8:00 P.M., I drove back to the club to get together with Stephen and Lillie, two of the friendlier waiters (and the only ones willing to socialize with a busboy), in Stephen's room on the grounds. We sat, ate Hostess donuts, drank wine, watched the Saturday-night NBC-TV lineup, and talked about what it would be like to be a rich member of the club.

Squeezed into the tiny room and sitting on the bed, which was pushed against the wall, we each promised to look out for and warn the others if anyone else tried to backstab us in the grill. Stephen was talking about his plans for the intercultural soccer league and what it could do for all eight clubs in the area.

"After spending a couple semesters in Japan," Stephen explained, "I realized how afraid Americans are of other cultures." Stephen told me that he was working at the club to pay for the rest of his college education. He was taking a two-year break between his sophomore and junior years at a midwestern university, where he was majoring in Japanese.

Lillie talked about the formal dinner that she had just worked at that evening. It was then that I learned she was half South American. Her father, who was from

Colombia, was an outdoor groundskeeper at the club. "I'm taking college courses now," she explained. "And maybe I'm crazy to say this, but I think I'd like to go into broadcasting." Given her nearly flawless English and her very white skin, I wondered if the members were aware of her Hispanic background. She felt very strong about her South American heritage, and she often acted as interpreter for some of the club workers who spoke only Spanish.

They were both such nice people, I felt terrible for intruding under such fraudulent circumstances.

■ ■ ■ APRIL 19 (SUNDAY)

It was Easter Sunday and the Easter-egg hunt began with dozens of small children scampering around the tulips and daffodils while well-dressed parents watched from the rear patio of the club. A giant Easter bunny gave out little baskets filled with jelly beans to parents and then hopped over to the bushes, where he hugged the children. As we peered out from the closed blinds in the grill, we saw women in mink, husbands in gray suits, children in Ralph Lauren and Laura Ashley. Hazel let out a sigh. "Aren't they beautiful?" she said. For just a moment, I found myself agreeing.

"So, Larry." Sam laughed as I poured fresh oil into the popcorn machine's heated pan. It was my second day at the machine in the Men's Grill. "When you decide to move on from the club, you'll be able to get yourself a job at the popcorn counter in one of those big movie theaters."

I forced a smile.

"And you can tell them," he continued, "that you just about have a master's degree in popcorn popping. Tell 'em you learned everything you know from Sam at the country club."

I laughed. "Sure, Sam."

"Yeah, tell them I awarded you a master's degree."

I had already become an expert at yucking it up with Sam.

As I raced around taking out orders of coffee and baskets of hot rolls, I got a chance to see groups of families. The men seemed to be uniformly taller than six feet. Most of them were wearing blue blazers, white shirts, and incredibly out-of-style silk ties—the kind with little blue whales or little green ducks floating downward. They were bespectacled and conspicuously clean-shaven.

The "ladies," as the club prefers to call them, almost invariably had straight blond hair. Whether or not they had brown roots and whether they were twenty-five or forty-eight, they wore their hair blond, straight, and off the face. No dangling earrings, five-carat diamonds, or designer handbags. Black velvet or pastel headbands were de rigueur.

There were also groups of high school kids who wore torn jeans, sneakers, or unlaced L.L. Bean shoes, and sweatshirts that said things like "Hotchkiss Lacrosse" or "Andover Crew." At one table, two boys sat talking to two girls.

"No way, J.C.," one of the girls cried in disbelief while playing with the straw in her diet Coke.

The strawberry blond girl next to her flashed her unpainted nails in the air. "Way. She said that if she didn't get her grades up by this spring, they were going to take her out altogether."

"And where would they send her?" one of the guys asked.

The strawberry blond's grin disappeared as she leaned in close. "Public school."

The group, in hysterics, shook the table. The guys stomped their feet.

"Oh, my God, J.C., oh, J.C., J.C.," the diet-Coke girl cried.

Sitting in a tableless corner of the room beneath the TV set was a young, dark-skinned black woman dressed in a white uniform and a thick wool coat. On her lap was a baby with silky white blond hair. The woman sat patiently, shifting the baby in her lap while glancing over to where the baby's family ate, two tables away.

I ran to the kitchen, brought back a glass of tea, and offered it to her. The woman looked up at me, shook her head, and then turned back to the gurgling infant.

■ ■ ■ APRIL 21 (TUESDAY)

The TV in the Men's Grill was tuned to one of the all-day cable news channels and was reporting on the violent confrontations between pro-choice marchers and right-to-life protesters in Buffalo, New York.

"Look at all those women running around," a man in his late forties commented as he sat by himself at one of the larger tables in the Men's Grill.

At 11:10 A.M., the grill wasn't even officially opened yet.

As I walked around doing a final wipe of the tables, the man cried out into the empty room. "That's just a damned shame," he said while shaking his head and pulling at his yellow polo shirt in disbelief.

I nodded as he looked at me over his bowl of peanuts. "I agree with you."

He removed his sun visor and dropped it onto a table closer to the television. We both watched images of police dragging women who lay sprawled in the middle of a Buffalo city street.

"You know, it just scares me to see all these women running around like that," the middle-aged member continued as we both watched screaming crowds of placard-carrying activists and hand-cuffed protesters. "Someone's gotta keep these women reined in. A good, hard law that forces them to have those babies when they get pregnant will teach them to be responsible."

I looked at the man as he sat there hypnotized by the screen.

"All this equal rights bull," he finally added. "Running around getting pregnant and then running around doing what they want. Enough to make you sick."

Later, while Hector and I stood inside a deep walk-in freezer, we scooped balls of butter into separate butter dishes and talked about our life plans. "Will you go finish school sometime?" he asked as I dug deep into a vat of frozen butter.

"Maybe. In a couple of years, when I save more money, but I'm not sure." I felt lousy about having to lie.

"Maybe? If I had money, I'd go now—and I'm twenty-three years old." He shook his head in disapproval. "In my country, I had education. But here I don't because I don't know much English. It's tough because we have no work in South America. And here, there's work, but you need English to get it and make money."

We agreed that since 75 percent of the club employees were Spanish-speaking South Americans, the club really needed a bilingual manager or someone on staff who understood their concerns.

"Well," I offered. "I'll help you with English if you teach me some Spanish."

He joked that my Spanish was a lot worse than his English. After all, I only knew the words *gracias, buenos dias,* and *por favor.* So, during an illegal twelve-minute break, he ran through a quick vocabulary lesson while we walked to his minuscule room just across the sweaty congested halls of the noisy squash courts.

The room he took me into overlooked the driving range and was the size of a walk-in closet. The single bed touched three walls of the room. The quarter-sized refrigerator served as a stand for a stereo. There were a small dresser and a small desk plastered with many different pictures of a young Spanish-looking woman and a cute baby girl.

"My family" is all Hector would say in explanation while simultaneously pushing me out of the room and into the sweaty hall. "We go now—before we lose our job."

Just as we were leaving for the day, Mr. Ryan came down to hand out the new policies for those who were going to live in the Monkey House. Amazingly, without a trace of discomfort, he and everyone else referred to the building as "the Monkey House." Many of the workers had been living temporarily in the squash building. Since it had recently been renovated, the club was requiring all new residents to sign the form. The policy included a rule that forbade the employees to have overnight guests. Rule 14 stated that the club management had the right to enter an employee's locked bedroom at any time, without permission and without giving notice.

As I was making rounds with my coffeepots, I overheard a raspy-voiced woman talking to a mother and daughter who were thumbing through a catalog of infants' clothing.

"The problem with au pairs is that they're usually only in the country for a year."

The mother and daughter nodded in agreement.

"But getting one that is a citizen has its own problems. For example, if you ever have to choose between a Negro and one of these Spanish people, always go for the Negro."

One of the women frowned, confused. "Really?"

"Yes," the raspy-voiced woman responded with cold logic, "Even though you can't trust either one, at least the Negroes can speak English and follow your directions."

Before I could refill the final cup, the raspy-voiced woman looked up at me and smiled. "Oh, thanks for the refill, Larry."

▪ ▪ ▪ APRIL 22 (WEDNESDAY)

"This is our country, and don't forget it. They came here and have to live by our rules!" Hazel pounded her fist into the palm of her pale white hand.

I had made the mistake of telling her I had learned a few Spanish phrases to help me communicate better with some of my coworkers. She wasn't impressed.

"I'll be damned if I'm going to learn or speak one word of Spanish. And I'd suggest you do the same," she said. She took a long drag on her cigarette while I loaded the empty shelves with clean glasses.

Today, the TV was tuned to testimony and closing arguments from the Rodney King police-beating trial in California.

"I am so sick of seeing this awful videotape," one woman said to friends at her table. "It shouldn't be on TV."

At around two, Lois, the club's official secretary, asked me to help her send out a mailing to six hundred members after my shift. It seemed that none of the waiters wanted to stay late. And since the only other choice was the non-English-speaking bus staff and dishwashers, I was it.

She took me up to her office on the main floor and introduced me to the two women who sat with her.

"Larry, this is Marge, whom you'll talk with in three months, because she's in charge of employee benefits."

I smiled at the brunette.

"And Larry, this is Sandy, whom you'll talk with after you become a member at the club, because she's in charge of members' accounts."

Both Sandy and I looked up at Lois with shocked expressions.

Lois winked, and at the same moment, the three jovial women burst out laughing.

Lois sat me down at a table in the middle of the club's cavernous ballroom and had me stamp "Annual Member Guest" on the bottom of small postcards and stuff them into envelopes.

As I sat in the empty ballroom, I looked around at the mirrors and the silver-and-crystal chandeliers that dripped from the high ceiling. I thought about all the beautiful weddings and debutante balls that must have taken place in that room. I could imagine members asking themselves, "Why would anybody who is not like us want to join a club where they're not wanted?"

I stuffed my last envelope, forgot to clock out, and drove back to the Merritt Parkway and into New York.

▪ ▪ ▪ APRIL 23 (THURSDAY)

"Wow, that's great," I said to Mr. Ryan as he posted a memo entitled "Employee Relations Policy Statement: Employee Golf Privileges."

After quickly reading the memo, I realized this "policy" was a crock. The memo opened optimistically. "The club provides golf privileges for staff. . . . Current employees will be allowed golf privileges as outlined below." Unfortunately, the only employees the memo listed "below" were department heads, golf-management personnel, teaching assistants, the general manager, and "key staff that appear on the club's organizational chart."

At the end of the day, Mr. Ryan handed me my first paycheck. Perhaps now the backbreaking work would seem worthwhile. When I opened the envelope and saw what I'd earned—$174.04 for five days—I laughed out loud.

Back in the security of a bathroom stall, where I had periodically been taking notes since my arrival, I studied the check and thought about how many hours—and how hard—I'd worked for so little money. It was less than one-tenth of what I'd make in the same time at my law firm. I went upstairs and asked Mr. Ryan about my paycheck.

"Well, we decided to give you $7 an hour," he said in a tone overflowing with generosity. I had never actually been told my hourly rate. "But if the check looks especially big, that's because you got some extra pay in there for all of your terrific work on Good Friday. And by the way, Larry, don't tell the others what you're getting, because we're giving you a special deal and it's really nobody else's business."

I nodded and thanked him for his largesse. I stuffed some more envelopes, emptied out my locker, and left.

The next morning, I was scheduled to work a double shift. Instead, I called and explained that I had a family emergency and would have to quit immediately. Mr. Ryan was very sympathetic and said I could return when things settled down. I told him, "No thanks," but asked that he send my last paycheck to my home. I put my uniform and the key to my locker in a brown padded envelope, and I mailed it all to Mr. Ryan.

Somehow it took two months of phone calls for me to get my final paycheck ($123.74 after taxes and a $30 deduction for my uniform).

I'm back at my law firm now, dressed in one of my dark gray Paul Stuart suits, sitting in a handsome office thirty floors above Midtown. While it's a long way from the Monkey House, we still have a long way to go.

Sick Societies

Robert B. Edgerton

introduction ▪ ▪ ▪ ▪ ▪

All human groups develop ways to rank their members. In each group, people also attempt to display the statuses they have achieved. We are familiar with some of these: wearing clothing with labels deemed prestigious, driving a Rolls Royce, sporting a Rolex watch, getting admitted to a "name" school. In New York City, many reputable businesses have managed to get Park Avenue addresses, even though they are not located on Park Avenue. People who do business by mail with these firms aren't aware that the company's location is actually on an adjoining side street.

Although such matters are of interest, in their studies of social stratification sociologists probe much more deeply than this. Of special interest to sociologists is power, especially the means by which more powerful groups oppress groups with less power. Around the world, gender is a basis for sorting people into groups, with men the group in power. And around the world, men have developed practices to keep women submissive. In some instances, such as those documented by Robert Edgerton in this selection, the means men use to maintain dominance are severely oppressive. Both the practices described here and their acceptance by the oppressed group—which can be termed the *internalization of oppression*—may surprise you.

Thinking Critically

As you read this selection, ask yourself:

1. Why have men-as-a-group dominated women-as-a-group in every society of the world?

2. Why can practices that are painful and disfiguring persist for centuries?

3. What right do the people of one culture (such as one in the West) have to judge (or to force changes in) the customs of another culture (such as one in the East)?

How people feel about the established customs and institutions of their society can be a powerful indicator of how adequately that society and its culture serve their needs. But between blissful contentment and open rebellion lie many complexities and contradictions of human emotion and behavior. For example, women and men alike have gone to remarkable lengths to beautify themselves. They tattoo themselves over their entire bodies, cover themselves with scars, mutilate their genitals, and blacken their teeth, file them into points, and knock some of them out, among other things. These are only a few examples of painful practices that have been, and in some quarters still are, eagerly pursued in the quest for beauty. As painful as these practices are, few things done in the quest for beauty were more extreme than the Chinese practice of binding the feet of women. Young girls, some still in infancy, suffered excruciating pain because their feet were bandaged so tightly that normal growth could not occur. So tightly, in fact, were the toes folded under the foot that the bones were often broken. Accounts of the anguish these children suffered during the process of replacing blood- and pus-soaked bandages with new and still tighter ones are truly harrowing. The pain was so severe that the girls could not walk or even sleep, and they were too young to understand why they were being made to suffer. Eventually, the acute pain subsided, but for the rest of their lives these women were barely able to hobble, and some were carried everywhere in a sedan chair.

Chinese men have admired small feet in women since before Confucian times, but the practice of footbinding apparently did not begin until around 1100 A.D. It was at first confined to the Chinese elite, but it eventually spread throughout society, even including some peasants and the urban poor. The reasons for the origin and spread of footbinding were complex, but in addition to aesthetic considerations, Chinese men said that they saw the practice as an effective way to control the sexual liaisons of their increasingly bold wives. Once women's feet were bound, they could no longer "run around," so to speak, because they could not even leave their houses without assistance. What is more, a woman with bound feet could not work; so her husband achieved prestige by demonstrating that he could afford to have a wife who did not need to work. Men also saw the practice as a clear and necessary expression of their dominance over women. Before long, men also saw fit to praise the erotic advantages of footbinding, saying that the tottering style of walking it produced created more beautiful buttocks and tightened the vagina. The naked bound foot itself—"the golden lotus"—became as much a focus of erotic desire for Chinese men as women's breasts were for Westerners.

The Manchu conquerors outlawed footbinding, but to such little effect that some members of the Manchu court adopted a modified version of the practice themselves. Footbinding endured for over a thousand years without any widespread social protest by women. For one thing, Chinese women lacked political power, but at the same time they could appreciate the advantages of footbinding. It could give them beauty and sensuality, lead to a good marriage, and offer a life of leisure. Of at least equal importance, parents who imposed the practice on their young daughters were not thinking only of their daughters' futures. A daughter's marriage to a wealthy man was of obvious benefit to the entire family.

With these benefits in mind, it is perhaps less surprising that footbinding lasted so long than that it ended as suddenly as it did. Opposed by Christian missionaries, the expansionist Japanese, and Westerners of all sorts, the reform-minded revolutionary governments of early twentieth-century China were able to eradicate footbinding in a decade or so among their urban population although it lasted until the 1930s in some traditional rural areas. That a practice so painful and disfiguring to women can nonetheless persist should not be surprising. In Victorian times, the same Western women (some of whom were the wives of missionaries in China) who deplored footbinding as a "barbaric" custom willingly had themselves cinched into steel- and whalebone-reinforced canvas corsets so tightly that they had difficulty breathing and their internal organs were sometimes damaged. Girls as young as three were corseted, and over time their corsets became progressively tighter. By adolescence many girls' back muscles had atrophied to such an extent that they could neither sit nor walk for more than a few minutes without someone's support. The pursuit of beauty may be directed by men, even imposed by them, but women can find it to their advantage to acquiesce. With the controversy about silicone breast implants so freshly in mind, we need hardly be reminded that many American women (and some men) today endure painful and expensive cosmetic surgery in an effort to "beautify" their faces or bodies.

These cautionary examples alert us to the need to proceed judiciously in evaluating how dissatisfied people may be with their culture. For example, the practice of sending widows or household slaves to the grave with their deceased husbands or masters was known in many parts of the world, including China, Africa, ancient Greece, Scandinavia, and Russia. The reasons for putting a man's wives or slaves to death varied. Sometimes it was said that the deceased would need his wives or slaves to provide him with earthly comforts in the hereafter. Sometimes it was said (more cynically) that this practice would encourage wives or slaves to do everything in their power to keep their husbands or masters alive as long as possible. There were other reasons, too, ranging from jealousy about the sexual activities of surviving wives to elaborate religious justifications. Nowhere did the practice become as widespread or take on such profound metaphysical meaning as in Hindu India, where a widow could achieve virtual divinity by voluntarily immolating herself on her husband's funeral pyre.

Known as *sati* in Sanskrit and Anglicized as "suttee," this practice was observed as early as the fourth century B.C. when Alexander the Great recorded it, and despite heated controversy it has continued to occur now and then in contemporary India. Originally practiced by the wives of kings and great warriors, sati spread first to Brahmins, then to members of lower castes. Although Hindu scriptural justifications for the practice (or practices, since a widow could choose to be buried alive instead of being burned to death) were contradictory, many indicated that by choosing sati she could reduce the pollution that endangered her husband's surviving relatives, absolve herself of sin (wives were thought to bear responsibility for their husbands' death), and rejoin her husband in a cycle of future rebirths. As Richard Shweder has commented, sati can be a heroic act that represents and confirms the "deepest properties of Hinduism's moral world."

Much like a wedding, the sati ceremony required elaborate ritual preparations. Priests, mourners, and an excited crowd followed the ornately dressed widow and her husband's corpse to the funeral pyre. After circling the fire, the widow distributed her jewels and money and looked into a mirror where she saw the past and the future; then a priest quoted scriptural passages that likened the pyre to a marriage bed. After the necessary ritual acts had been completed and the widow had joined her husband's corpse on the pyre, it was set alight by her son (who sometimes collapsed in grief after doing so). After the ceremony, the spot where the sati died became a shrine, and she was revered as a heroine and goddess.

As improbable as the spectacle of a woman willingly, even eagerly, burning herself to death may seem, there are numerous eyewitness reports to the effect that sometimes, at least, that is exactly what took place. William Carey witnessed a sati in 1798 in which the widow actually danced on the pyre to show her contempt for death before lying down next to the corpse of her husband and being consumed by flames. In 1829 a British magistrate named Halliday attempted to convince a widow not to become a sati. "At length she showed some impatience and asked to be allowed to proceed to the site." Horrified, Halliday tried once again to dissuade her by asking if she understood how much pain she was about to suffer. The woman looked scornfully at the Englishman, then demanded that a lamp be brought to her and lighted. "Then steadfastly looking at me with an air of grave defiance she rested her right elbow on the ground and put her finger in the flame of the lamp. The finger scorched, blistered, and blackened and finally twisted up . . . this lasted for some time, during which she never moved her hand, uttered a sound, or altered the expression of her countenance." Halliday gave permission for the ceremony to proceed.

Over the centuries, many Hindu widows must have chosen sati deaths sublimely and reverently. But there was another reality to sati, one that falls well short of sublimity. First, it will not have escaped the reader's attention that sati was for women only; widowers had no duty to join their deceased wives in the divine devotion of a fiery death. Second, despite great pressure, very few widows actually chose sati. Even in Bengal where sati was most common, only a small minority of widows—less than 10 percent—chose sati although the prospect of widowhood was a dismal one at best. Widows were not only forbidden to remarry but were compelled to live in socially isolated asceticism—praying, fasting, reading holy books, and avoiding any hint of worldly pleasure. Because widows were thought to endanger others and often were accused of being witches, they were also scorned and feared. Despite the wretched conditions of widowhood, the promised rewards of sati, and the often relentless pressure exerted by the deceased husband's relatives on the widow to choose this supreme act of devotion, the great majority of widows preferred to live. Sometimes, however, they were given no choice. Because many women were married as infants, they became widows and "chose" sati while still children. One wife burned with the corpse of her adult husband was only four years old; others were scarcely older.

Sometimes the pressures imposed on a widow to choose sati were anything but subtle; indeed, they amounted to murder. In 1827 a British observer witnessed a sati ceremony in which the fire had no sooner been lighted than the widow leapt off the pyre and tried to flee; several men seized her and flung her back into the blaze. Once again the widow fled, and although badly burned she managed to outdistance her pursuers and throw herself into a nearby stream where she lay "weeping bitterly."

She swore that she would not go through with the ceremony. Seeming to take pity on her, a man promised that if she would sit on a large cloth he had spread on the ground, he would carry her home. When she did so, she was once again seized, sewn into the cloth, and thrown back into the inferno. The cloth was immediately consumed by the flames, and the wretched victim once again tried to flee. This time she was beheaded with a sword, and her body was thrown back onto the pyre. Not exactly a serene act of wifely devotion.

It was not just tormented widows who frequently wanted no part of sati; some Hindu scriptures sharply criticized the custom. In *Mahamivantantra* (verses 79 and 80) it is said that a woman who accepts sati will go to hell. And there was a vigorous anti-sati movement in India even before the British attempted to abolish the practice (the movement was not led by women but by a Brahmin man). It was also observed that there were economic reasons for sati. It was most common in Bengal, and it was only in Bengal that a widow without a son had the same rights to the family property formerly possessed by her deceased husband. Surviving family members therefore attempted to protect family property by convincing the widow that it was her duty to join her husband in death (thereby conveniently leaving the property to her husband's family).

In recent years opposition to sati in India has grown, but the ceremony has not been abandoned. In 1987 Roop Kanwar, a beautiful eighteen-year-old, college-educated woman, immolated herself with her dead husband's head on her lap while a crowd estimated at 300,000 watched in admiration. But many Indians were outraged at the death of this young woman, partly because it was reported that she had been injected with morphine before the ceremony, which raised questions about undue influence on the part of her husband's relatives. Following Kanwar's death the government of Rajasthan, where the sati took place, made it a crime punishable by seven years in prison to "glorify" sati by collecting funds, building a temple, or performing a ceremony to preserve the memory of a person who committed sati; it also decreed that any attempt made to abet an act of sati was punishable by death. Many Indians were indignant about this criminalization of the ritual, arguing that a widow's immolation was a courageous, inspirational tradition that reaffirmed marital devotion and belief in rebirth.

The point of this example, perhaps overlong in the telling even though greatly oversimplified, is that people in a society can take quite different views of their customs and institutions. It is not only we outsiders who have differing views of sati; so have Indians themselves. A similar disagreement has existed, and indeed still does, in many parts of Africa with regard to the practice of female genital mutilation, generally known as female infibulation, circumcision, or clitoral excision. In parts of the Sudan, for example, the genitalia of young Nubian girls are still almost completely cut away, and the vaginal opening is sutured closed except for an opening the size of a matchstick for the passage of urine and menstrual blood. Done without anesthesia, the operation is excruciatingly painful, there can be dangerous complications, and some girls die. Nubian men are sometimes squeamish about the practice, but women have continued to support infibulation despite governmental efforts to abolish it. Farther south, in East Africa, the operation does not involve closing the vaginal opening, but it does require excision of the clitoris and both sets of labia—as in Nubia, the pain is terrible. There the operation does not take place until the girls are adolescents, and not every girl is able to stand the pain. Some have to be excised while they are held down by men. For many years, educated East Africans have deplored the practice, and it has been illegal in Kenya for some years. It nevertheless still takes place both in Kenya and elsewhere in Africa. . . .

The extent to which women accept and value their culturally prescribed roles varies from society to society, but in a good many of them, women have been quite unhappy and have (not without justification, I might add) blamed men for their plight. Women have launched spirited verbal and even physical assaults against their husbands in various parts of the world, but with rare exceptions men physically dominate women, and they are often far from gentle about it. As a result, when women protest, they usually do so indirectly. Sometimes women consciously adopt a sick role, as in *susto* (or fright sickness, common in Latin America), to escape, if only temporarily, from the burdens of their lives. Writing about the Zapotec of Oaxaca, Douglas Uzzell concluded that women who claimed to suffer from *susto* were able to withdraw from ordinary relationships—including beatings from their husbands—because the illness was thought to be fatal unless the patient was indulged. . . .

Another form of indirect protest was practiced by women among the Awald' Ali Bedouin in Egypt's western desert. Distressed by the cultural constraints of arranged marriage and enforced segregation, these women indulged in various kinds of irreverent discourse about men and masculinity, including oral lyric poetry that discreetly but pointedly ridiculed, chided, and sometimes excoriated men.

Women have also taken aggressive action against what they have perceived as intolerable behavior on the part of men. From Ulithi Atoll in Micronesia to the Inuit of the far north, aggrieved women sometimes gathered together to direct obscene and abusive taunts and songs against men. Women among the Andean people who were first incorporated into the Inca Empire and later subjugated to Spanish colonial rule protested against the misery of their lives in a number of ways. Sometimes they became so desperate that they preferred suicide to a tormented life. Other Andean women preferred killing their own children to allowing a new generation to suffer under the rule of colonial officials. Those who did so killed their sons rather than their daughters to protest the manifold ways in which men had betrayed them. Still other women fled with their children to inaccessible regions where they established an underground culture of resistance to colonial rule.

Among the Samburu [of Africa] . . . bands of twenty or so women would sing ribaldly abusive and threatening songs outside the house of an elder who, for instance, was unusually harsh with his wives. In other parts of Africa women's protests could become particularly overt and even painful. When women among the Igbo of Nigeria were offended by something a man did (such as mistreating his wife or infringing on women's economic rights), they would gather at his household where they danced and sang abusive songs that detailed his offenses (and not infrequently questioned his masculinity). They would also pound on the walls of his house, and if he came outside to object, they would even rough him up a bit. All this would continue until the man apologized and promised not to repeat his offenses. Among the Bakweri of West Cameroon, if a woman was offended by a man, she might call out all the women of the village, who then descended on the culprit and demanded an apology and recompense. A similar phenomenon occurred among the Kamba of Kenya, whose women were ordinarily quite subservient to their harshly domineering husbands. However, when Kamba women felt that something had taken place to endanger their crops or their general well-being and that the all-male council of elders had failed to remedy the problem, they would gather together and take direct action. Beating large drums and flailing thorny boughs about them, they would march on the offender to make their demands. Any man who was incautious enough to get in their way would become the target of verbal abuse, and some were even assaulted physically. In apparent recognition of the legitimacy of the women's indignation, the usually dominant Kamba men meekly acquiesced.

Like the Kamba, men among the Pokot of Kenya thoroughly dominated women during the course of everyday life; indeed, a husband rarely hesitated to beat his wife, sometimes severely, and it was considered his right to do so. Pokot women often expressed their anger to one another but typically seemed resigned to a life of subservience. It was common for them to remark, with as much fatalism as anger, that "we cannot rule men; we can only hate them." But sometimes when a man's abuse of his wife went beyond the very generous bounds of husbandly rights, the wife could and did organize other women to "shame" her husband, as the Pokot put it. If, for example, a man beat his wife excessively or failed to have sexual intercourse with her, she and the other women could tie him up while he slept; they then not only ridiculed and reviled him with every imaginable obscenity, but one woman after another showed their genitals to him—something that was ordinarily unthinkable among the Pokot—then urinated and even defecated on him before beating his testicles with small sticks. Finally, they would cut larger sticks and threaten to beat him even more severely. It was not until his wife intervened to halt the beating (no doubt with crocodile tears in her eyes) and the now thoroughly chastened man agreed to allow the women to slaughter and eat his favorite ox (something else that was ordinarily unthinkable) that the women would finally agree to release the man. Throughout this public event, men would make no attempt to intervene. Instead, they found that they were needed elsewhere. . . .

■ ■ ■ CONCLUSION*

[Throughout history, the subjugation of women by men has taken many forms. In control of society, males have set the standards of beauty and loyalty that women have had to meet in order to achieve social status. We reviewed footbinding as an example of how the male idea of beauty was forced upon women, female circumcision as a way of enforcing male standards of sexuality, and sati as a final act of male dominance. For some women, the consequence has been extreme pain; for others, death. We also reviewed examples of societies in which women banded together to rebel against their subjugation.]

*Conclusion by the editor.

PART

IV   Social Institutions

■ ■

The previous parts have examined some of the social forces that influence our lives, that twist and turn us in one direction or another. You have read about culture and socialization, social control and deviance, and various forms of social stratification. In this part, we turn our focus onto *social institutions,* the standard ways that society has set up to meet its basic needs.

To exist, every society must solve certain recurrent problems. Babies must be nourished and children taught how to take responsibility. The sex drive must also be held within bounds. To help meet these needs, every society has set up some form of marriage and family, the first social institution we meet on the stage of life. Social order—keeping people from robbing, raping, cheating, injuring, and killing one another—also has to be established. To accomplish this, each social group sets up some form of politics. Goods and services also have to be produced and distributed. This leads to what is called the economy. The new generation also has to be taught to view the world in ways that match the dominant orientation, as well as to learn the skills needed to participate in the economy. For this, we have some form of education. Then there are views of the spiritual world, of God and morality, perhaps of an afterlife. For this, we have religion.

We are immersed in social institutions, and we never escape from them. We are born into one (the family), we attend school in another (education), and we make our living in still another (economy). Even if we don't vote, the political institution surrounds us with the demands of its laws. Even if we don't worship at a church, synagogue, or mosque, we can't avoid religion, for religious principles are the foundation of many of our laws. Even closing most offices, schools, and factories on Sunday is based on religion.

Social institutions, then, are another way that society nudges us to fit in. Like a curb or median is to an automobile, so social institutions are to humans. They set boundaries around us, pushing us to turn one way instead of another, directing us to think, act, and even feel along approved avenues.

Social institutions are so significant that many sociologists specialize in them. Some focus on marriage and family, others study politics or the economy, while still others do research on religion, education, or the military. After this introductory course—which is sort of a survey of sociology—students usually can take courses on specific social institutions. Most departments of sociology teach a course on marriage and family. In large departments, there may be a course on each social institution, one on the sociology of religion, another on the sociology of education, and so on. In very large departments, the social institutions may be broken down into smaller components, and there may be several specialized courses on the sociology of politics, education, and so on.

To focus on social institutions, we open this part with an article that has become a classic in sociology. C. Wright Mills analyzes the ruling elite of the United States. What he calls the *power elite* is the group that makes the major decisions that affect our lives. Annette Lareau then compares middle-class and lower-class families, examining how the internal dynamics of families set children on separate class-based courses in life. We conclude this part with a research report by Jonathan Kozol on the social inequality that plagues our educational system and how this, too, sets children on class-based courses in life.

The Power Elite

C. Wright Mills

introduction

A theme that has run through many of the preceding selections is how groups influence us—how in some instances they even control our behavior. Our membership in some of these groups (as with gender in the immediately preceding selection) comes with birth and is involuntary. Other groups, we join because we desire the membership. All groups—whether our membership is voluntary or involuntary—try to control our behavior. The broad, overarching groups, which lay the general boundaries for our actions and even our thinking, are the *social institutions* of our society. We are born and we die within social institutions. And between birth and death, we live within them—from family and school to politics and religion.

A central question that sociologists ask concerns power. Who has it, and how is it exercised? In this selection, C. Wright Mills says that power in U.S. society has become concentrated in our political, military, and economic institutions. Not only have these three grown larger, but also they have become more centralized and interconnected. As a result, their power has outstripped those of our other social institutions. Together, these three form a "triangle of power." The interests of the top political, military, and business leaders have coalesced, says Mills, and in his term, they now form a *power elite*. It is this power elite that makes the major decisions that so vitally affect our welfare—and, increasingly, with the dominance of the United States in global affairs, the welfare of the world.

Thinking Critically

As you read this selection, ask yourself:

1. If the members of the power elite don't meet together as a group, how can they be considered the primary source of power in the United States?

2. Mills identifies the top leaders of the top corporations as the pinnacle of power. Why doesn't he identify the top military or political leaders as this pinnacle?

3. Use Mills' analysis to explain why in *Essentials* war is classified as an aspect of politics. Why do you think that the power elite often calls the waging of war by the United States by terms other than war, such as "interventions," "helping a people or government," even—and my favorites—"establishing democracy" or "establishing peace"?

The powers of ordinary men* are circumscribed by the everyday worlds in which they live, yet even in these rounds of job, family, and neighborhood they often seem driven by forces they can neither understand nor govern. "Great changes" are beyond their control, but affect their conduct and outlook nonetheless. The very framework of modern society confines them to projects not their own, but from every side, such changes now press upon the men and women of the mass society, who accordingly feel that they are without purpose in an epoch in which they are without power.

But not all men are in this sense ordinary. As the means of information and of power are centralized, some men come to occupy positions in American society from which they can look down upon, so to speak, and by their decisions mightily affect, the everyday worlds of ordinary men and women. They are not made by their jobs; they set up and break down jobs for thousands of others; they are not confined by simple family responsibilities; they can escape. They may live in many hotels and houses, but they are bound by no one community. They need not merely "meet the demands of the day and hour"; in some part, they create these demands, and cause others to meet them. Whether or not they profess their power, their technical and political experience of it far transcends that of the underlying population. What Jacob Burckhardt said of "great men," most Americans might well say of their elite: "They are all that we are not."

The power elite is composed of men whose positions enable them to transcend the ordinary environments of ordinary men and women; they are in positions to make decisions having major consequences. Whether they do or do not make such decisions is less important than the fact that they do occupy such pivotal positions: Their failure to act, their failure to make decisions, is itself an act that is often of greater consequence than the decisions they do make. For they are in command of the major hierarchies and organizations of modern society. They rule the big corporations. They run the machinery of the state and claim its prerogatives. They direct the military establishment. They occupy the strategic command posts of the social structure, in which are now centered the effective means of the power and the wealth and the celebrity which they enjoy.

The power elite are not solitary rulers. Advisers and consultants, spokesmen and opinion-makers are often the captains of their higher thought and decision. Immediately below the elite are the professional politicians of the middle levels of power, in the Congress and in the pressure groups, as well as among the new and old upper classes of town and city and region. Mingling with them, in curious ways which we shall explore, are those professional celebrities who live by being continually displayed but are never, so long as they remain celebrities, displayed enough. If such celebrities are not at the head of any dominating hierarchy, they do often have the power to distract the attention of the public or afford sensations to the masses, or,

---

*As with the first article in this anthology, when Mills wrote, "men" was used to refer to both men and women and "his" to both hers and his. Although the writing style has changed, the sociological ideas are as significant as ever.

more directly, to gain the ear of those who do occupy positions of direct power. More or less unattached, as critics of morality and technicians of power, as spokesmen of God and creators of mass sensibility, such celebrities and consultants are part of the immediate scene in which the drama of the elite is enacted. But that drama itself is centered in the command posts of the major institutional hierarchies.

The truth about the nature and the power of the elite is not some secret which men of affairs know but will not tell. Such men hold quite various theories about their own roles in the sequence of event and decision. Often they are uncertain about their roles, and even more often they allow their fears and their hopes to affect their assessment of their own power. No matter how great their actual power, they tend to be less acutely aware of it than of the resistances of others to its use. Moreover, most American men of affairs have learned well the rhetoric of public relations, in some cases even to the point of using it when they are alone, and thus coming to believe it. The personal awareness of the actors is only one of the several sources one must examine in order to understand the higher circles. Yet many who believe that there is no elite, or at any rate none of any consequence, rest their argument upon what men of affairs believe about themselves, or at least assert in public.

There is, however, another view: those who feel, even if vaguely, that a compact and powerful elite of great importance does now prevail in America often base that feeling upon the historical trend of our time. They have felt, for example, the domination of the military event, and from this they infer that generals and admirals, as well as other men of decision influenced by them, must be enormously powerful. They hear that the Congress has again abdicated to a handful of men decisions clearly related to the issue of war or peace. They know that the bomb was dropped over Japan in the name of the United States of America, although they were at no time consulted about the matter. They feel that they live in a time of big decisions; they know that they are not making any. Accordingly, as they consider the present as history, they infer that at its center, making decisions or failing to make them, there must be an elite of power.

On the one hand, those who share this feeling about big historical events assume that there is an elite and that its power is great. On the other hand, those who listen carefully to the reports of men apparently involved in the great decisions often do not believe that there is an elite whose powers are of decisive consequence.

Both views must be taken into account, but neither is adequate. The way to understand the power of the American elite lies neither solely in recognizing the historic scale of events nor in accepting the personal awareness reported by men of apparent decision. Behind such men and behind the events of history, linking the two, are the major institutions of modern society. *These hierarchies of state [politics] and corporation [business] and army [military] constitute the means of power* [italics added]; as such they are now of a consequence not before equaled in human history—and at their summits, there are now those command posts of modern society which offer us the sociological key to an understanding of the role of the higher circles in America.

Within American society, major national power now resides in the economic, the political, and the military domains. Other institutions seem off to the side of modern history, and, on occasion, duly subordinated to these. No family is as directly powerful in national affairs as any major corporation; no church is as directly powerful in the external biographies of young men in America today as the military establishment; no college is as powerful in the shaping of momentous events as the National Security Council. Religious, educational, and family institutions are not autonomous centers of national power; on the contrary, these decentralized areas are increasingly shaped by the big three, in which developments of decisive and immediate consequence now occur.

Families and churches and schools adapt to modern life; governments and armies and corporations shape it; and, as they do so, they turn these lesser institutions into means for their ends. Religious institutions provide chaplains to the armed forces where they are used as a means of increasing the effectiveness of its morale to kill. Schools select and train men for their jobs in corporations and their specialized tasks in the armed forces. The extended family has, of course, long been broken up by the industrial revolution, and now the son and the father are removed from the family, by compulsion if need be, whenever the army of the state sends out the call. And the symbols of all these lesser institutions are used to legitimate the power and the decisions of the big three.

The life-fate of the modern individual depends not only upon the family into which he was born or which he enters by marriage, but increasingly upon the corporation in which he spends the most alert hours of his best years; not only upon the school where he is educated as a child and adolescent, but also upon the state which touches him throughout his life; not only upon the church in which on occasion he hears the word of God, but also upon the army in which he is disciplined.

If the centralized state could not rely upon the inculcation of nationalist loyalties in public and private schools, its leaders would promptly seek to modify the decentralized educational system. If the bankruptcy rate among the top five hundred corporations were as high as the general divorce rate among the [57] million married couples, there would be economic catastrophe on an international scale. If members of armies gave to them no more of their lives than do believers to the churches to which they belong, there would be a military crisis.

Within each of the big three, the typical institutional unit has become enlarged, has become administrative, and, in the power of its decisions, has become centralized. Behind these developments there is a fabulous technology, for as institutions, they have incorporated this technology and guide it, even as it shapes and paces their developments.

The economy—once a great scatter of small productive units in autonomous balance—has become dominated by two or three hundred giant corporations, administratively and politically interrelated, which together hold the keys to economic decisions.

The political order, once a decentralized set of several dozen states with a weak spinal cord, has become a centralized, executive establishment which has taken up into itself many powers previously scattered, and now enters into each and every cranny of the social structure.

The military order, once a slim establishment in a context of distrust fed by state militia, has become the largest and most expensive feature of government, and, although well versed in smiling public relations, now has all the grim and clumsy efficiency of a sprawling bureaucratic domain.

In each of these institutional areas, the means of power at the disposal of decision makers have increased enormously; their central executive powers have been enhanced; within each of them modern administrative routines have been elaborated and tightened up.

As each of these domains becomes enlarged and centralized, the consequences of its activities become greater, and its traffic with the others increases. The decisions of a handful of corporations bear upon military and political as well as upon economic developments around the world. The decisions of the military establishment rest upon and grievously affect political life as well as the very level of economic activity. The decisions made within the political domain determine economic activities and military programs. There is no longer, on the one hand, an economy, and, on the other hand, a political order containing a military establishment unimportant to politics and to money-making. There is a political economy linked, in a thousand ways, with military institutions and decisions. On each side of the world-split running through central Europe and around the Asiatic rimlands, there is an ever-increasing inter-locking of economic, military, and political structures. If there is government intervention in the corporate economy, so is there corporate intervention in the governmental process. In the structural sense, this triangle of power is the source of the interlocking directorate that is most important for the historical structure of the present.

The fact of the interlocking is clearly revealed at each of the points of crisis of modern capitalist society—slump, war, and boom. In each, men of decision are led to an awareness of the interdependence of the major institutional orders. In the nineteenth century, when the scale of all institutions was smaller, their liberal integration was achieved in the automatic economy, by an autonomous play of market forces, and in the automatic political domain, by the bargain and the vote. It was then assumed that out of the imbalance and friction that followed the limited decisions then possible a new equilibrium would in due course emerge. That can no longer be assumed, and it is not assumed by the men at the top of each of the three dominant hierarchies.

For given the scope of their consequences, decisions—and indecisions—any one of these ramify into the others, and hence top decisions tend either to become coordinated or to lead to a commanding indecision. It has not always been like this. When numerous small entrepreneurs made up the economy, for example, many of them could fail and the consequences still remain local; political and military authorities did not intervene. But now, given political expectations and military commitments, can they afford to allow key units of the private corporate economy to break down in slump? Increasingly, they do intervene in economic affairs, and as they do so, the controlling decisions in each order are inspected by agents of the other two, and economic, military, and political structures are interlocked.

At the pinnacle of each of the three enlarged and centralized domains, there have arisen those higher circles which make up the economic, the political, and the military elites. At the top of the economy, among the corporate rich, there are the chief executives; at the top of the political order, the members of the political directorate; at the top of the military establishment, the elite of soldier-statesmen clustered in and around the Joint Chiefs of Staff and the upper echelon. As each of these domains has coincided with the others, as decisions tend to become total in their consequence, the leading men in each of the three domains of power—the warlords, the corporation chieftains, the political directorate—tend to come together, to form the power elite of America.

The higher circles in and around these command posts are often thought of in terms of what their members possess: They have a greater share than other people of the things and experiences that are most highly valued. From this point of view, the elite are simply those who have the most of what there is to have, which is generally held to include money, power, and prestige—as well as all the ways of life to which these lead. But the elite are not simply those who have the most, for they could not "have the most" were it not for their positions in the great institutions. For such institutions are the necessary bases of power, of wealth, and of prestige, and at the same time, the chief means of exercising power, of acquiring and retaining wealth, and of cashing in the higher claims for prestige.

By the powerful we mean, of course, those who are able to realize their will, even if others resist it. No one, accordingly, can be truly powerful unless he has access to the command of major institutions, for it is over these institutional means of power that the truly powerful are, in the first instance, powerful. Higher politicians and key officials of government command such institutional power; so do admirals and generals, and so do the major owners and executives of the larger corporations. Not all power, it is true, is anchored in and exercised by means of such institutions, but only within and through them can power be more or less continuous and important.

Wealth also is acquired and held in and through institutions. The pyramid of wealth cannot be understood merely in terms of the very rich; for the great inheriting families, as we shall see, are now supplemented by the corporate institutions of modern society: Every one of the very rich families has been and is closely connected—always legally and frequently managerially as well—with one of the multimillion-dollar corporations.

The modern corporation is the prime source of wealth, but, in latter-day capitalism, the political apparatus also opens and closes many avenues to wealth. The amount as well as the source of income, the power over consumers' goods as well as over productive capital, are determined by position within the political economy. If our interest in the very rich goes beyond their lavish or their miserly consumption, we must examine their relations to modern forms of corporate property as well as to the state; for such relations now determine the chances of men to secure big property and to receive high income.

Great prestige increasingly follows the major institutional units of the social structure. It is obvious that prestige depends, often quite decisively, upon access to the publicity machines that are now a central and normal feature of all the big institutions of modern America. Moreover, one feature of these hierarchies of corporation, state, and military establishment is that their top positions are increasingly interchangeable. One result of this is the accumulative nature of prestige. Claims for prestige, for example, may be initially based on military roles, then expressed in and augmented by an educational institution run by corporate executives; and cashed in, finally, in the political order, where, for [top military leaders who become president, such as] General Eisenhower and those [they represent], power and prestige finally meet at the very peak. Like wealth and power, prestige tends to be cumulative: The more of it you have, the more you can get. These values also tend to be translatable into one another: The wealthy find it easier than the poor to gain power; those with status find it easier than those without it to control opportunities for wealth.

If we took the one-hundred most powerful men in America, the one-hundred wealthiest, and the one-hundred most celebrated away from the institutional positions they now occupy, away from their resources of men and women and money, away from the media of mass communication that are now focused upon them— then they would be powerless and poor and uncelebrated. For power is not of a man. Wealth does not center in the person of the wealthy. Celebrity is not inherent in any personality. To be celebrated, to be wealthy, to have power requires access to major institutions, for the institutional positions men occupy determine in large part their chances to have and to hold these valued experiences.

The people of the higher circles may also be conceived as members of a top social stratum, as a set of groups whose members know one another, see one another socially and at business, and so, in making decisions, take one another into account. The elite, according to this conception, feel themselves to be, and are felt by others to be, the inner circle of "the upper social classes." They form a more or less compact social and psychological entity; they have become self-conscious members of a social class. People are either accepted into this class or they are not, and there is a qualitative split, rather than merely a numerical scale, separating them from those who are not elite. They are more or less aware of themselves as a social class and they behave toward one another differently from the way they do toward members of other classes. They accept one another, understand one another, marry one another, tend to work and to think if not together at least alike.

Now, we do not want by our definition to prejudge whether the elite of the command posts are conscious members of such a socially recognized class, or whether considerable proportions of the elite derive from such a clear and distinct class. These are matters to be investigated. Yet in order to be able to recognize what we intend to investigate, we must note something that all biographies and memoirs of the wealthy and the powerful and the eminent make clear: No matter what else they may be, the people of these higher circles are involved in a set of overlapping "crowds" and intricately connected "cliques." There is a kind of mutual attraction among those who "sit on the same terrace"—although this often becomes clear to them, as well as to others, only at the point at which they feel the need to draw the line; only when, in their common defense, they come to understand what they have in common, and so close their ranks against outsiders.

The idea of such ruling stratum implies that most of its members have similar social origins, that throughout their lives they maintain a network of internal connections, and that to some degree there is an interchangeability of position between the various hierarchies of money and power and celebrity. We must, of course, note at once that if such an elite stratum does exist, its social visibility and its form, for very solid historical reasons, are quite different from those of the noble cousin-hoods that once ruled various European nations.

That American society has never passed through a feudal epoch is of decisive importance to the nature of the American elite, as well as to American society as a historic whole. For it means that no nobility or aristocracy, established before the capitalist era, has stood in tense opposition to the higher bourgeoisie. It means that this bourgeoisie has monopolized not only wealth but prestige and power as well. It means that no set of noble families has commanded the top positions and monopolized the values that are generally held in high esteem; and certainly that no set has done so explicitly by inherited right. It means that no high church dignitaries or court nobilities, no entrenched landlords with honorific accouterments, no monopolists of high army posts have opposed the enriched bourgeoisie and in the name of birth and prerogative successfully resisted its self-making.

But this does *not* mean that there are no upper strata in the United States. That they emerged from a "middle class" that had no recognized aristocratic superiors does not mean they remained middle class when enormous increases in wealth made their own superiority possible. Their origins and their newness may have made the upper strata less visible in America than elsewhere. But in America today there are in fact tiers and ranges of wealth and power of which people in the middle and lower ranks know very little and may not even dream. There are families who, in their well-being, are quite insulated from the economic jolts and lurches felt by the merely prosperous and those farther down the scale. There are also men of power who in quite small groups make decisions of enormous consequence for the underlying population. . . .

Social Class and Childrearing

Annette Lareau

introduction ▪ ▪ ▪ ▪

It is difficult to overstate the significance of the family in our lives. It is here that we learn our basic orientations to life, the foundation that envelops our experiences. In our family we are introduced to gender, to how males and females should act and feel, to basic ideas about God, authority, the value of education, how to interact with others, and how to view the self. Here begin our aspirations, our ideas of what we want to attain in life. Unwitting as it may be, our family places an initial veil over our eyes through which we evaluate our self and the world. It is not without reason that the family is called the basic building block of society.

Largely hidden from view is the influence of social class. Although as children we gradually become aware that there are richer and poorer neighborhoods and that some families have more material goods than others, apart from gross differences such as two-parent and single-parent families, for the most part family seems to be family. Permeating family in ways beyond our perception, however, is social class. The differences are often subtle, but they are significantly cumulative. As this research by Lareau makes evident, we need to look beyond the physical differences (type of house or apartment, amount of income, and so on) to explore what happens within families.

Thinking Critically

As you read this selection, ask yourself:

1. How do my own childhood experiences compare with the findings reported here?

2. The author documents significant differences in middle-class and lower-class use of language. What is the impact of this language use on the children's future?

3. Why are the terms "natural growth" and "concerted cultivation" appropriate?

In recent decades, sociological knowledge about inequality in family life has increased dramatically. Yet, debate persists, especially about the transmission of class advantages to children. Kingston (2000) and others question whether disparate aspects of family life cohere in meaningful patterns. Pointing to a "thin evidentiary base" for claims of social class differences in the interior of family life, Kingston also asserts that "class distinguishes neither distinctive parenting styles [n]or distinctive involvement of kids" in specific behaviors (p. 134).

. . . I draw on findings from a small, intensive data set collected using ethnographic methods. I map the connections between parents' resources and their children's daily lives. My first goal, then, is to challenge Kingston's (2000) argument that social class does not distinguish parents' behavior or children's daily lives. I seek to show empirically that social class does indeed create distinctive parenting styles. I demonstrate that parents differ by class in the ways they define their own roles in their children's lives as well as in how they perceive the nature of childhood. The middle-class parents, both white *and* black, tend to conform to a cultural logic of childrearing I call "concerted cultivation." They enroll their children in numerous age-specific organized activities that dominate family life and create enormous labor, particularly for mothers. The parents view these activities as transmitting important life skills to children. Middle-class parents also stress language use and the development of reasoning and employ talking as their preferred form of discipline. This "cultivation" approach results in a wider range of experiences for children but also creates a frenetic pace for parents, a cult of individualism within the family, and an emphasis on children's performance.

The childrearing strategies of white and black working-class and poor parents emphasize the "accomplishment of natural growth." These parents believe that as long as they provide love, food, and safety, their children will grow and thrive. They do not focus on developing their children's special talents. Compared to the middle-class children, working-class and poor children participate in few organized activities and have more free time and deeper, richer ties within their extended families. Working-class and poor parents issue many more directives to their children and, in some households, place more emphasis on physical discipline than do the middle-class parents. These findings extend Kohn and Schooler's (1983) observation of class differences in parents' values, showing that differences also exist in the *behavior* of parents *and* children. . . .

I trace the connections between the class position of family members—including children—and the uneven outcomes of their experiences outside the home as they interact with professionals in dominant institutions. The pattern of concerted cultivation encourages an *emerging sense of entitlement* in children. All parents and children are not equally assertive, but the pattern of questioning and intervening among the white and black middle-class parents contrasts sharply with the definitions of how to be helpful and effective observed among the white and black working-class and poor adults. The pattern of the accomplishment of natural growth encourages an *emerging sense of constraint*. Adults as well as children in these social classes tend to be deferential and outwardly accepting in their interactions with professionals such as doctors and educators. At the same time, however, compared to their middle-class counterparts, white and black working-class and poor family members are more distrustful of professionals. These are differences with potential long-term consequences. In an historical moment when the dominant society privileges active, informed, assertive clients of health and educational services, the strategies employed by children and parents are not equally effective across classes. In sum, differences in family life lie not only in the advantages parents obtain for their children, but also in the skills they transmit to children for negotiating their own life paths.

■ ■ ■ METHODOLOGY

Study Participants

This study is based on interviews and observations of children, aged 8 to 10, and their families. The data were collected over time in three research phases. Phase one involved observations in two third-grade classrooms in a public school in the Midwestern community of "Lawrenceville."[1] . . .

Phase two took place at two sites in a northeastern metropolitan area. One school, "Lower Richmond," although located in a predominantly white, working-class urban neighborhood, drew about half of its students from a nearby all-black housing project. I observed one third-grade class at Lower Richmond about twice a week for almost six months. The second site, "Swan," was located in a suburban neighborhood about 45 minutes from the city center. It was 90 percent white; most of the remaining 10 percent were middle-class children.[2] . . . A team of research assistants and I interviewed the parents and guardians . . . Thus, the total number of children who participated in the study was 88 (32 from the Midwest and 56 from the Northeast). . . .

Phase three, the most intensive research phase of the study, involved home observations of 12 children and their families in the Northeast who had been previously interviewed. Some themes, such as language use and families' social connections, surfaced mainly during this phase. . . .

■ ■ ■ CONCERTED CULTIVATION AND NATURE GROWTH

The interviews and observations suggested that crucial aspects of family life *cohered*. Within the concerted cultivation and accomplishment of natural growth approaches, three key dimensions may be distinguished: the organization of daily life, the use of language, and social connections. . . . These dimensions do not capture all important parts of family life, but they do incorporate core aspects of childrearing. Moreover, our field observations revealed that behaviors and activities related to these dimensions dominated the rhythms of family life. Conceptually, the organization of daily life and the use of language are crucial dimensions. Both must be present for the family to be described as engaging in one childrearing approach rather than the other. Social connections are significant but less conceptually essential.

All three aspects of childrearing were intricately woven into the families' daily routines, but rarely remarked upon. As part of everyday practice, they were invisible to parents and children. Analytically, however, they are useful means for comparing and contrasting ways in which social class differences shape the character of family life. I now examine two families in terms of these three key dimensions. I "control" for race and gender and contrast the lives of two black boys—one from an (upper) middle-class family and one from a family on public assistance. I could have focused on almost any of the other 12 children, but this pair seemed optimal, given the limited number of studies reporting on black middle-class families, as well as the aspect of my argument that suggests that race is less important than class in shaping childrearing patterns.

Developing Alexander Williams

Alexander Williams and his parents live in a predominantly black middle-class neighborhood. Their six-bedroom house is worth about $150,000. Alexander is an only child. Both parents grew up in small towns in the South, and both are from large families. His father, a tall, handsome man, is a very successful trial lawyer who earns about $125,000 annually in a small firm specializing in medical malpractice cases. Two weeks each month, he works very long hours (from about 5:30 A.M. until midnight) preparing for trials. The other two weeks, his workday ends around 6:00 P.M. He rarely travels out of town. Alexander's mother, Christina, is a positive, bubbly woman with freckles and long, black, wavy hair. A high-level manager in a major corporation, she has a corner office, a personal secretary, and responsibilities for other offices across the nation. She tries to limit her travel, but at least once a month she takes an overnight trip.

Alexander is a charming, inquisitive boy with a winsome smile. Ms. Williams is pleased that Alexander seems interested in so many things:

> Alexander is a joy. He's a gift to me. He's a very energetic, very curious, loving, caring person, that um . . . is outgoing and who, uh, really loves to be with people. And who love to explore, and loves to read and . . . just do a lot of fun things.

The private school Alexander attends has an on-site after-school program. There, he participates in several activities and receives guitar lessons and photography instruction.

Organization of Daily Life.   Alexander is busy with activities during the week and on weekends (Table 1). His mother describes their Saturday morning routine. The day starts early with a private piano lesson for Alexander downtown, a 20-minute drive from the house:

Table 1   Participation in Activities Outside of School: Boys

Boy's Name/ Race/Class	Activated Organized by Adults	Informal Activities
Middle Class Alexander Williams (black)	Soccer team Baseball team Community choir Church choir Sunday school Piano (Suzuki) School plays Guitar (through school)	Restricted television Plays outside occasionally with two other boys Visits friends from school
Poor Harold McAllister (black)	Bible study in neighbor's house (occasionally) Bible camp (1 week)	Visits relatives Plays ball with neighborhood kids Watches television Watches videos

> *It's an 8:15 class. But for me, it was a tradeoff. I am very adamant about Saturday morning TV. I don't know what it contributes. So . . . it was . . . um . . . either stay at home and fight on a Saturday morning* [laughs] *or go do something constructive. . . . Now Saturday mornings are pretty booked up. You know, the piano lesson, and then straight to choir for a couple of hours. So, he has a very full schedule.*

Ms. Williams' vehement opposition to television is based on her view of what Alexander needs to grow and thrive. She objects to TV's passivity and feels it is her obligation to help her son cultivate his talents.

Sometimes Alexander complains that "my mother signs me up for everything!" Generally, however, he likes his activities. He says they make him feel "special," and without them life would be "boring." His sense of time is thoroughly entwined with his activities: He feels disoriented when his schedule is not full. This unease is clear in the following field-note excerpt. The family is driving home from a Back-to-School night. The next morning, Ms. Williams will leave for a work-related day trip and will not return until late at night. Alexander is grumpy because he has nothing planned for the next day. He wants to have a friend over, but his mother rebuffs him. Whining, he wonders what he will do. His mother, speaking tersely, says:

> *You have piano and guitar. You'll have some free time.* [Pause] *I think you'll survive for one night.* [Alexander does not respond but seems mad. It is quiet for the rest of the trip home.]

Alexander's parents believe his activities provide a wide range of benefits important for his development. In discussing Alexander's piano lessons, Mr. Williams notes that as a Suzuki student,[3] Alexander is already able to read music. Speculating about more diffuse benefits of Alexander's involvement with piano, he says:

I don't see how any kid's adolescence and adulthood could not but be enhanced by an awareness of who Beethoven was. And is that Bach or Mozart? I don't know the difference between the two! I don't know Baroque from Classical—but he does. How can that not be a benefit in later life? I'm convinced that this rich experience will make him a better person, a better citizen, a better husband, a better father—certainly a better student.

Ms. Williams sees music as building her son's "confidence" and his "poise." In interviews and casual conversation, she stresses "exposure." She believes it is her responsibility to broaden Alexander's worldview. Childhood activities provide a learning ground for important life skills:

Sports provide great opportunities to learn how to be competitive. Learn how to accept defeat, you know. Learn how to accept winning, you know, in a gracious way. Also it gives him the opportunity to learn leadership skills and how to be a team player. . . . Sports really provides a lot of really great opportunities.

Alexander's schedule is constantly shifting; some activities wind down and others start up. Because the schedules of sports practices and games are issued no sooner than the start of the new season, advance planning is rarely possible. Given the sheer number of Alexander's activities, events inevitably overlap. Some activities, though short-lived, are extremely time consuming. Alexander's school play, for example, requires rehearsals three nights the week before the opening. In addition, in choosing activities, the Williamses have an added concern—the group's racial balance. Ms. Williams prefers that Alexander not be the only black child at events. Typically, one or two other black boys are involved, but the groups are predominantly white and the activities take place in predominantly white residential neighborhoods. Alexander is, however, part of his church's youth choir and Sunday School, activities in which all participants are black.

Many activities involve competition. Alex must audition for his solo performance in the school play, for example. Similarly, parents and children alike understand that participation on "A," "B," or "All-Star" sports teams signal different skill levels. Like other middle-class children in the study, Alexander seems to enjoy public performance. According to a field note, after his solo at a musical production in front of over 200 people, he appeared "contained, pleased, aware of the attention he's receiving."

Alexander's commitments do not consume *all* his free time. Still, his life is defined by a series of deadlines and schedules interwoven with a series of activities that are organized and controlled by adults rather than children. Neither he nor his parents see this as troublesome.

Language Use.   Like other middle-class families, the Williamses often engage in conversation that promotes reasoning and negotiation. An excerpt from a field note (describing an exchange between Alexander and his mother during a car ride home after summer camp) shows the kind of pointed questions middle-class parents ask children. Ms. Williams is not just eliciting information. She is also giving Alexander the opportunity to develop and practice verbal skills, including how to summarize, clarify, and amplify information:

> As she drives, [Ms. Williams] asks Alex, "So, how was your day?"
> Alex: "Okay. I had hot dogs today, but they were burned! They were all black!"
> Mom: "Oh, great. You shouldn't have eaten any."
> Alex: "They weren't all black, only half were. The rest were regular."
> Mom: "Oh, okay. What was that game you were playing this morning? . . .
> Alex: "It was [called] 'Whatcha doin?'"
> Mom: "How do you play?"
>
> Alexander explains the game elaborately—fieldworker doesn't quite follow. Mom asks Alex questions throughout his explanation, saying, "Oh, I see," when he answers. She asks him about another game she saw them play; he again explains. . . . She continues to prompt and encourage him with small giggles in the back of her throat as he elaborates.

Not all middle-class parents are as attentive to their children's needs as this mother, and none are *always* interested in negotiating. But a general pattern of reasoning and accommodating is common.

Social Connections.   Mr. and Ms. Williams consider themselves very close to their extended families. Because the Williamses' aging parents live in the South, visiting requires a plane trip. Ms. Williams takes Alexander with her to see his grandparents twice a year. She speaks on the phone with her parents at least once a week and also calls her siblings several times a week. Mr. Williams talks with his mother regularly by phone (he has less contact with his stepfather). With pride, he also mentions his niece, whose Ivy League education he is helping to finance.

Interactions with cousins are not normally a part of Alexander's leisure time. . . . Nor does he often play with neighborhood children. The huge homes on the Williams's street are occupied mainly by couples without children. Most of Alexander's playmates come from his classroom or his organized activities. Because most of his school events, church life, and assorted activities are organized by the age (and sometimes gender) of the participants, Alexander interacts almost exclusively with children his own age, usually boys. Adult-organized activities thus define the context of his social life.

Mr. and Ms. Williams are aware that they allocate a sizable portion of time to Alexander's activities. What they stress, however, is the time they *hold back*. They mention activities the family has chosen *not* to take on (such as traveling soccer).

Summary.   Overall, Alexander's parents engaged in concerted cultivation. They fostered their son's growth through involvement in music, church, athletics, and academics. They talked with him at length, seeking his opinions and encouraging his ideas. Their approach involved considerable direct expenses (e.g., the cost of lessons and equipment) and large indirect expenses (e.g., the cost of taking time off from work, driving to practices, and foregoing adult leisure activities). Although Mr. and Ms. Williams acknowledged the importance of extended family, Alexander spent relatively little time with relatives. His social interactions occurred almost exclusively with children his own age and with adults. Alexander's many activities significantly shaped the organization of daily life in the family. Both parents' leisure time was tailored to their son's commitments. Mr. and Ms. Williams felt that the strategies they cultivated with Alexander would result in his having the best possible chance at a happy and productive life. They couldn't imagine themselves not investing large amounts of time and energy in their son's life. But, as I explain in the next section, which focuses on a black boy from a poor family, other parents held a different view.

Supporting the Natural Growth of Harold McAllister

Harold McAllister, a large, stocky boy with a big smile, is from a poor black family. He lives with his mother and his 8-year-old sister, Alexis, in a large apartment. Two cousins often stay overnight. Harold's 16-yearold sister and 18-year-old brother usually live with their grandmother, but sometimes they stay at the McAllister's home. Ms. McAllister, a high school graduate, relies on public assistance. Hank, Harold and Alexis's father, is a mechanic. He and Ms. McAllister have never married. He visits regularly, sometimes weekly, stopping by after work to watch television or nap. Harold (but not Alexis) sometimes travels across town by bus to spend the weekend with Hank.

The McAllisters' apartment is in a public housing project near a busy street. The complex consists of rows of two- and three-story brick units. The buildings, blocky and brown, have small yards enclosed by concrete and wood fences. Large floodlights are mounted on the corners of the buildings, and wide concrete sidewalks cut through the spaces between units. The ground is bare in many places; paper wrappers and glass litter the area.

Inside the apartment, life is humorous and lively, with family members and kin sharing in the daily routines. Ms. McAllister discussed, disdainfully, mothers who are on drugs or who abuse alcohol and do not "look after" their children. Indeed, the previous year Ms. McAllister called Child Protective Services to report her twin sister, a cocaine addict, because she was neglecting her children. Ms. McAllister is actively involved in her twin's daughters' lives. Her two nephews also frequently stay with her. Overall, she sees herself as a capable mother who takes care of her children and her extended family.

Organization of Daily Life.   Much of Harold's life and the lives of his family members revolve around home. Project residents often sit outside in lawn chairs or on front stoops, drinking beer, talking, and watching children play. During summer, windows are frequently left open, allowing breezes to waft through the units and providing vantage points from which residents can survey the neighborhood. A large deciduous tree in front of the McAllister's apartment unit provides welcome shade in the summer's heat.

Harold loves sports. He is particularly fond of basketball, but he also enjoys football, and he follows televised professional sports closely. Most afternoons, he is either inside watching television or outside playing ball. He tosses a football with cousins and boys from the neighboring units and organizes pick-up basketball games. Sometimes he and his friends use a rusty, bare hoop hanging from a telephone pole in the housing project; other times, they string up an old, blue plastic crate as a make-shift hoop. One obstacle to playing sports, however, is a shortage of equipment. Balls are costly to replace, especially given the rate at which they disappear—theft of children's play equipment, including balls and bicycles, is an ongoing problem. During a field observation, Harold asks his mother if she knows where the ball is. She replies with some vehemence, "They stole the blue and yellow ball, and they stole the green ball, and they stole the other ball."

Hunting for balls is a routine part of Harold's leisure time. One June day, with the temperature and humidity in the high 80s, Harold and his cousin Tyrice (and a fieldworker) wander around the housing project for about an hour, trying to find a basketball:

> We head to the other side of the complex. On the way . . . we passed four guys sitting on the step. Their ages were 9 to 13 years. They had a radio blaring. Two were working intently on fixing a flat bike tire. The other two were dribbling a basketball.

> Harold: "Yo! What's up, ya'll."
> Group: "What's up, Har." "What's up?" "Yo."

> They continued to work on the tire and dribble the ball. As we walked down the hill, Harold asked, "Yo, could I use your ball?"

> The guy responded, looking up from the tire, "Naw, man. Ya'll might lose it."

Harold, Tyrice, and the fieldworker walk to another part of the complex, heading for a makeshift basketball court where they hope to find a game in progress:

> No such luck. Harold enters an apartment directly in front of the makeshift court. The door was open. . . . Harold came back. "No ball. I guess I gotta go back."

The pace of life for Harold and his friends ebbs and flows with the children's interests and family obligations. The day of the basketball search, for example, after spending time listening to music and looking at baseball cards, the children join a water fight Tyrice instigates. It is a lively game, filled with laughter and with efforts to get the adults next door wet (against their wishes). When the game winds down, the kids ask their mother for money, receive it, and then walk to a store to buy chips and soda. They chat with another young boy and then amble back to the apartment, eating as they walk. Another afternoon, almost two weeks later, the children—Harold, two of his cousins, and two children from the neighborhood— and the fieldworker play basketball on a makeshift court in the street (using the fieldworker's ball). As Harold bounces the ball, neighborhood children of all ages wander through the space.

Thus, Harold's life is more free-flowing and more child-directed than is Alexander Williams'. The pace of any given day is not so much planned as emergent, reflecting child-based interests and activities. Parents intervene in specific areas, such as personal grooming, meals, and occasional chores, but they do not continuously direct and monitor their children's leisure activities. Moreover, the leisure activities Harold and other working-class and poor children pursue require them to develop a repertoire of skills for dealing with much older and much younger children as well as with neighbors and relatives.

Language Use.   Life in the working-class and poor families in the study flows smoothly without extended verbal discussions. The amount of talking varies, but overall, it is considerably less than occurs in the middle-class homes.[4] Ms. McAllister jokes with the children and discusses what is on television. But she does not appear to cultivate conversation by asking the children questions or by drawing them out. Often she is brief and direct in her remarks. For instance, she coordinates the use of the apartment's only bathroom by using one-word directives. She sends the children (there are almost always at least four children home at once) to wash up by pointing to a child, saying one word, "bathroom," and handing him or her a washcloth. Wordlessly, the designated child gets up and goes to the bathroom to take a shower.

Similarly, although Ms. McAllister will listen to the children's complaints about school, she does not draw them out on these issues or seek to determine details, as Ms. Williams would. For instance, at the start of the new school year, when I ask Harold about his teacher, he tells me she is "mean" and that "she lies." Ms. McAllister, washing dishes, listens to her son, but she does not encourage Harold to support his opinion about his new teacher with more examples, nor does she mention any concerns of her own. Instead, she asks about last year's teacher, "What was the name of that man teacher?" Harold says, "Mr. Lindsey?" She says, "No, the other one." He says, "Mr. Terrene." Ms. McAllister smiles and says, "Yeah. I liked him." Unlike Alexander's mother, she seems content with a brief exchange of information.

Social Connections.   Children, especially boys, frequently play outside. The number of potential playmates in Harold's world is vastly higher than the number in Alexander's neighborhood. When a fieldworker stops to count heads, she finds 40 children of elementary school age residing in the nearby rows of apartments. With so many children nearby, Harold could choose to play only with others his own age. In fact, though, he often hangs out with older and younger children and with his cousins (who are close to his age).

The McAllister family, like other poor and working-class families, is involved in a web of extended kin. As noted earlier, Harold's older siblings and his two male cousins often spend the night at the McAllister home. Celebrations such as birthdays involve relatives almost exclusively. Party guests are not, as in middle-class families, friends from school or from extracurricular activities. Birthdays are celebrated enthusiastically, with cake and special food to mark the occasion; presents, however, are not offered. Similarly, Christmas at Harold's house featured a tree and special food but no presents. At these and other family events, the older children voluntarily look after the younger ones: Harold plays with his 16-month-old niece, and his cousins carry around the younger babies.

The importance of family ties—and the contingent nature of life in the McAllisters' world—is clear in the response Alexis offers when asked what she would do if she were given a million dollars:

> *Oh, boy! I'd buy my brother, my sister, my uncle, my aunt, my nieces and my nephews, and my grandpop, and my grandmom, and my mom, and my dad, and my friends, not my friends, but mostly my best friend—I'd buy them all clothes . . . and sneakers. And I'd buy some food, and I'd buy my mom some food, and I'd get my brothers and my sisters gifts for their birthdays.*

Summary.   In a setting where everyone, including the children, was acutely aware of the lack of money, the McAllister family made do. Ms. McAllister rightfully saw herself as a very capable mother. She was a strong, positive influence in the lives of the children she looked after. Still, the contrast with Ms. Williams is striking. Ms. McAllister did not seem to think that Harold's opinions needed to be cultivated and developed. She, like most parents in the working-class and poor families, drew strong and clear boundaries between adults and children. Adults gave directions to children. Children were given freedom to play informally unless they were needed for chores. Extended family networks were deemed important and trustworthy.

The Intersection of Race and Class in Family Life

I expected race to powerfully shape children's daily schedules, but this was not evident (also see Conley 1999; Pattillo-McCoy 1999). This is not to say that race is unimportant. Black parents were particularly concerned with monitoring their children's lives outside the home for signs of racial problems.[5] Black middle-class fathers, especially, were likely to stress the importance of their sons understanding "what it means to be a black man in this society" (J. Hochschild 1995). Mr. Williams, in summarizing how he and his wife orient Alexander, said:

> *[We try to] teach him that race unfortunately is the most important aspect of our national life. I mean people look at other people and they see a color first. But that isn't going to define who he is. He will do his best. He will succeed, despite racism. And I think he lives his life that way.*

Alexander's parents were acutely aware of the potential significance of race in his life. Both were adamant, however, that race should not be used as "an excuse" for not striving to succeed. Mr. Williams put it this way:

> *I discuss how race impacts on my life as an attorney, and I discuss how race will impact on his life. The one teaching that he takes away from this is that he is never to use discrimination as an excuse for not doing his best.*

Thus far, few incidents of overt racism had occurred in Alexander's life, as his mother noted:

> *Those situations have been far and few between. . . . I mean, I can count them on my fingers.*

Still, Ms. Williams recounted with obvious pain an incident at a birthday party Alexander had attended as a preschooler. The grandparents of the birthday child repeatedly asked, "Who is that boy?" and exclaimed, "He's so dark!" Such experiences fueled the Williams's resolve always to be "cautious":

> *We've never been, uh, parents who drop off their kid anywhere. We've always gone with him. And even now, I go in and—to school in the morning—and check [in]. . . . The school environment, we've watched very closely.*

Alexander's parents were not equally optimistic about the chances for racial equality in this country. Ms. Williams felt strongly that, especially while Alexander was young, his father should not voice his pessimism. Mr. Williams complained that this meant he had to "watch" what he said to Alexander about race relations. Still, both parents agreed about the need to be vigilant regarding potential racial problems in Alexander's life. Other black parents reported experiencing racial prejudice and expressed a similar commitment to vigilance.

Issues surrounding the prospect of growing up black and male in this society were threaded through Alexander's life in ways that had no equivalent among his middleclass, white male peers. Still, in fourth grade there were no signs of racial experiences having "taken hold" the way that they might as Alexander ages. . . . The research assistants and I saw no striking differences in the ways in which white parents and black parents in the working-class and poor homes socialized their children. . . .

Impact of Childrearing Strategies on Interactions with Institutions

Social scientists sometimes emphasize the importance of reshaping parenting practices to improve children's chances of success. Explicitly and implicitly, the literature exhorts parents to comply with the views of professionals (Bronfenbrenner 1966; Epstein 2001; Heimer and Staffen 1998). Such calls for compliance do not, however, reconcile professionals' judgments regarding the intrinsic value of current childrearing standards with the evidence of the historical record, which shows regular shifts in such standards over time (Aries 1962; Wrigley 1989; Zelizer 1985). Nor are the stratified, and limited, possibilities for success in the broader society examined.

I now follow the families out of their homes and into encounters with representatives of dominant institutions—institutions that are directed by middle-class professionals. Again, I focus on Alexander Williams and Harold McAllister. Across all social classes, parents and children interacted with teachers and school officials, healthcare professionals, and assorted government officials. Although they often addressed similar problems (e.g., learning disabilities, asthma, traffic violations), they typically did not achieve similar resolutions. The pattern of concerted cultivation fostered an *emerging sense of entitlement* in the life of Alexander Williams and other middle-class children. By contrast, the commitment to nurturing children's natural growth fostered an *emerging sense of constraint* in the life of Harold McAllister and other working-class or poor children.

Both parents and children drew on the resources associated with these two childrearing approaches during their interactions with officials. Middle-class parents and children often customized these interactions; working-class and poor parents were more likely to have a "generic" relationship. When faced with problems, middle-class parents also appeared better equipped to exert influence over other adults compared with working-class and poor parents. Nor did middle-class parents or children display the intimidation or confusion we witnessed among many working-class and poor families when they faced a problem in their children's school experience.

Emerging Signs of Entitlement

Alexander Williams' mother, like many middle-class mothers, explicitly teaches her son to be an informed, assertive client in interactions with professionals. For example, as she drives Alexander to a routine doctor's appointment, she coaches him in the art of communicating effectively in healthcare settings:

> Alexander asks if he needs to get any shots today at the doctor's. Ms. Williams says he'll need to ask the doctor. . . . As we enter Park Lane, Mom says quietly to Alex: "Alexander, you should be thinking of questions you might want to ask the doctor. You can ask him anything you want. Don't be shy. You can ask anything."
>
> Alex thinks for a minute, then: "I have some bumps under my arms from my deodorant."
>
> Mom: "Really? You mean from your new deodorant?"
> Alex: "Yes."
> Mom: "Well, you should ask the doctor."

Alexander learns that he has the right to speak up (e.g., "don't be shy") and that he should prepare for an encounter with a person in a position of authority by gathering his thoughts in advance. . . .

Middle-class parents and children were also very assertive in situations at the public elementary school most of the middle-class children in the study attended. There were numerous conflicts during the year over matters small and large. For example, parents complained to one another and to the teachers about the amount of homework the children were assigned. A black middle-class mother whose daughters had not tested into the school's gifted program negotiated with officials to have the girls' (higher) results from a private testing company accepted instead. The parents of a fourth-grade boy drew the school superintendent into a battle over religious lyrics in a song scheduled to be sung as part of the holiday program. The superintendent consulted the district lawyer and ultimately "counseled" the principal to be more sensitive, and the song was dropped.

Children, too, asserted themselves at school. Examples include requesting that the classroom's blinds be lowered so the sun wasn't in their eyes, badgering the teacher for permission to retake a math test for a higher grade, and demanding to know why no cupcake had been saved when an absence prevented attendance at a classroom party. In these encounters, children were not simply complying with adults' requests or asking for a repeat of an earlier experience. They were displaying an emerging sense of entitlement by urging adults to permit a customized accommodation of institutional processes to suit their preferences. . . .

Emerging Signs of Constraint

The interactions the research assistants and I observed between professionals and working-class and poor parents frequently seemed cautious and constrained. This unease is evident, for example, during a physical Harold McAllister has before going to Bible camp. Harold's mother, normally boisterous and talkative at home, is quiet. Unlike Ms. Williams, she seems wary of supplying the doctor with accurate information:

> Doctor: *"Does he eat something each day—either fish, meat, or egg?"*
>
> Mom, response is low and muffled: *"Yes."*
>
> Doctor, attempting to make eye contact but mom stares intently at paper: *"A yellow vegetable?"*
>
> Mom, still no eye contact, looking at the floor: *"Yeah."*
>
> Doctor: *"A green vegetable?"*
>
> Mom, looking at the doctor: *"Not all the time."* [Fieldworker has not seen any of the children eat a green or yellow vegetable since visits began.]
>
> Doctor: *"No. Fruit or juice?"*
>
> Mom, low voice, little or no eye contact, looks at the doctor's scribbles on the paper he is filling out: *"Ummh humn."*
>
> Doctor: *"Does he drink milk everyday?"*
>
> Mom, abruptly, in considerably louder voice: *"Yeah."*
>
> Doctor: *"Cereal, bread, rice, potato, anything like that?"*
>
> Mom, shakes her head: *"Yes, definitely."* [Looks at doctor.]

Ms. McAllister's knowledge of developmental events in Harold's life is uneven. She is not sure when he learned to walk and cannot recall the name of his previous doctor. And when the doctor asks, "When was the last time he had a tetanus shot?" she counters, gruffly, "What's a tetanus shot?" . . .

Still, neither Harold nor his mother seemed as comfortable as Alexander had been. Alexander was used to extensive conversation at home; with the doctor, he was at ease initiating questions. Harold, who was used to responding to directives at home, primarily answered questions from the doctor, rather than posing his own.

Alexander, encouraged by his mother, was assertive and confident with the doctor. Harold was reserved. Absorbing his mother's apparent need to conceal the truth about the range of foods he ate, he appeared cautious, displaying an emerging sense of constraint.

We observed a similar pattern in school interactions. Overall, the working-class and poor adults had much more distance or separation from the school than their middle-class counterparts. Ms. McAllister, for example, could be quite assertive in some settings (e.g., at the start of family observations, she visited the local drug dealer, warning him not to "mess with" the black male fieldworker). But throughout the fourth-grade parent-teacher conference, she kept her winter jacket zipped up, sat hunched over in her chair, and spoke in barely audible tones. She was stunned when the teacher said that Harold did not do homework. Sounding dumbfounded, she said, "He does it at home." The teacher denied it and continued talking. Ms. McAllister made no further comments and did not probe for more information, except about a letter the teacher said he had mailed home and that she had not received. The conference ended, having yielded Ms. McAllister few insights into Harold's educational experience.[6]

Other working-class and poor parents also appeared baffled, intimidated, and subdued in parent-teacher conferences. . . . Working-class and poor children seemed aware of their parents' frustration and witnessed their powerlessness. Billy Yanelli, [a working-class boy], for example, asserted in an interview that his mother "hate[d]" school officials.

At times, these parents encouraged their children to resist school officials' authority. The Yanellis told Billy to "beat up" a boy who was bothering him. Wendy Driver's mother advised her to punch a male classmate who pestered her and pulled her ponytail. Ms. Driver's boyfriend added, "Hit him when the teacher isn't looking."

In classroom observations, working-class and poor children could be quite lively and energetic, but we did not observe them try to customize their environments. They tended to react to adults' offers or, at times, to plead with educators to repeat previous experiences, such as reading a particular story, watching a movie, or going to the computer room. Compared to middle-class classroom interactions, the boundaries between adults and children seemed firmer and clearer. Although the children often resisted and tested school rules, they did not seem to be seeking to get educators to accommodate their own *individual* preferences.

Overall, then, the behavior of working-class and poor parents cannot be explained as a manifestation of their temperaments or of overall passivity; parents were quite energetic in intervening in their children's lives in other spheres. Rather, working-class and poor parents generally appeared to depend on the school (Lareau 2000), even as they were dubious of the trustworthiness of the professionals. This suspicion of professionals in dominant institutions is, at least in some instances, a reasonable response.[7] The unequal level of trust, as well as differences in the amount and quality of information divulged, can yield unequal *profits* during an historical moment when professionals applaud assertiveness and reject passivity as an inappropriate parenting strategy (Epstein 2001). Middle-class children and parents often (but not always) accrued advantages or profits from their efforts. Alexander Williams succeeded in having the doctor take his medical concerns seriously. Ms. Marshall's children ended up in the gifted program, even though they did not technically qualify. Middle-class children expect institutions to be responsive to *them* and to accommodate their individual needs. By contrast, when Wendy Driver is told to hit the boy who is pestering her (when the teacher isn't looking) or Billy Yanelli is told to physically defend himself, despite school rules, they are not learning how to make bureaucratic institutions work to their advantage. Instead, they are being given lessons in frustration and powerlessness.

■ ■ ■ WHY DOES SOCIAL CLASS MATTER?

Parents' economic resources helped create the observed class differences in childrearing practices. Enrollment fees that middle-class parents dismissed as "negligible" were formidable expenses for less affluent families. Parents also paid for clothing, equipment, hotel stays, fast food meals, summer camps, and fundraisers. . . . Moreover, families needed reliable private transportation and flexible work schedules to get children to and from events. These resources were disproportionately concentrated in middle-class families.

Differences in educational resources also are important. Middle-class parents' superior levels of education gave them larger vocabularies that facilitated concerted cultivation, particularly in institutional interventions. Poor and working-class parents were not familiar with key terms professionals used, such as "tetanus shot." Furthermore, middle-class parents' educational backgrounds gave them confidence when criticizing educational professionals and intervening in school matters. Working-class and poor parents viewed educators as their social superiors.

. . . Middle-class parents . . . tended to view childhood as a dual opportunity: a chance for play and for developing talents and skills of value later in life. Mr. Tallinger noted that playing soccer taught Garrett to be "hard nosed" and "competitive," valuable workplace skills. Ms. Williams mentioned the value of Alexander learning to work with others by playing on a sports team. Middle-class parents, aware of the "declining fortunes" of the middle class, worried about their own economic futures and those of their children (Newman 1993). This uncertainty increased their commitment to helping their children develop broad skills to enhance their future possibilities.

Working-class and poor parents' conceptions of adulthood and childhood also appeared to be closely connected to their lived experiences. For the working class, it was the deadening quality of work and the press of economic shortages that defined their experience of adulthood and influenced their vision of childhood. It was dependence on public assistance and severe economic shortages that most shaped poor parents' views. . . .

Thus, childrearing strategies are influenced by more than parents' education. It is the interweaving of life experiences and resources, including parents' economic resources, occupational conditions, and educational backgrounds, that appears to be most important in leading middle-class parents to engage in concerted cultivation and working-class and poor parents to engage in the accomplishment of natural growth.

NOTES

1. All names of people and places are pseudonyms. The Lawrenceville school was in a white suburban neighborhood in a university community a few hours from a metropolitan area. The student population was about half white and half black; the (disproportionately poor) black children were bused from other neighborhoods.

2. Over three-quarters of the students at Lower Richmond qualified for free lunch; by contrast, Swan did not have a free lunch program.

3. The Suzuki method is labor intensive. Students are required to listen to music about one hour per day. Also, both child and parent(s) are expected to practice daily and to attend every lesson together.

4. Hart and Risley (1995) reported a similar difference in speech patterns. In their sample, by about age three, children of professionals had larger vocabularies and spoke more utterances per hour than the *parents* of similarly aged children on welfare.

5. This section focuses primarily on the concerns of black parents. Whites, of course, also benefited from race relations, notably in the scattering of poor white families in working-class neighborhoods rather than being concentrated in dense settings with other poor families (Massey and Denton 1993).

6. Middle-class parents sometimes appeared slightly anxious during parent-teacher conferences, but overall, they spoke more and asked educators more questions than did working-class and poor parents.

7. The higher levels of institutional reports of child neglect, child abuse, and other family difficulties among poor families may reflect this group's greater vulnerability to institutional intervention (e.g., see L. Gordon 1989).

REFERENCES

Aries, Philippe. 1962. *Centuries of Childhood: A Social History of the Family.* Translated by R. Baldick. London: Cape.

Bronfenbrenner, Urie. 1966. "Socialization and Social Class through Time and Space." Pp. 362–77 in *Class, Status and Power,* edited by R. Bendix and S. M. Lipset. New York: Free Press.

Conley, Dalton. 1999. *Being Black, Living in the Red: Race, Wealth, and Social Policy in America.* Berkeley, CA: University of California Press.

Epstein, Joyce. 2001. *Schools, Family, and Community Partnerships.* Boulder, CO: Westview.

Gordon, Linda. 1989. *Heroes of Their Own Lives: The Politics and History of Family Violence.* New York: Penguin.

Hart, Betty and Todd Risley. 1995. *Meaningful Differences in the Everyday Experience of Young American Children.* Baltimore, MD: Paul Brooks.

Heimer, Carol A. and Lisa Staffen. 1998. *For the Sake of the Children: The Social Organization Responsibility in the Hospital and at Home.* Chicago, IL: University of Chicago Press.

Hochschild, Jennifer L. 1995. *Facing Up to The American Dream.* Princeton, NJ: Princeton University Press.

Kingston, Paul. 2000. *The Classless Society.* Stanford, CA: Stanford University Press.

Kohn, Melvin and Carmi Schooler, eds. 1983. *Work and Personality: An Inquiry into the Impact of Social Stratification.* Norwood, NJ: Ablex.

Lareau, Annette. 2000. *Home Advantage: Social Class and Parental Intervention in Elementary Education.* 2d ed. Lanham, MD: Rowman and Littlefield.

————. 2002. "Doing Multi-Person, Multi-Site 'Ethnographic' Work: A Reflective, Critical Essay." Department of Sociology, Temple University, Philadelphia, PA. Unpublished manuscript.

Massey, Douglas and Nancy Denton. 1993. *American Apartheid.* Cambridge, MA: Harvard University Press.

Newman, Kathleen. 1993. *Declining Fortunes: The Withering of the American Dream.* New York: Basic Books.

Pattillo-McCoy. Mary 1999. *Black Picket Fences: Privilege and Peril among the Black Middle-Class.* Chicago, IL: University of Chicago Press.

Wrigley, Julia. 1989. "Do Young Children Need Intellectual Stimulation? Experts' Advice to Parents, 1900–1985." *History of Education* 29:41–75.

Zelizer, Viviana. 1985. *Pricing the Priceless Child: The Changing Social Value of Children.* New York: Basic Books.

Still Separate, Still Unequal

Jonathan Kozol

introduction

Social inequality so pervades our society that it leaves no area of life untouched. Because we are immersed in social inequality, much of it is invisible to us. Most lies beneath our radar, part of our taken-for-granted, unquestioned reality. When we do become aware of social inequality, seldom are we conscious of its *social* origins. We tend to see social inequality as part of the *natural* ordering of life, often explaining it on the bases of individual characteristics. ("They are lazier than us. That's the reason they have less than we do." You can fill in "lazier" with a variety of terms that people use in these individualistic explanations: less intelligent, less moral, less thrifty, whatever.) This selection, in contrast, looks at the *social* base of inequality—how the ways society is arranged keep even intelligent, hardworking people down.

In his ongoing examination and critique of the U.S. educational system, Kozol has traveled around the country and observed schools in poor, middle-class, and rich communities. In his articles and books, he has documented the tremendous disparity in the quality of education among communities. Because schools are financed largely by local property taxes, wealthier communities are able to offer teachers higher salaries, purchase newer textbooks and equipment, and teach what some call "fringe" courses in language, music, and the arts. Others cannot.

Thinking Critically

As you read this selection, ask yourself:

1. How is the social stratification reported here likely to have an impact on the future of the United States?

2. Why does this social inequality exist?

3. What can be done to change the situation?

Many Americans who live far from our major cities and who have no firsthand knowledge of the realities to be found in urban public schools seem to have the rather vague and general impression that the great extremes of racial isolation that were matters of grave national significance some thirty-five or forty years ago have gradually but steadily diminished in more recent years. The truth, unhappily, is that the trend, for well over a decade now, has been precisely the reverse. Schools that were already deeply segregated twenty-five or thirty years ago are no less segregated now, while thousands of other schools around the country that had been integrated either voluntarily or by the force of law have since been rapidly resegregating.

In Chicago, by the academic year 2002–2003, 87 percent of public-school enrollment was black or Hispanic; less than 10 percent of children in the schools were white. In Washington, D.C., 94 percent of children were black or Hispanic; less than 5 percent were white. In St. Louis, 82 percent of the student population were black or Hispanic; in Philadelphia and Cleveland, 79 percent; in Los Angeles, 84 percent; in Detroit, 96 percent; in Baltimore, 89 percent. In New York City, nearly three quarters of the students were black or Hispanic.

Even these statistics, as stark as they are, cannot begin to convey how deeply isolated children in the poorest and most segregated sections of these cities have become. In the typically colossal high schools of the Bronx, for instance, more than 90 percent of students (in most cases, more than 95 percent) are black or Hispanic. At John F. Kennedy High School in 2003, 93 percent of the enrollment of more than 4,000 students were black and Hispanic; only 3.5 percent of students at the school were white. At Harry S. Truman High School, black and Hispanic students represented 96 percent of the enrollment of 2,700 students; 2 percent were white. At Adlai Stevenson High School, which enrolls 3,400 students, blacks and Hispanics made up 97 percent of the student population; a mere eight-tenths of one percent were white.

A teacher at P.S. 65 in the South Bronx once pointed out to me one of the two white children I had ever seen there. His presence in her class was something of a wonderment to the teacher and to the other pupils. I asked how many white kids she had taught in the South Bronx in her career. "I've been at this school for eighteen years," she said. "This is the first white student I have ever taught."

One of the most disheartening experiences for those who grew up in the years when Martin Luther King Jr. and Thurgood Marshall were alive is to visit public schools today that bear their names, or names of other honored leaders of the integration struggles that produced the temporary progress that took place in the three decades after *Brown v. Board of Education,* and to find out how many of these schools are bastions of contemporary segregation. It is even more disheartening when schools like these are not in deeply segregated inner-city neighborhoods but in racially mixed areas where the integration of a public school would seem to be most natural, and where, indeed, it takes a conscious effort on the part of parents or school officials in these districts to avoid the integration option that is often right at their front door.

In a Seattle neighborhood that I visited in 2002, for instance, where approximately half the families were Caucasian, 95 percent of students at the Thurgood Marshall Elementary School were black, Hispanic, Native American, or of Asian origin. An African-American teacher at the school told me—not with bitterness but wistfully—of seeing clusters of white parents and their children each morning on the corner of a street close to the school, waiting for a bus that took the children to a predominantly white school. . . .

There is a well-known high school named for Martin Luther King Jr. in New York City. This school, which I've visited repeatedly in recent years, is located in an upper-middle-class white neighborhood, where it was built in the belief—or hope—that it would draw large numbers of white students by permitting them to walk to school, while only their black and Hispanic classmates would be asked to ride the bus or come by train. When the school was opened in 1975, less than a block from Lincoln Center in Manhattan, "it was seen," according to the *New York Times,* "as a promising effort to integrate white, black and Hispanic students in a thriving neighborhood that held one of the city's cultural gems." Even from the start, however, parents in the neighborhood showed great reluctance to permit their children to enroll at Martin Luther King, and, despite "its prime location and its name, which itself creates the highest of expectations," notes the *Times,* the school before long came to be a destination for black and Hispanic students who could not obtain admission into more successful schools. It stands today as one of the nation's most visible and problematic symbols of an expectation rapidly receding and a legacy substantially betrayed.

Perhaps most damaging to any serious effort to address racial segregation openly is the refusal of most of the major arbiters of culture in our northern cities to confront or even clearly name an obvious reality they would have castigated with a passionate determination in another section of the nation fifty years before—and which, moreover, they still castigate today in retrospective writings that assign it to a comfortably distant and allegedly concluded era of the past. There is, indeed, a seemingly agreed-upon convention in much of the media today not even to use an accurate descriptor like "racial segregation" in a narrative description of a segregated school. Linguistic sweeteners, semantic somersaults, and surrogate vocabularies are repeatedly employed. Schools in which as few as 3 or 4 percent of students may be white or Southeast Asian or of Middle Eastern origin, for instance—and where *every other child* in the building is black or Hispanic—are referred to as "diverse." Visitors to schools like these discover quickly the eviscerated meaning of the word, which is no longer a proper adjective but a euphemism for a plainer word that has apparently become unspeakable.

School systems themselves repeatedly employ this euphemism in describing the composition of their student populations. In a school I visited in the fall of 2004 in Kansas City, Missouri, for example, a document distributed to visitors reports that the school's curriculum "addresses the needs of children from diverse backgrounds." But as I went from class to class, I did not encounter any children who were white or Asian—or Hispanic, for that matter—and when I was later provided with precise statistics for the demographics of the school, I learned that 99.6 percent of students there were African American. In a similar document, the school board of another district, this one in New York State, referred to "the diversity" of its student population and "the rich variations of ethnic backgrounds." But when I looked at the racial numbers that the district had reported to the state, I learned that there were 2,800 black and Hispanic children in the system, 1 Asian child, and 3 whites. Words, in these cases, cease to have real meaning; or, rather, they mean the opposite of what they say.

High school students whom I talk with in deeply segregated neighborhoods and public schools seem far less circumspect than their elders and far more open in their willingness to confront these issues. "It's more like being hidden," said a fifteen-year-old girl named Isabel[1] I met some years ago in Harlem, in attempting to explain to me the ways in which she and her classmates understood the racial segregation of their neighborhoods and schools. "It's as if you have been put in a garage where, if they don't have room for something but aren't sure if they should throw it out, they put it there where they don't need to think of it again."

I asked her if she thought America truly did not "have room" for her or other children of her race. "Think of it this way," said a sixteen-year-old girl sitting beside her. "If people in New York woke up one day and learned that we were gone, that we had simply died or left for somewhere else, how would they feel?"

"How do you think they'd feel?" I asked. "I think they'd be relieved," this very solemn girl replied.

Many educators make the argument today that given the demographics of large cities like New York and their suburban areas, our only realistic goal should be the nurturing of strong, empowered, and well-funded schools in segregated neighborhoods. Black school officials in these situations have sometimes conveyed to me a bitter and clear-sighted recognition that they're being asked, essentially, to mediate and render functional an uncontested separation between children of their race and children of white people living sometimes in a distant section of their town and sometimes in almost their own immediate communities. Implicit in this mediation is a willingness to set aside the promises of *Brown* and—though never stating this or even thinking of it clearly in these terms—to settle for the promise made more than a century ago in *Plessy v. Ferguson,* the 1896 Supreme Court ruling in which "separate but equal" was accepted as a tolerable rationale for the perpetuation of a dual system in American society.

Equality itself—equality alone—is now, it seems, the article of faith to which most of the principals of inner-city public schools subscribe. And some who are perhaps most realistic do not even dare to ask for, or expect, complete equality, which seems beyond the realm of probability for many years to come, but look instead for only a sufficiency of means—"adequacy" is the legal term most often used today—by which to win those practical and finite victories that appear to be within their reach. Higher standards, higher expectations, are repeatedly demanded of these urban principals, and of the teachers and students in their schools, but far lower standards—

certainly in ethical respects—appear to be expected of the dominant society that isolates these children in unequal institutions.

"Dear Mr. Kozol," wrote the eight-year-old, "we do not have the things you have. You have Clean things. We do not have. You have a clean bathroom. We do not have that. You have Parks and we do not have Parks. You have all the thing and we do not have all the thing. Can you help us?"

The letter, from a child named Alliyah, came in a fat envelope of twenty-seven letters from a class of third-grade children in the Bronx. Other letters that the students in Alliyah's classroom sent me registered some of the same complaints. "We don't have no gardens," "no Music or Art," and "no fun places to play," one child said. "Is there a way to fix this Problem?" Another noted a concern one hears from many children in such overcrowded schools: "We have a gym but it is for lining up. I think it is not fair." Yet another of Alliyah's classmates asked me, with a sweet misspelling, if I knew the way to make her school into a "good" school—"like the other kings have"—and ended with the hope that I would do my best to make it possible for "all the kings" to have good schools.

The letter that affected me the most, however, had been written by a child named Elizabeth. "It is not fair that other kids have a garden and new things. But we don't have that," said Elizabeth. "I wish that this school was the most beautiful school in the whole why world."

"The whole why world" stayed in my thoughts for days. When I later met Elizabeth, I brought her letter with me, thinking I might see whether, in reading it aloud, she'd change the "why" to "wide" or leave it as it was. My visit to her class, however, proved to be so pleasant, and the children seemed so eager to bombard me with their questions about where I lived, and why I lived there rather than in New York, and who I lived with, and how many dogs I had, and other interesting questions of that sort, that I decided not to interrupt the nice reception they had given me with questions about usages and spelling. I left "the whole why world" to float around unedited and unrevised in my mind. The letter itself soon found a resting place on the wall above my desk.

In the years before I met Elizabeth, I had visited many other schools in the South Bronx and in one northern district of the Bronx as well. I had made repeated visits to a high school where a stream of water flowed down one of the main stairwells on a rainy afternoon and where green fungus molds were growing in the office where the students went for counseling. A large blue barrel was positioned to collect rainwater coming through the ceiling. In one makeshift elementary school housed in a former skating rink next to a funeral establishment in yet another nearly all-black-and-Hispanic section of the Bronx, class size rose to thirty-four and more; four kindergarten classes and a sixth-grade class were packed into a single room that had no windows. The air was stifling in many rooms, and the children had no place for recess because there was no outdoor playground and no indoor gym.

In another elementary school, which had been built to hold 1,000 children but was packed to bursting with some 1,500, the principal poured out his feelings to me in a room in which a plastic garbage bag had been attached somehow to cover part of the collapsing ceiling. "This," he told me, pointing to the garbage bag, then gesturing around him at the other indications of decay and disrepair one sees in ghetto schools much like it elsewhere, "would not happen to white children."

Libraries, once one of the glories of the New York City school system, were either nonexistent or, at best, vestigial in large numbers of the elementary schools. Art and music programs had also for the most part disappeared. "When I began to teach in 1969," the principal of an elementary school in the South Bronx reported to me, "every school had a full-time licensed art and music teacher and librarian." During the subsequent decades, he recalled, "I saw all of that destroyed."

School physicians also were removed from elementary schools during these years. In 1970, when substantial numbers of white children still attended New York City's public schools, 400 doctors had been present to address the health needs of the children. By 1993 the number of doctors had been cut to 23, most of them part-time—a cutback that affected most severely children in the city's poorest neighborhoods, where medical facilities were most deficient and health problems faced by children most extreme. Teachers told me of asthmatic children who came into class with chronic wheezing and who at any moment of the day might undergo more serious attacks, but in the schools I visited there were no doctors to attend to them.

In explaining these steep declines in services, political leaders in New York tended to point to shifting economic factors, like a serious budget crisis in the middle 1970s, rather than to the changing racial demographics of the student population. But the fact of economic ups and downs from year to year, or from one decade to the next, could not convincingly explain the permanent shortchanging of the city's students, which took place routinely in good economic times and bad. The bad times were seized upon politically to justify the cuts, and the money was never restored once the crisis years were past.

"If you close your eyes to the changing racial composition of the schools and look only at budget actions and political events," says Noreen Connell, the director of the nonprofit Educational Priorities Panel in New York, "you're missing the assumptions that are underlying these decisions." When minority parents ask for something better for their kids, she says, "the assumption is that these are parents who can be discounted. These are kids who just don't count—children we don't value."

This, then, is the accusation that Alliyah and her classmates send our way: "You have. . . . We do not have." Are they right or are they wrong? Is this a case of naive and simplistic juvenile exaggeration? What does a third-grader know about these big-time questions of fairness and justice? Physical appearances apart, how in any case do you begin to measure something so diffuse and vast and seemingly abstract as having more, or having less, or not having at all?

Around the time I met Alliyah in the school year 1997–1998, New York's Board of Education spent about $8,000 yearly on the education of a third-grade child in a New York City public school. If you could have scooped Alliyah up out of the neighborhood where she was born and plunked her down in a fairly typical white suburb of New York, she would have received a public education worth about $12,000 a year. If you were to lift her up once more and set her down in one of the wealthiest white suburbs of New York, she would have received as much as $18,000 worth of public education every year and would likely have had a third-grade teacher paid approximately $30,000 more than her teacher in the Bronx was paid.

The dollars on both sides of the equation have increased since then, but the discrepancies between them have remained. The present per-pupil spending level in the New York City schools is $11,700, which may be compared with a per-pupil spending level in excess of $22,000 in the well-to-do suburban district of Manhasset, Long Island. The present New York City level is, indeed, almost exactly what Manhasset spent per pupil eighteen years ago, in 1987, when that sum of money bought a great deal more in services and salaries than it can buy today. In dollars adjusted for inflation, New York City has not yet caught up to where its wealthiest suburbs were a quarter-century ago.

Gross discrepancies in teacher salaries between the city and its affluent white suburbs have remained persistent as well. In 1997 the median salary for teachers in Alliyah's neighborhood was $43,000, as compared with $74,000 in suburban Rye, $77,000 in Manhasset, and $81,000 in the town of Scarsdale, which is only about eleven miles from Alliyah's school. Five years later, in 2002, salary scales for New York City's teachers rose to levels that approximated those within the lower-spending districts in the suburbs, but salary scales do not reflect the actual salaries that teachers typically receive, which are dependent upon years of service and advanced degrees. Salaries for first-year teachers in the city were higher than they'd been four years before, but the differences in median pay between the city and its upper-middle-income suburbs had remained extreme. The overall figure for New York City in 2002–2003 was $53,000, while it had climbed to $87,000 in Manhasset and exceeded $95,000 in Scarsdale.

"There are expensive children and there are cheap children," writes Marina Warner, an essayist and novelist who has written many books for children, "just as there are expensive women and cheap women." The governmentally administered diminishment in value of the children of the poor begins even before the age of five or six, when they begin their years of formal education in the public schools. It starts during their infant and toddler years, when hundreds of thousands of children of the very poor in much of the United States are locked out of the opportunity for preschool education for no reason but the accident of birth and budgetary choices of the government, while children of the privileged are often given veritable feasts of rich developmental early education. . . .

There are remarkable exceptions to this pattern in some sections of the nation. In Milwaukee, for example, virtually every four-year-old is now enrolled in a preliminary kindergarten program, which amounts to a full year of preschool education, prior to a second kindergarten year for five-year-olds. More commonly in urban neighborhoods, large numbers of low-income children are denied these opportunities and come into their kindergarten year without the minimal social skills that children need in order to participate in class activities and without even such very modest early-learning skills as knowing how to hold a crayon or a pencil, identify perhaps a couple of shapes and colors, or recognize that printed pages go from left to right.

Three years later, in third grade, these children are introduced to what are known as "high-stakes tests," which in many urban systems now determine whether students can or cannot be promoted. Children who have been in programs like those offered by the "Baby Ivies" since the age of two have, by now, received the benefits of six or seven years of education, nearly twice as many as the children who have been denied these opportunities; yet all are required to take, and will be measured by, the same examinations. Which of these children will receive the highest scores? The ones who spent the years from two to four in lovely little Montessori programs and in other pastel-painted settings in which tender and attentive and well-trained instructors read to them from beautiful storybooks and introduced them very gently for the first time to the world of numbers and the shapes of letters, and the sizes and varieties of solid objects, and perhaps taught them to sort things into groups or to arrange them in a sequence, or to do those many other interesting things that early childhood specialists refer to as prenumeracy skills? Or the ones who spent those years at home in front of a TV or sitting by the window of a slum apartment gazing down into the street? There is something deeply hypocritical about a society that holds an eight-year-old inner-city child "accountable" for her performance on a high-stakes standardized exam but does not hold the high officials of our government accountable for robbing her of what they gave their own kids six or seven years earlier.

Perhaps in order to deflect these recognitions, or to soften them somewhat, many people, even while they do not doubt the benefit of making very large investments in the education of their own children, somehow—paradoxical as it may seem—appear to be attracted to the argument that money may not really matter that much at all. No matter with what regularity such doubts about the worth of spending money on a child's education are advanced, it is obvious that those who have the money, and who spend it lavishly to benefit their own kids, do not do it for no reason. Yet shockingly large numbers of well-educated and sophisticated people whom I talk with nowadays dismiss such challenges with a surprising ease. "Is the answer really to throw money into these dysfunctional and failing schools?" I'm often asked. "Don't we have some better ways to make them 'work'?" The question is posed in a variety of forms. "Yes, of course, it's not a perfectly fair system as it stands. But money alone is surely not the sole response. The values of the parents and the kids themselves must have a role in this as well you know, housing, health conditions, social factors." "Other factors"—a term of overall reprieve one often hears—"have got to be considered, too." These latter points are obviously true but always seem to have the odd effect of substituting things we know we cannot change in the short run for obvious solutions like cutting class size and constructing new school buildings or providing universal preschool that we actually could put in place right now if we were so inclined.

Frequently these arguments are posed as questions that do not invite an answer because the answer seems to be decided in advance. "Can you really buy your way to better education for these children?" "Do we know enough to be quite sure that we will see an actual return on the investment that we make?" "Is it even clear that this is the right starting point to get to where we'd like to go? It doesn't always seem to work, as I am sure that you already know," or similar questions that somehow assume I will agree with those who ask them.

Some people who ask these questions, although they live in wealthy districts where the schools are funded at high levels, don't even send their children to these public schools but choose instead to send them to expensive private day schools. At some of the well-known private prep schools in the New York City area, tuition and associated costs are typically more than $20,000 a year. During their children's teenage years, they sometimes send them off to very fine New England schools like Andover or Exeter or Groton, where tuition, boarding, and additional expenses rise to more than $30,000. Often a family has two teenage children in these schools at the same time, so they may be spending more than $60,000 on their children's education every year. Yet here I am one night, a guest within their home, and dinner has been served and we are having coffee now; and this entirely likable, and generally sensible, and beautifully refined and thoughtful person looks me in the eyes and asks me whether you can really buy your way to better education for the children of the poor.

As racial isolation deepens and the inequalities of education finance remain unabated and take on new and more innovative forms, the principals of many inner-city schools are making choices that few principals in public schools that serve white children in the mainstream of the nation ever need to contemplate. Many have been dedicating vast amounts of time and effort to create an architecture of adaptive strategies that promise incremental gains within the limits inequality allows.

New vocabularies of stentorian determination, new systems of incentive, and new modes of castigation, which are termed "rewards and sanctions," have emerged. Curriculum materials that are alleged to be aligned with governmentally established goals and standards and particularly suited to what are regarded as "the special needs and learning styles" of low-income urban children have been introduced. Relentless emphasis on raising test scores, rigid policies of nonpromotion and nongraduation, a new empiricism and the imposition of unusually detailed lists of named and numbered "outcomes" for each isolated parcel of instruction, an oftentimes fanatical insistence upon uniformity of teachers in their management of time, an openly conceded emulation of the rigorous approaches of the military and a frequent use of terminology that comes out of the world of industry and commerce—these are just a few of the familiar aspects of these new adaptive strategies.

Although generically described as "school reform," most of these practices and policies are targeted primarily at poor children of color; and although most educators speak of these agendas in broad language that sounds applicable to all, it is understood that they are valued chiefly as responses to perceived catastrophe in deeply segregated and unequal schools.

"If you do what I tell you to do, how I tell you to do it, when I tell you to do it, you'll get it right," said a determined South Bronx principal observed by a reporter for the *New York Times*. She was laying out a memorizing rule for math to an assembly of her students. "If you don't, you'll get it wrong." This is the voice, this is the tone, this is the rhythm and didactic certitude one hears today in inner-city schools that have embraced a pedagogy of direct command and absolute control. "Taking their inspiration from the ideas of B. F. Skinner . . . ," says the *Times,* proponents of scripted rote-and-drill curricula articulate their aim as the establishment of "fault-less communication" between "the teacher, who is the stimulus," and "the students, who respond."

The introduction of Skinnerian approaches (which are commonly employed in penal institutions and drug-rehabilitation programs), as a way of altering the attitudes and learning styles of black and Hispanic children, is provocative, and it has stirred some outcries from respected scholars. To actually go into a school where you know some of the children very, very well and see the way that these approaches can affect their daily lives and thinking processes is even more provocative.

On a chilly November day four years ago in the South Bronx, I entered P.S. 65, a school I had been visiting since 1993. There had been major changes since I'd been there last. Silent lunches had been instituted in the cafeteria, and on days when children misbehaved, silent recess had been introduced as well. On those days the students were obliged to sit in rows and maintain perfect silence on the floor of a small indoor room instead of going out to play. The words SUCCESS FOR ALL, the brand name of a scripted curriculum—better known by its acronym, SFA—were prominently posted at the top of the main stairway and, as I would later find, in almost every room. . . .

I entered the fourth grade of a teacher I will call Mr. Endicott, a man in his mid-thirties who had arrived here without training as a teacher, one of about a dozen teachers in the building who were sent into this school after a single summer of short-order preparation. Now in his second year, he had developed a considerable sense of confidence and held the class under a tight control. . . .

My attention was distracted by some whispering among the children sitting to the right of me. The teacher's response to this distraction was immediate: his arm shot out and up in a diagonal in front of him, his hand straight up, his fingers flat. The young co-teacher did this, too. When they saw their teachers do this, all the children in the classroom did it, too.

"Zero noise," the teacher said, but this instruction proved to be unneeded. The strange salute the class and teachers gave each other, which turned out to be one of a number of such silent signals teachers in the school were trained to use, and children to obey, had done the job of silencing the class.

"Active listening!" said Mr. Endicott. "Heads up! Tractor beams!" which meant, "Every eye on me." . . .

A well-educated man, Mr. Endicott later spoke to me about the form of class-room management that he was using as an adaptation from a model of industrial efficiency. "It's a kind of 'Taylorism' in the classroom," he explained, referring to a set of theories about the management of factory employees introduced by Frederick Taylor in the early 1900s. "Primitive utilitarianism" is another term he used when we met some months later to discuss these management techniques with other teachers from the school. His reservations were, however, not apparent in the classroom. Within the terms of what he had been asked to do, he had, indeed, become a master of control. It is one of the few classrooms I had visited up to that time in which almost nothing even hinting at spontaneous emotion in the children or the teacher surfaced while I was there.

The teacher gave the "zero noise" salute again when someone whispered to another child at his table. "In two minutes you will have a chance to talk and share this with your partner." Communication between children in the class was not prohibited but was afforded time slots and, remarkably enough, was formalized in an expression that I found included in a memo that was posted on the wall beside the door: "An opportunity . . . to engage in Accountable Talk."[2] . . .

In speaking of the drill-based program in effect at P.S. 65, Mr. Endicott told me he tended to be sympathetic to the school administrators, more so at least than the other teachers I had talked with seemed to be. He said he believed his principal had little choice about the implementation of this program, which had been mandated for all elementary schools in New York City that had had rock-bottom academic records over a long period of time. "This puts me into a dilemma," he went on, "because I love the kids at P.S. 65." And even while, he said, "I know that my teaching SFA is a charade . . . if I don't do it I won't be permitted to teach these children."

Mr. Endicott, like all but two of the new recruits at P.S. 65—there were about fifteen in all—was a white person, as were the principal and most of the administrators at the school. As a result, most of these neophyte instructors had had little or no prior contact with the children of an inner-city neighborhood; but, like the others I met, and despite the distancing between the children and their teachers that resulted from the scripted method of instruction, he had developed close attachments to his students and did not want to abandon them. At the same time, the class- and race-specific implementation of this program obviously troubled him. "There's an expression now," he said. " 'The rich get richer, and the poor get SFA.' " He said he was still trying to figure out his "professional ethics" on the problem that this posed for him.

White children made up "only about one percent" of students in the New York City schools in which this scripted teaching system was imposed,[3] according to the *New York Times,* which also said that "the prepackaged lessons" were intended "to ensure that all teachers—even novices or the most inept"—would be able to teach reading. As seemingly pragmatic and hardheaded as such arguments may be, they are desperation strategies that come out of the acceptance of inequity. If we did not have a deeply segregated system in which more experienced instructors teach the children of the privileged and the least experienced are sent to teach the children of minorities, these practices would not be needed and could not be so convincingly defended. They are confections of apartheid, and no matter by what arguments of urgency or practicality they have been justified, they cannot fail to further deepen the divisions of society.

There is no misery index for the children of apartheid education. There ought to be; we measure almost everything else that happens to them in their schools. Do kids who go to schools like these enjoy the days they spend in them? Is school, for most of them, a happy place to be? You do not find the answers to these questions in reports about achievement levels, scientific methods of accountability, or structural revisions in the modes of governance. Documents like these don't speak of happiness. You have to go back to the schools themselves to find an answer to these questions. You have to sit down in the little chairs in first and second grade, or on the reading rug with kindergarten kids, and listen to the things they actually say to one another and the dialogue between them and their teachers. You have to go down to the basement with the children when it's time for lunch and to the playground with them, if they have a playground, when it's time for recess, if they still have recess at their school. You have to walk into the children's bathrooms in these buildings. You have to do what children do and breathe the air the children breathe. I don't think that there is any other way to find out what the lives that children lead in school are really like.

High school students, when I first meet them, are often more reluctant than the younger children to open up and express their personal concerns; but hesitation on the part of students did not prove to be a problem when I visited a tenth-grade class at Fremont High School in Los Angeles. The students were told that I was a writer, and they took no time in getting down to matters that were on their minds.

"Can we talk about the bathrooms?" asked a soft-spoken student named Mireya.

In almost any classroom there are certain students who, by the force of their directness or the unusual sophistication of their way of speaking, tend to capture your attention from the start. Mireya later spoke insightfully about some of the serious academic problems that were common in the school, but her observations on the physical and personal embarrassments she and her schoolmates had to undergo cut to the heart of questions of essential dignity that kids in squalid schools like this one have to deal with all over the nation.

Fremont High School, as court papers filed in a lawsuit against the state of California document, has fifteen fewer bathrooms than the law requires. Of the limited number of bathrooms that are working in the school, "only one or two . . . are open and unlocked for girls to use." Long lines of girls are "waiting to use the bathrooms," which are generally "unclean" and "lack basic supplies," including toilet paper. Some of the classrooms, as court papers also document, "do not have air conditioning," so that students, who attend school on a three-track schedule that runs year-round, "become red-faced and unable to concentrate" during "the extreme heat of summer." The school's maintenance records report that rats were found in eleven classrooms. Rat droppings were found "in the bins and drawers" of the high school's kitchen, and school records note that "hamburger buns" were being "eaten off [the] bread-delivery rack."

No matter how many tawdry details like these I've read in legal briefs or depositions through the years, I'm always shocked again to learn how often these unsanitary physical conditions are permitted to continue in the schools that serve our poorest students—even after they have been vividly described in the media. But hearing of these conditions in Mireya's words was even more unsettling, in part because this student seemed so fragile and because the need even to speak of these indignities in front of me and all the other students was an additional indignity.

"It humiliates you," said Mireya, who went on to make the interesting statement that "the school provides solutions that don't actually work," and this idea was taken up by several other students in describing course requirements within the school. A tall black student, for example, told me that she hoped to be a social worker or a doctor but was programmed into "Sewing Class" this year. She also had to take another course, called "Life Skills," which she told me was a very basic course—"a retarded class," to use her words—that "teaches things like the six continents," which she said she'd learned in elementary school.

When I asked her why she had to take these courses, she replied that she'd been told they were required, which as I later learned was not exactly so. What was required was that high school students take two courses in an area of study called "The Technical Arts," and which the Los Angeles Board of Education terms "Applied Technology." At schools that served the middle class or upper-middle class, this requirement was likely to be met by courses that had academic substance and, perhaps, some relevance to college preparation. At Beverly Hills High School, for example, the technical-arts requirement could be fulfilled by taking subjects like residential architecture, the designing of commercial structures, broadcast journalism, advanced computer graphics, a sophisticated course in furniture design, carving and sculpture, or an honors course in engineering research and design. At Fremont High, in contrast, this requirement was far more often met by courses that were basically vocational and also obviously keyed to low-paying levels of employment.

Mireya, for example, who had plans to go to college, told me that she had to take a sewing class last year and now was told she'd been assigned to take a class in hairdressing as well. When I asked her teacher why Mireya could not skip these subjects and enroll in classes that would help her to pursue her college aspirations, she replied, "It isn't a question of what students want. It's what the school may have available. If all the other elective classes that a student wants to take are full, she has to take one of these classes if she wants to graduate."

A very small girl named Obie, who had big blue-tinted glasses tilted up across her hair, interrupted then to tell me with a kind of wild gusto that she'd taken hairdressing *twice!* When I expressed surprise that this was possible, she said there were two levels of hairdressing offered here at Fremont High. "One is in hairstyling," she said. "The other is in braiding."

Mireya stared hard at this student for a moment and then suddenly began to cry. "I don't *want* to take hairdressing. I did not need sewing either. I knew how to sew. My mother is a seamstress in a factory. I'm trying to go to college. I don't need to sew to go to college. My mother sews. I hoped for something else."

"What would you rather take?" I asked.

"I wanted to take an AP class," she answered.

Mireya's sudden tears elicited a strong reaction from one of the boys who had been silent up till now: a thin, dark-eyed student named Fortino, who had long hair down to his shoulders. He suddenly turned directly to Mireya and spoke into the silence that followed her last words.

"Listen to me," he said. "The owners of the sewing factories need laborers. Correct?"

"I guess they do," Mireya said.

"It's not going to be their own kids. Right?"

"Why not?" another student said.

"So they can grow beyond themselves" Mireya answered quietly. "But we remain the same."

"You're ghetto," said Fortino, "so we send you to the factory." He sat low in his desk chair, leaning on one elbow, his voice and dark eyes loaded with a cynical intelligence. "You're ghetto—so you sew!"

"There are higher positions than these," said a student named Samantha.

"You're ghetto," said Fortino unrelentingly. "So sew!"

Admittedly, the economic needs of a society are hound to be reflected to some rational degree within the policies and purposes of public schools. But, even so, there must be *something* more to life as it is lived by six-year-olds or ten-year-olds, or by teenagers, for that matter, than concerns about "successful global competition." Childhood is not merely basic training for utilitarian adulthood. It should have some claims upon our mercy, not for its future value to the economic interests of competitive societies but for its present value as a perishable piece of life itself.

Very few people who are not involved with inner-city schools have any real idea of the extremes to which the mercantile distortion of the purposes and character of education have been taken or how unabashedly proponents of these practices are willing to defend them. The head of a Chicago school, for instance, who was criticized by some for emphasizing rote instruction that, his critics said, was turning children into "robots," found no reason to dispute the charge. "Did you ever stop to think that these robots will never burglarize your home?" he asked, and "will never snatch your pocketbooks. . . . These robots are going to be producing taxes."

Corporate leaders, when they speak of education, sometimes pay lip-service to the notion of "good critical and analytic skills," but it is reasonable to ask whether they have in mind the critical analysis of *their* priorities. In principle, perhaps some do; but, if so, this is not a principle that seems to have been honored widely in the schools I have been visiting. In all the various business-driven inner-city classrooms I have observed in the past five years, plastered as they are with corporation brand names and managerial vocabularies, I have yet to see the two words "labor unions." Is this an oversight? How is that possible? Teachers and principals themselves, who are almost always members of a union, seem to be so beaten down that they rarely even question this omission.

It is not at all unusual these days to come into an urban school in which the principal prefers to call himself or herself "building CEO" or "building manager." In some of the same schools teachers are described as "classroom managers."[4] I have never been in a suburban district in which principals were asked to view themselves or teachers in this way. These terminologies remind us of how wide the distance has become between two very separate worlds of education.

It has been more than a decade now since drill-based literacy methods like Success For All began to proliferate in our urban schools. It has been three and a half years since the systems of assessment that determine the effectiveness of these and similar practices were codified in the federal legislation, No Child Left Behind, that President

Bush signed into law in 2002. Since the enactment of this bill, the number of standardized exams children must take has more than doubled. It will probably increase
again after the year 2006, when standardized tests, which are now required in grades
three through eight, may be required in Head Start programs and, as President Bush
has now proposed, in ninth, tenth, and eleventh grades as well.

The elements of strict accountability, in short, are solidly in place; and in many
states where the present federal policies are simply reinforcements of accountability
requirements that were established long before the passage of the federal law, the
same regimen has been in place since 1995 or even earlier. The "tests-and-standards"
partisans have had things very much their way for an extended period of time, and
those who were convinced that they had ascertained "what works" in schools that
serve minorities and children of the poor have had ample opportunity to prove that
they were right.

What, then, it is reasonable to ask, are the results?

The achievement gap between black and white children, which narrowed for
three decades up until the late years of the 1980s—the period in which school segregation steadily decreased—started to widen once more in the early 1990s when
the federal courts began the process of resegregation by dismantling the mandates
of the *Brown* decision. From that point on, the gap continued to widen or remained
essentially unchanged; and while recently there has been a modest narrowing of the
gap in reading scores for fourth-grade children, the gap in secondary school remains
as wide as ever.

The media inevitably celebrate the periodic upticks that a set of scores may
seem to indicate in one year or another in achievement levels of black and Hispanic
children in their elementary schools. But if these upticks were not merely temporary
"testing gains" achieved by test-prep regimens and were instead authentic education
gains, they would carry over into middle school and high school. Children who know
how to read—and read with comprehension—do not suddenly become nonreaders
and hopelessly disabled writers when they enter secondary school. False gains evapo-
rate; real gains endure. Yet hundreds of thousands of the inner-city children who
have made what many districts claim to be dramatic gains in elementary school, and
whose principals and teachers have adjusted almost every aspect of their school days
and school calendars, forfeiting recess, canceling or cutting back on all the so-called
frills (art, music, even social sciences) in order to comply with state demands—those
students, now in secondary school, are sitting in subject-matter classes where they
cannot comprehend the texts and cannot set down their ideas in the kind of sentences
expected of most fourth- and fifth-grade students in the suburbs. Students in this
painful situation, not surprisingly, tend to be most likely to drop out of school.

In 48 percent of high schools in the nation's 100 largest districts, which are
those in which the highest concentrations of black and Hispanic students tend to be
enrolled, less than half the entering ninth-graders graduate in four years. Nationwide,
from 1993 to 2002, the number of high schools graduating less than half their ninth-
grade class in four years has increased by 75 percent. In the 94 percent of districts
in New York State where white children make up the majority, nearly 80 percent of
students graduate from high school in four years. In the 6 percent of districts where

black and Hispanic students make up the majority, only 40 percent do so. There are 120 high schools in New York, enrolling nearly 200,000 minority students, where less than 60 percent of entering ninth-graders even make it to twelfth grade.

The promulgation of new and expanded inventories of "what works," no matter the enthusiasm with which they're elaborated, is not going to change this. The use of hortatory slogans chanted by the students in our segregated schools is not going to change this. Desperate historical revisionism that romanticizes the segregation of an older order (this is a common theme of many separatists today) is not going to change this. Skinnerian instructional approaches, which decapitate a child's capability for critical reflection, are not going to change this. Posters about "global competition" will certainly not change this. Turning six-year-olds into examination soldiers and denying eight-year-olds their time for play at recess will not change this.

"I went to Washington to challenge the soft bigotry of low expectations," said President Bush in his campaign for reelection in September 2004. "It's working. It's making a difference." Here we have one of those deadly lies that by sheer repetition is at length accepted by surprisingly large numbers of Americans. But it is not the truth; and it is not an innocent misstatement of the facts. It is a devious appeasement of the heartache of the parents of the black and brown and poor, and if it is not forcefully resisted it will lead us further in a very dangerous direction.

Whether the issue is inequity alone or deepening resegregation or the labyrinthine intertwining of the two, it is well past the time for us to start the work that it will take to change this. If it takes people marching in the streets and other forms of adamant disruption of the governing civilities, if it takes more than litigation, more than legislation, and much more than resolutions introduced by members of Congress, these are prices we should be prepared to pay. "We do not have the things you have," Alliyah told me when she wrote to ask if I would come and visit her school in the South Bronx. "Can you help us?" America owes that little girl and millions like her a more honorable answer than they have received.

NOTES

1. The names of children mentioned in this article have been changed to protect their privacy.

2. Since that day at P.S. 65, I have visited nine other schools in six different cities where the same Skinnerian curriculum is used. The signs on the walls, the silent signals, the curious salute, the same insistent naming of all cognitive particulars, became familiar as I went from one school to the next.

3. SFA has since been discontinued in the New York City public schools, though it is still being used in 1,300 U.S. schools, serving as many as 650,000 children. Similar scripted systems are used in schools (overwhelmingly minority in population) serving several million children.

4. A school I visited three years ago in Columbus, Ohio, was littered with "Help Wanted" signs. Starting in kindergarten, children in the school were being asked to think about the jobs that they might choose when they grew up. In one classroom there was a poster that displayed the names of several retail stores: J.C. Penney, Wal-Mart, Kmart, Sears, and a few others. "It's like working in a store," a classroom aide explained. "The children are learning to pretend

they're cashiers." At another school in the same district, children were encouraged to apply for jobs in their classrooms. Among job positions open to the children in this school, there was an "Absence Manager" and a "Behavior Chart Manager," a "Form Collector Manager," a "Paper Passer Outer Manager," a "Paper Collecting Manager," a "Paper Returning Manager," an "Exit Ticket Manager," even a "Learning Manager," a "Reading Corner Manager," and a "Score Keeper Manager." I asked the principal if there was a special reason why those two words "management" and "manager" kept popping up throughout the school. "We want every child to be working as a manager while he or she is in this school," the principal explained. "We want to make them understand that, in this country, companies will give you opportunities to work, to prove yourself, no matter what you've done." I wasn't sure what she meant by "no matter what you've done," and asked her if she could explain it. "Even if you have a felony arrest," she said, "we want you to understand that you can be a manager someday."

PART

V Social Change

■■■■ ■

Like it or not, change is one of the chief characteristics of our society, and our birth during this particular historical era has destined us to live in the midst of shifting norms and technological innovation. Social change is so swift that it can be difficult to adjust to the new expectations suddenly forced on us. Change is so extensive that little remains the same from one generation to the next. We must constantly refine old skills or learn new ones. Although U.S. physicians receive a top-notch education and become familiar with the latest developments in their profession, if they fail to continue taking courses in their specialties, in a short time they fall woefully behind.

Some changes are small and of little consequence for our lives. A fast food outlet opens where a gas station used to be. The new models of cars sprout new lines—ever so slightly. Computers appear in new colors. Our college adds a course and drops another. A band, singer, or actor becomes an overnight sensation, then quickly drops from sight.

Other changes are large, and have a huge impact on us. Cities expand so greatly that they bump into one another, and no longer can you tell where one ends and the other leaves off. These megacities increasingly influence U.S. culture, changing the way we view life. Latinos immigrate to the United States in such vast numbers that they become the largest U.S. minority group and significantly influence U.S. politics. Upset about some social condition, people band together in social movements, their protests echoing throughout the society.

Social change is not something abstract, but a social force that has a fundamental impact on our own lives. Our own economic future changes as the globalization of capitalism sweeps jobs away from us, transplanting them into other parts of the world. As the mass media become more powerful, they increasingly shape public opinion—and our own—and with it, the affairs of the nation. Computers change the way we work, get educated, find spouses and lovers, and even how we worship and fight wars. Computers even change the way we think, though this fundamental impact is so recent—and though extensive, yet so subtle—that we currently have little understanding of it.

To conclude this book, then, we shall focus on social change. Farai Chideya opens this final part by giving us background on understanding the many changes that Latino immigration is bringing. George Ritzer then examines how changes in the economy are affecting our lives, how society is being McDonaldized. The final selection that closes this part, written by a team of researchers, examines changes in the sex lives of Americans.

Border Blues: The Dilemma of Illegal Immigration

Farai Chideya

introduction ▪ ▪ ▪ ▪

Changes in urbanization and population ordinarily seem remote, something occurring at a distance that has little relevance for our own lives. These changes, however, are two of the most significant events that the world is experiencing. They are so significant that it is difficult to exaggerate their impact not only on society but also on our own future. As our society has urbanized—as increasing numbers of people have moved from village and farm to the city—the city has expanded its influence. Today, U.S. culture so revolves around urban life that even rural life has been urbanized. To say *U.S. culture* is to say *urban* culture. Similarly significant are changes in population, which sociologists call *demographic shifts.* On a global level, population growth and population shrinkage affect the welfare of nations. They set up conditions for vast migrations, bringing ethnic changes that transform nations—and conflicts that reverberate around the world.

A demographic shift that is having a major impact on the United States is migration from Mexico and South America. This migration has been so extensive in the past decade that Latinos have replaced African Americans as the largest ethnic group in the country. It is too early to tell what changes this demographic shift will bring to U.S. social institutions and to popular culture, but we can be certain that they will be extensive. In this selection, Farai Chideya provides a background for understanding this fundamental shift in our population, as well as an insider's perspective into some of the experiences of illegal immigrants.

Thinking Critically

As you read this selection, ask yourself:

1. Why is this vast migration occurring? Look for both social and personal factors.

2. What changes to U.S. social institutions and culture is this demographic shift likely to bring?

3. What solutions would you propose to solve the problem of illegal immigration? What problems would your solution solve? What problems would it create? In formulating your answer, be sure to take the main points of this article into consideration.

The land around El Paso, Texas, is an imposing desert scene painted in tones of ochre and red clay—stark mountains, vast sky, arid plains. It's so far west that it's the only major Texas city in the mountain, rather than the central, time zone. Atop a nearby mountain is the massive Christo Rey—an imposing figure of Jesus hewn out of tons of stone. It seems like a peaceful vista, but this land is the staging ground for a colossal clash of cultures—the meeting of Mexico and the United States at the border. The biggest clash is not between Mexico and the United States per se, but between many competing visions of what Mexican immigration means to the United States. Mexican immigration has been decried as an "illegal alien invasion," an erosion of America's job base, even the beginnings of a plot to return the Southwest to Mexican hands. And sometimes Mexican Americans themselves are perceived with suspicion, in the belief their allegiance is pledged to Mexico, not the United States.

What's the reality behind these perceptions? And what's life on the border like?. . . I've spent virtually my whole life living on the East Coast, where the Latino communities are dominated by Puerto Ricans, Dominicans, Cubans. I groove to Latin hip-hop and Afro-Cuban sounds, but I hadn't heard much Mexican-American music like ranchero and Tejano. I know a good plate of *pernil* when I eat one, but I couldn't tell you from *tortas*. And I've heard more opinions over whether Puerto Rico should become independent than I've heard firsthand accounts of life on the border. In other words, when I came to El Paso I was starting at ground zero. Why did I choose El Paso? Well, first, this border city has been the site of a well-publicized crackdown on illegal immigration. Second, it's been deeply impacted by government policies like NAFTA. But third, and most important to me, El Paso is not majority Anglo but 70 percent Latino and Mexican American, a place where there are bound to be differences of opinion between members of the Latino community. . . .

[W]hile trade with Mexico has been good for Texas in general, the NAFTA free trade treaty has hit El Paso's economy hard. The city already has an unemployment rate double the national average. Now plants that used to pay workers five dollars an hour in El Paso can pay them five dollars a day just across the border in Juarez—and not pay duty on the goods shipped back to the United States. Among the issues I want to explore here in El Paso are not just questions of Mexican-American identity—how they see themselves—but also how they see their (real or distant) cousins across the border. Do the residents of El Paso look upon the Mexicans as brothers, economic competitors—or a bit of both?

One of the first people I meet in El Paso gives me a hint of the differences in opinion about border issues. Nora is chic, almost out of place in the grungy alternative bar we're both sitting in, with high cheekbones, light skin, and curly black hair cut in a bob. "I hate to say it, but I agree with him," she says. "They need to learn English." The "him" Nora is talking about is a black city councilman who chewed out a citizen who addressed a town hall meeting in Spanish. The "they"—an implicit "they"—are recent Mexican immigrants. Nora, who used to model in New York and now works in the local clothing industry, takes the councilman's side. But some local cartoonists lampooned the politician's outrage, and many residents wrote letters of protest to the newspaper.

Many El Paso residents are from first- or second-generation immigrant families, people who remember life in Mexico and have direct family ties across the border. But it's a mistake to think that they encompass all of El Paso's Latinos. A large proportion of El Paso families, like Nora's, are *Tejano,* a term which means that her forebears have lived in Texas for generations—i.e., even before it was part of the United States. (As many Tejanos like to say, "We didn't cross the border. The border crossed us.") The unique Tex-Mex culture of the Tejanos gave rise to one of the biggest Latina singing sensations, Selena, whose premature death in 1995 woke America up to the size of the Latino community. And one lesson America has yet to learn about the Latino community is how many different cultural and political perspectives there are—even within a single group, like Mexican Americans.

Those different perspectives come into direct conflict when it comes to an issue as controversial as the border. I focused on two groups of people familiar with El Paso: the enforcers who try to keep people out, and the border crossers desperate to stay in America.

■ ■ ■ THE ENFORCERS

Melissa Lucio gets the radio call at noon on a scorching summer day. An electric sensor just inside the U.S. border's been tripped; agents are looking around but they haven't found anyone yet. She heads for the sensor's coordinates and pulls up alongside a couple of agents. They're beating the bushes around a splotch of water halfway between a pond and a puddle. After a minute, a guy about thirty-five years old steps out of a thicket with a resigned look on his face and a satchel slung over his shoulder. A Mexican worker who's crossed illegally into the States, he also happens to be wearing an OFFICIAL U.S. TAXPAYER baseball cap. When I laughingly point this out to Melissa, she goes me one better. "We had a guy who walked in with a Border Patrol hat the other day. We asked him where he got it and he said he found it on the bank of the river. The officer's name was still written on the inside—he'd lost it over a year ago."

Melissa's just one of the thousands of U.S. Border Patrol agents charged with the thankless (and some would say impossible) task of keeping illegal immigrants out of America and catching them once they come in. A Mexican-American El Paso native, she's also the wife of another Mexican-American Border Patrol agent. Just thirty years old, she's also the mother of five sons. With her thick black hair pulled back in a neat French braid, her brown uniform replete with two-way radio and gun, Melissa rides the Texas–Mexico–New Mexico border tracking and detaining border crossers. Sometimes she gets help from the electronic signals of hidden sensors, but much of the time she relies on her own eyes, scanning the horizon and bending toward the earth to interpret "signs"—the scant marks and footprints in the dry earth which she reads for vital clues of time and direction. The day is hot and clear. Recent rains have made it easier to track signs—and have also put desert flowers into bloom. Melissa's comments as she navigates the covered-cab truck around bumps and gullies are punctuated with interjections about the wildlife—"Beautiful bird!" "Really cool lizard!" "Check out that jackrabbit!" But her ear is always tuned to the radio, and she's tough when she has to be. If her truck gets stuck, she breaks off branches and digs it out; if a suspect in a vehicle takes off into a residential area, she pursues and radios the local police. As we traverse highways, dirt roads, and long stretches of pristine desert, we don't run into any other female agents out in the field.

The man Melissa has just picked up doesn't protest when she puts him in the covered back area of the truck. In fact, he reaches into his satchel, pulls out a newspaper, and starts to read. At my request, she asks him where he was going and what he was going to do.

"¿Para dónde vas?" she asks.

"Para Coronado," he answers.

Coronado is an affluent area, replete with a country club, where he was headed to cut yards. "He was actually closer to the east side of Juarez," Melissa translates, "and I asked him why he didn't cross over there. And he said there's a lot of *cholos* [bandits] stealing and robbing in that area. He says it's easier to cross over here. He says he doesn't come often, but every once in a while when he needs money."

One stereotype of illegal immigrants is that they're a bunch of welfare cheats. But this crosser, and most of the ones that Melissa picks up, are coming in strictly to work—sometimes to stay for the day and go back that night. The economics are clear cut. The starting wage in the *maquiladoras,* or twin plants—so named because they're owned by U.S. corporations who maintain both Mexican factories and their "twins" across the border—is about five dollars a day. The wages for yard work are far, far higher. "If they have their own tools, they could make sixty bucks a day," Melissa says. "If not, it could be thirty or forty." In other words, one day per week of work in the United States earns more than an entire week's labor in Mexico. Of course, there'd be no point crossing the border if U.S. employers weren't willing, even eager, to give undocumented workers jobs. If a border crosser makes it in every day, the payoff is good even relative to U.S. workers. "If you think about minimum wage, four sixty per hour with taxes taken out, [the border crossers] are going to make more," she says. "Even the Mexican police officers, some of them make four hundred dollars per month if they're lucky."

I ask Melissa if the people she picks up ever give her flack for being Mexican American and picking up Mexicans. "I've only had one person say, 'Don't you think you're being mean?'" she says. "And I say, if you had a job, you would do it to the best of your ability, right? They say 'Yeah.'"—she draws the word out to give it a dubious inflection. "And I say that's just what I'm doing. I've got five children. I want to maintain my household. And they understand."

"Like this education issue," she continues. "Let's say you educate them, and then what? They're illegal in the United States so they can't obtain work. Or let's say they become legal, then they're going to be competing against my children or me for a job that could have very well been mine." She's no fan of NAFTA, which she believes has knocked the wind out of an already weakened local economy. "Not a month goes by that you don't hear about a local company that's up and relocating to Mexico," she says. "It may be a good law, but not for the people who live paycheck to paycheck."

We drop our passenger off at the Paso Del Norte processing station, a short-term holding area that seems appropriately located in the middle of nowhere. Inside the plain building is a bullpen of officers at their desks, surrounded by large cells where individuals are sorted by gender, age, and area of origin. Locals—people from Juarez and nearby border areas—are the easiest to process and return. People from the interior of Mexico, farther south, are interviewed by Mexican officials and given bus fare home. And last of all are detainees from Central America, some of whom have traveled hundreds upon hundreds of miles from Honduras and points south, only to be caught on the final leg of their journey. There are men and women, old and young—really young. One of the kids in the pen, who flashes me an impish grin when I check him out, looks about twelve.

"Oh, we get kids who are eight, nine, ten. I ask them, 'Your Mom, doesn't she worry about you?' And some of their parents do, but they really run wild. If they know a lady at a bakery [in the United States] will give them sweet-breads, stuff like that, they'll come. Some of them have friends they come to goof off with. This is what they do. This is recreation."

By the time they're sixteen—which is the age of the next border crosser we pick up—they're usually crossing to work. The teenager has tan skin and hair bleached nearly blond by the sun; he's carrying yard tools.

"*¿Con qué te posito entro los Estados Unidos?*" Melissa asks.

"*Trabajo.*"

"*¿Qué clase trabajo?*"

"*En yardas,*" he answers. He was headed to Coronado as well.

An Economic Judgment

Melissa Lucio is not only a Border Patrol agent, but a mother and a taxpayer as well. She believes the influx of illegal immigrants could curtail her children's chances at prosperity. "When people talk about immigration issues as being racial," she says, "you have Hispanics as well as Anglos as well as other ethnic groups that will say the same thing: 'We need to be strong on immigration issues.' Why should my tax dollars and my anything be funding someone else?"

Melissa's family immigrated from Mexico a couple of generations ago. "My grandma jokes that I'm going to send her back over the border," Melissa says. She had what she describes as a typical, happy coming of age in El Paso. She met her first love, Rick, who's also Mexican American, in high school, and married him right after she graduated. Like several members of both of their families, Rick went into law enforcement, joining the Border Patrol. Melissa dreamed about the same thing for ten years before she decided to take the plunge. "I had thought about going to college and to the FBI behavioral science department, to pursue some forensics. But the more and more children I started having, I just started to see that dream being pushed further and further away," she says.

Melissa found out the Border Patrol was hiring when Rick told her about a career day he was coordinating—but he tried to discourage her from trying out. It was an arduous process. First she had to take a written test to get admitted to the academy. Then she had to get in shape. After seven years of bearing and raising five sons (Daniel, David, Derek, Dario, and Andrew—"we ran out of Ds," she says), she was two hundred and twenty pounds. She quit her job and lost forty before going into the academy, and another ten once she was there. When it came time for the induction ceremony, she received her badge from an officer who'd specially requested the honor—her husband. "As he's pinning me he whispers in my ear, 'Oh Melissa, I never thought you would make it. You've never made me so proud.'" She beams. "It was absolutely great. It was amazing."

Now Melissa works just past the El Paso line in the Christo Rey area of New Mexico. Standing atop the hill that supports the huge statue of Christ, you can see Mexico, New Mexico, and Texas in panorama. You can also see the latest attempts to keep the border clamped down. Along the length of the border, construction crews are putting up an immense fence designed to eventually cover the entire U.S.-Mexico line. But Melissa for one is skeptical it will stop the crossings. "They'll just have to walk a little further," she says, to where mesas break the fence line.

Her division, which contains forty to sixty agents per day depending on scheduling, picks up about a hundred and fifty people per day, a thousand per week. It's labor-intensive work, particularly given the nature of the terrain. The El Paso Border Patrol region gained prominence in 1991 when Silvestre Reyes, the chief at the time, implemented a policy he called Operation Hold the Line. Instead of chasing border crossers after they walked over train tracks or through the Rio Grande (at the Juarez–El Paso border, the river is little more than a trickle in a concrete culvert), Reyes posted agents in vehicles along large stretches of the border. Their presence dropped the number of crossers at that juncture from eight thousand a day to virtually zero. But that meant more Mexicans who wanted to come to Texas chose to go through the New Mexico mountains. "You can't do that here. You'd have to have a ton of agents to watch every side of every hill. We have to be mobile," Melissa says.

It seems like an awful lot of work for each agent on an eight-hour shift to pick up the equivalent of three border jumpers a day. But the political stakes are far higher than those numbers would suggest. Tensions about immigration characterize the turn of this century as deeply as they marked the turn of the last one. But instead of Italians, Irish, and Jews who received a lukewarm welcome disembarking at Ellis Island in the late 1800s and early 1900s, Mexican Americans crossing into the border for points as far flung as New York and the Midwest are the immigrants under scrutiny today. . . .

The pickups don't always go smoothly. Some of the border crossers have passed out and nearly died from heat stroke or dehydration as they're being taken in; other times agents just find the bodies. (One agent tells me a gruesome, perhaps apocryphal tale of finding a body whose eyes had literally popped out of the scorched head.) Sometimes people resist or carry weapons. The agents also have to watch out for *cholos*—gang members who can come from either side of the border, and who often prey on those crossing the border to work. In a Wild West twist, some of the *cholos* rob trains passing through the region. "A bandit will board the trains out West and pilfer through first, and say, 'The Nike tennis shoes are here.' Then they have their buddies, twenty or thirty or forty guys, shunt the track so the little computer tells the train to stop. As soon as it stops, these guys start throwing the stuff down. They don't care if the nine hundred ninety-nine dollar television cracks open because the good ones will land somewhere and they will grab it and sell it. Or on the other hand, in the next two weeks you'll arrest a bunch of people that are all wearing brand new Nike tennis shoes."

Sometimes they prey on the individuals working along the border fence line. As our day together draws to a close, Melissa gets a radio call from one of the men erecting the new fence. He's worried because four men are approaching and he's alone. "Ten-four. Horse patrol and myself will thirteen over there and check it out," Melissa radios back. As we approach, two men on powerful horses gallop parallel, about twenty yards away. "I'm on the list for horseback," Melissa says. "I think it's so cool." She surveys the situation as we approach. "These guys are definitely up to no good." I ask how she can tell. "They don't have any bags, which means they're not crossing. They don't have any water and they're just hanging around with no attempt to go north." They might have wanted to get their hands on some of the construction supplies, she figures.

Every eight weeks Melissa and the other agents change shift—days, evenings, overnights (which start at midnight). Now she's working days and her husband is working evenings, making it easy for him to take the kids to and from school. They try to avoid both doing the evening shift, "because we've noticed that our kids' grades drop."

To help out, Rick and Melissa have hired a live-in housekeeper, which is a drama in and of itself. "I advertised for a housekeeper two years ago, [and] the first thing off the bat was, 'Are you a U.S. citizen or a legal resident? If not, I work for immigration and I can't hire you.' And half the people would hang up. A quarter of the people would say, 'I'm a border crosser,' but they were not permitted to work. The lady we hired, she's late forties, great with the kids, teaching the kids Spanish, and she's a legal resident, so it worked out really, really, well."

"So what's funny, a neighbor came up and said, 'Do you realize your house is under surveillance?' I was like 'Excuse me?'" One day, when both husband and wife were gone, an agent came to the home and asked their housekeeper for documents. Neighbors came out to watch, and she waved right back at them to say "I'm still here because I'm legal," Melissa says. The couple learned why the Immigration and Naturalization Service suspected them when they talked the matter over with their chief. A neighbor had phoned in with an elaborate tale how the housekeeper, supposedly illegal, had begged up and down the street for work and found it with the Lucios. "It's just someone being vindictive. I thought, that is really terrible," Melissa says. "At the time we lived in the Coronado Country Club area. They were really unhappy about Hold the Line because their maids couldn't come in illegally." As we head back into the station, I think again about the economics of the illegal immigration debate. The reality is that for every undocumented immigrant who finds low-wage work in America, there is somebody willing to hire that person. And some of the same people benefiting from below-market labor loudly decry illegal immigration at the same time.

The Politics of the Border

America likes to think its immigration laws are tough. And while they're arguably harsh on people who cross the border, most penalties on the businesses that hire illegal immigrants are modest. And people like the border crossers Melissa Lucio picked up often don't work for "businesses" at all, but everyday U.S. citizens who usually suspect the person they've hired to cut their lawn or babysit their kids doesn't hold a green card. America decries the waves of illegal immigration. But some Americans on the border and throughout the United States profit from the cheap labor these immigrants provide.

The economics of the border are full of conflict and duplicity, people who profit, people who lose, and people who lie about which camp they're in. Most important, the economics are deeply intertwined. Downtown El Paso, an unremarkable collection of modest office buildings and low-priced shops, is tethered by a bridge to downtown Juarez, Mexico. The Mexicans who cross the bridge come to work, visit, and shop. The Anglos going the other way often buy cheap groceries and pharmaceuticals (you can purchase Valium and Prozac without a prescription there), and college students hit the bars, where the words "drinking age" are meaningless. What happens when the Border Patrol cracks down on illegal crossings? Many downtown El Paso businessmen say their shops suffer, deprived of the day workers that used to buy clothes and consumer goods.

Many Mexican residents of Juarez aren't happy about the increasingly fortified border, either. El Paso and Juarez are separated by an unimpressive trickle of water that, amazingly enough, is part of the mighty Rio Grande river. A cement aqueduct, fenced on both sides, contains the water and separates the people. Painted on the concrete are signs decrying the border fortifications:

One reads OJO MIGRA (eyes are painted into the o's) ¡¡YA BASTA!!

Another says: POR CADA ILEGAL QUE NOS MALTRATEN EN LOS ESTADOS UNIDOS DE N. A. VAMOS A MALTRATAR UN VISITANTE GAVACHO. BIENVENIDOS LOS PAISANOS.

Their translations: "Look, Immigration—enough already!" and "For every illegal they mistreat in the United States, we are going to mistreat a visiting gringo. Welcome, countrymen."

It sounds like a bit of useless bravado, the "welcome, countrymen" sign. But the history of the Southwest is the history of what Mexico founded and America fought to win—not particularly fairly, either. Writes biographer Hugh Pearson:

> In 1845, hewing to the strictures of Manifest Destiny we annexed the Republic of Texas, which had been part of Mexico. Its American settlers decided to introduce slavery into the territory, which was illegal in Mexico. Then, as gratitude for the Mexican government's inviting them to settle the territory and because they wanted to keep their slaves, they fought for independence. As former President and Gen. Ulysses S. Grant wrote in his memoirs, "The occupation, separation and annexation were, from the inception of the movement to its final consummation, a conspiracy to acquire territory out of which slave states might be formed for the American union."
>
> After accepting the Texas republic's petition to be annexed by the United States, a dispute between the United States and Mexico ensued, regarding where the exact boundary of Texas lay. Mexican and U.S. patrols clashed somewhere along the disputed

territory and the United States declared war on Mexico. In the process of fighting the war, U.S. troops captured from Mexico what is now New Mexico and what the Mexicans called Upper California. As conditions for surrender, Mexico was forced to cede all of the captured territory north of the Rio Grande River, and an agreed upon jagged imaginary line that now separates California, Arizona and New Mexico from Mexico. So today, Mexicans crossing into U.S. California are treated as illegal aliens if they don't go through the proper channels for entering territory that was originally theirs.

I didn't learn any of this in high school, and I'd wager that many Americans don't know it today. What happened doesn't change the fact that America has the right to control its borders, but it does cast into sharper relief the interconnectedness of these two nations. Texas was birthed from Mexico. But—defying the stereotypes that pervade much of the news coverage about the border—many Mexican Americans are now the ones guarding the border.

Silvestre Reyes headed the Border Patrol for the entire El Paso region. . . . I meet the solid, handsome fifty-year-old in the offices where he's running his campaign [for U.S. Congress] with the help of his twenty-five-year-old daughter. Even in his civilian clothes, he's got the demeanor of a law enforcement officer. Reyes grew up in a small farming town where his high school graduating class was made up of just twenty-six students. When he was a child, he served as a lookout against *la migra*—the Border Patrol—in the fields where Mexicans worked. He served in Vietnam, then worked as a Border Patrol agent for over twenty-five years. He believes that people's opinions about the border don't have anything to do with ethnic loyalty, but quality of life. "Hispanics, like every ethnic group in the country, have an expectation to be safe and secure in their neighborhoods," he says. "A Hispanic no more than anybody else appreciates undocumented people flowing through their backyards, creating a chaotic situation."

Still, Reyes says he'd like to find a way to benefit both Mexicans and Americans at the same time. "Mexican citizens don't want to come up here," he says. "They would rather stay home. But they stay home, they starve. We've got forces down in Mexico that want jobs, and people up here that want them to come up here. But the whole problem is, let's find a system that does it legally."

Despite its adverse effect on the El Paso economy, Reyes supports NAFTA as a way of increasing employment opportunities in Mexico. If things don't get better there, he reasons, illegal immigration will never stop. "Mexico has a surplus of manpower. I think 60 percent of Mexican citizens are under the age of twenty, if I remember my statistics right," he says. . . .

One policy he doesn't support is California's Proposition 187, which voters passed in 1994 in an effort, among other things, to prevent illegal immigrants from receiving government medical care or public education. Reyes calls the measure "illegal and unconstitutional. . . . Should we amend the Constitution in order to deny children born in this country their citizenships? I think we're crazy," he says. "What's gonna keep someone from going back retroactively and saying, 'You know, your father was born to illegal parents back in 1924. Therefore he was illegal, therefore you're illegal.'" (Such logic recalls a joke by Mexican-American comedian Paul Rodriguez, who says he supports making deportations for illegal immigration retroactive and shipping the Anglos back home.) The idea of barring education to undocumented children is "insanity running amok. The way that people enslave whole segments of our society is by keeping them ignorant. . . . To me it doesn't matter whether it's black or Hispanics or Chinese or whites or who it is. I think it's just wrong for any country to guarantee a subculture of ignorance. And that's what you're doing when you don't educate the kids."

The wording of California's Proposition 187 was also openly militaristic, reading:

> WE CAN STOP ILLEGAL ALIENS. If the citizens and the taxpayers of our state wait for the politicians in Washington and Sacramento to stop the incredible flow of ILLEGAL ALIENS, California will be in economic and social bankruptcy. We have to act and ACT NOW! On our ballot, Proposition 187 will be the first giant stride in ultimately ending the ILLEGAL ALIEN invasion.

Some advocates say the border has already become militarized, infringing upon the rights of citizens and legal immigrants. El Paso's Border Rights Coalition says that . . . half of the individuals who complained to their group about mistreatment by the Border Patrol, Immigration and Naturalization Service, and U.S. Customs were U.S. citizens, not legal or illegal immigrants. The group helped students at El Paso's Bowie High School file a class action suit. They alleged that Border Patrol agents were routinely harassing individuals on and near campus—in one case, arresting a group of students, U.S. citizens, who were driving to school. Today, the Border Patrol is operating under a settlement that requires they meet higher standards before detaining individuals, and limits searches at schools and churches.

Of course, the ultimate military-style solution would be to create a physical wall between Mexico and the United States. Reyes strongly disagrees with such a plan. "That's impractical, you know. The Berlin wall didn't seal, and that was using mines and barbed wire and guards and concrete, and all of that, and still people got out of there," he says. Yet as Reyes and I talk, construction on just such a wall is happening along the border near El Paso. While I'm out with Melissa Lucio, she shows me the early stages of the construction site. It's impossible to cover the whole border, of course. But . . . several miles of what Reyes calls the "impractical" solution stand completed.

▪ ▪ ▪ THE BORDER CROSSERS

A Family Full of Contradictions

Gilberto, an eighteen-year-old undocumented immigrant from Chihuahua, has few marketable skills but one strong advantage on his side. He has family legally in the United States who are willing to help him. Gilberto is the brother-in-law of a naturalized U.S. citizen who emigrated from Hong Kong. Chiu, who went to college in the United States, met his wife Lorena, in a Juarez nightclub. Now they have two children, baby Jenny Anna and Andy, who turned three the day after I spoke with them. Both attend the University of Texas at El Paso, and they earn a living by running a home care facility for the elderly.

Gilberto helps out with the home care, meaning he's guaranteed a job as well as a place to stay far from the eyes of the Border Patrol. Like virtually all illegal immigrants, he's an unskilled laborer. Like many Mexicans, he finished the "secondario" level of schooling at fifteen and then started working. His first job was in a junkyard—hot, heavy work for very little money. Still, like a teenager, he used the remaining money he had to party rather than save. Asked if he's worried *la migra* will find him—something they did once before, as he was out and about—he shakes his head confidently, "No."

Chiu and Lorena's generous brick house is nestled in a pristine, upper-middle-class enclave undergoing rapid development. Bold and self-assured, Chiu strongly opposes illegal immigration, a position it's hard not to think deeply about when you see Gilberto sitting sheepishly on the other side of the table. "My brother-in-law, he's an illegal alien. He come and go whenever he wants. When you're talking about Hold the Line, it's only to make the government look good," Chiu scolds. "Washington, D.C., will furnish a lot of money for this project because it's very successful—you catch ten billion illegal aliens. Oh great job!" he sneers. "Now they have this Hold the Line thing, OK, and then they say, 'Nobody coming across.' But in the reality it's not true. In Mexico, if the people over there are making three to five dollars a day and if they cannot support their kids, do you think they would just sit there and die?"

Gilberto isn't in the dire straits many border crossers are. In fact, he originally entered not to stay but to fulfill teenage longings. "All the boys, they have the same dream: you know, they wanted to come and get some money and buy a truck, a nice truck," his sister Lorena translates, "and then go back to Mexico and spend one or two months or whatever on the money they saved up. Then after that, they come back to the United States again and work and get some more money. That's the way they think." Now Gilberto's changed his mind. He wants to stay in the United States and become a nurse. "It's very important to learn to speak English, otherwise there's no way to find a job—well, maybe in El Paso a very low job. But I want to go further," he says. He's enrolled in a local high school, where his legal status proved no problem. "As a matter of fact, they are not allowed to ask you whether you have papers or not or whether you have a Social Security number or not, because if they do that they have violated federal law," Chiu says. "So they have to let him register although he's an illegal alien." In a clear example of how self-interest overrides politics, Chiu says that he's happy his brother-in-law can be enrolled, but that he is opposed to educating undocumented children. "When they do that they are inviting illegal immigrants to come to school here, you see. I would say no illegal immigrants to go to school in this country for free."

Neither Mexican nor American

A pensive seventeen-year-old named Diana finds herself in the opposite situation from Gilberto: with her near-perfect English and years of schooling in the United States, she seems culturally American, but this undocumented immigrant has no one to advocate for her or protect her. She's been caught between two worlds most of her life. Four years ago, Diana crossed into the United States at the Juarez–El Paso bridge that symbolizes the border so well. Now she's a senior at Fremont High School in Oakland, California. . . . Before crossing the Rio Grande, she spent her junior high school years near Durango, Mexico. And before that, from the ages of two until nine, she lived in the United States—attending American schools, playing with American toys, speaking both English and Spanish. Without a green card or citizenship, but with a keen understanding of American culture and her precarious position in it, she is neither fully American nor fully Mexican.

Diana remembers the day her family crossed over from Juarez to El Paso. "We used a raft to get across. It was really sunny that day. People were on the bridge watching us. They were like 'Oh look!'" she says. "I remember I saw this man with a little boy in his arms pointing at us." Once they got to El Paso, her family tried to blend in with the rest of the crowds in the downtown shopping area. "We crossed the street right in front of a Border Patrol car," Diana remembers. "The car stopped so we could cross the street! My Mom was praying and I was like, 'Mom, they're not going to do anything to us now.' They didn't."

While her experience in crossing the Rio Grande was a common one until recently, Diana's reasons for going back and forth between the United States and Mexico are personal and complex. Like most families who cross over from Mexico, Diana's came to work and make a better life for their children. Her father has a green card, so he was able to live and work legally; but he brought Diana, her mother, and Diana's older brother into the country without papers. Diana's father began drinking too much, and after living in the United States for several years, he decided to move the family back to Mexico and pull himself together. But there's little work near Durango, so he ended up going back to the United States to earn a living (taking Diana's teenage brother along with him) and sending money to the family back home. It was only once her father had stopped drinking that he decided to reunite the family, arranging for a "coyote"—or someone who smuggles people across the border—to bring Diana and the rest of the family north through Mexico, on a raft over the Rio Grande, and by truck out of Texas.

Diana was too young to remember the first time she crossed the border. She was only two years old, and friends of the family who had papers for their own toddler smuggled her in as their child. "People told me I kept saying, 'I want my mother.' They needed me to be quiet," she says. From two on, Diana lived in Chico, California, as a normal Mexican-American kid—almost. When I ask her if she knew she was an "illegal immigrant," she says, "That question really bothered me and came into my head in, I think, the second grade. Most of my friends would go to Mexico on their summer vacations to see their grandparents, and I would ask, 'Why aren't we going to Mexico?' My mother would say, 'We can't.' Then," she continues, "one time in school I said, 'Um, I'm illegal.' And my teacher said, 'Honey, don't say that out loud. You could get your parents in a lot of trouble.' That's when I started feeling a little inferior to other kids."

Sometimes she still does. "Not because of who I am but because of what I can't do," she says, quietly breaking into tears. One thing she can't do is apply to college, even though she's a solid student. Without legal residence papers, she has little hope of attending school or getting anything but the most menial of jobs. Her older brother tried enrolling in college, but after they repeatedly asked him for a Social Security number, he simply left. Now he plays in a band. "I want to get a green card so I can work, so I can go to school, so I don't need to worry about getting deported and everything. But we have to pay a lawyer seven hundred dollars for each person applying for the green card," money her struggling family doesn't have. After she gets a green card, she wants to become a citizen "because I would like to be heard in this country. I would like to vote and be part of the process."

The most wrenching part of her experience is that Diana knows she could have been a legal resident by now. In 1987, she says, "we could have gotten our papers through the National Amnesty Program," a one-shot chance for illegal immigrants to declare themselves to officials in exchange for a green card. "My mother applied for us, but my Dad [who was drinking] felt that if we went back to Mexico, everything would be for the best." She remembers the day they left the United States. "I had to leave all my friends and the things I had. We left everything: the furniture, my toys, my Barbies. I had to practically leave my life there."

Yet Diana credits the time she spent in Mexico with helping her reconnect with her heritage. She became close with her grandmother, was in the Mexican equivalent of junior ROTC, and won dramatic speaking contests, reciting poetry. "In Mexico, I always wanted to be the one with the best grades—always wanted to be the center of attention," she says. "Maybe because I believed in myself and what I did," she says. That sense of confidence is lacking in Diana today. But if she had stayed in Mexico, it would have been difficult for her to continue her education considering how little money her family had. Most of the girls Diana knew stopped going to school at fourteen or fifteen, got married to a farmer or laborer, and started a family.

So, in one sense, Diana feels she was lucky to return to the United States. But when she first arrived, she had a difficult time readjusting. She returned in time for ninth grade, which in Oakland at the time was still a part of junior high school. Teachers put her in an English as a second language program, probably because her shyness inhibited her from talking much. "It wasn't very helpful," she says. Luckily, as soon as one of her teachers found out how good Diana's English really was, Diana was moved into the regular track.

But Diana was dealing not only with educational displacement but ethnic culture shock. "In the ninth grade, there was only my Mexican friends . . . and we felt a little inferior to the rest." In her opinion, the Mexican kids broke down into two cliques: the "Mexican Mexicans," or hard-working immigrants, and the "little gangsters," or tough, Americanized teens. She hung out with the former—until tenth grade, when she went to Fremont and joined the Media Academy. There she made friends of several races. "When I got to Fremont there was African Americans, Asians, and Mexicans and everybody hangs out together and it was cool," she says.

What is heartbreaking to Diana today is that, though she loves school, she has little hope of continuing her education. She remembers a time that her teacher was leading them through an exercise in filling out college applications. "Everybody was like: 'Oh, I want to go to this place and I wanna go such and such and oh, my grades are good and everything.' My teacher was like, 'Aren't you going to fill out your applications?' And I was like, 'What for?'" Another girl in the class asked the question Diana was desperate to, but just couldn't. "What if you're not a legal resident?" Her teacher said to leave the Social Security number slot blank, but Diana says, dejected, "I didn't want to continue it.". . .

Still, "Regardless of all the barriers that are put between you and other people, America *is* the Land of Opportunity," says Diana. "No matter where you go, you will never find another place where even when you're not legal you can still get a job that pays you. There's no other place like it. In Mexico you can't even get a job. You depend on the crops on your land and live on what grows. There's nowhere for you to go, no McDonald's for you to hang out at. To me, it's better in America."

■ ■ ■ MEXICANIZING AMERICA?

The unspoken fear that underlies much of our policy about the border is that an influx of immigrants will "Mexicanize" America. But my journey through El Paso illustrates the complex culture of Mexican Americans, and just how unfounded the fears about "Mexicanization" are. Those living on the U.S.-Mexican border face some difficult political and economic questions: whether Americans can compete with the low-wage workers in Mexico; whether Washington lawmakers can truly understand the issues facing Americans on the border; and, for Mexican Americans in particular, whether they should feel some connection to the problems facing Mexicans, or simply focus on their own issues. The influence of Mexican culture on America's should be seen as part of a continuum. Just as every immigration wave has shaped this country, so will the rise of the Latino population. In a best-case scenario, border towns like El Paso would help foster a rich appreciation for Mexican culture as *part* of American-style diversity.

The McDonaldization
of Society

George Ritzer

introduction ∎ ∎ ∎ ∎

A key term in sociology is *rationalization*. This term refers to choosing the most efficient means to accomplish tasks. In business it refers to the bottom line, calculating costs to produce the most gain. With rationalization, profit becomes king, while people, evaluated according to what they bring to the bottom line, become expendable.

The rationalization of society, said Max Weber, the sociologist who first analyzed this process, is extremely significant, for it tends to ensnare us all. The traditional ways of doing things—which may be inefficient but which are also the source of satisfactions that come from personal relationships—are passing. In their place come bureaucracies with time and motion studies, cold analyses of every act, with profits placed higher than the people who make up the work setting. Weber didn't know how far reaching and accurate his analysis would prove. Rationalization threatens to engulf all of society, locking us all in what Weber called an iron cage of rationality. College administrators, for example, want to evaluate instructors not by how they challenge students to think or by how they open their minds to new perceptions, but, rather, by the sheer number of students they turn out each semester. Even traditional, routine, everyday aspects of family life are not impervious to this change, as becomes evident in Ritzer's analysis.

Thinking Critically

As you read this selection, ask yourself:

1. How is your own life being rationalized?

2. What further rationalizations of everyday life do you think the future will bring?

3. In what ways is the rationalization of life good? Bad? Indifferent?

McDonald's has sought to construct highly efficient systems, and *McDonaldization* implies the search for maximum efficiency in increasingly numerous and diverse social settings. *Efficiency* means the choice of the optimum means to a given end, but this definition requires some clarification. Although we use the term *optimum*, it is rare that the truly optimum means to an end is ever found. Rather, there is a search for a . . . far better means to an end than would be employed under ordinary circumstances. . . .

■ ■ ■ ■ WIRELESS KEYBOARDS AND SELF-SERVICE SLURPEES

The emphasis of McDonaldization on efficiency implies that contrasting, nonrational systems are less efficient, or even inefficient. The fast-food restaurant grew as a result of its greater efficiency in comparison to alternative methods of obtaining a meal. In the early 1950s, at the dawning of the era of the fast-food restaurant, the major alternative was the home-cooked meal made largely from ingredients previously purchased at various markets. . . .

But the home-cooked meal was, and still is, a relatively inefficient way of obtaining a meal. The restaurant has long been a more efficient alternative. But restaurants can be inefficient in that it may take several hours to go to the restaurant, consume a meal, and then return home. The desire for more efficient restaurants led to the rise of some of the ancestors of the fast-food restaurant—diners, cafeterias, and early drive-through or drive-in restaurants. The modern fast-food restaurant can be seen as being built on the latter models and as a further step in the direction of more efficient food consumption. . . .

Above all else, it was the efficiency of the McDonald brothers' operation that impressed Ray Kroc [the individual behind the franchising of McDonald's], as well as the enormous profit potential of such a system if it were applied in a large number of sites. Here is how Kroc described his initial reactions to the McDonald's system:

> I was fascinated by the simplicity and effectiveness of the system. . . . Each step in producing the limited menu was stripped down to its essence and accomplished with a minimum of effort. They sold hamburgers and cheeseburgers only. The burgers were . . . all fried the same way.

Kroc and his associates looked at each component of the hamburger in order to increase the efficiency with which it could be produced and served. For example, they started with only partially sliced buns that were attached to one another. However, it was found that buns could be used more efficiently if they were sliced all the way through and separated from one another. At first, the buns arrived in cardboard boxes and the griddle workers had to spend time opening the boxes, separating the buns, slicing them, and discarding the leftover paper and cardboard. In addition to separating and preslicing them, buns were made efficient to use by having them shipped in reusable boxes. Similar attention was devoted to the meat patty. For example, the paper between the patties had to have just the right amount of wax so that the patties would readily slide off the paper and onto the grill.

Kroc makes it clear that the goal of these kinds of refinements was greater efficiency:

> The purpose of all these refinements, and we never lost sight of it, was to make our griddle man's job easier to do quickly and well. And the other considerations of cost cutting, inventory control, and so forth were important to be sure, but they were secondary to the critical detail of what happened there at the smoking griddle. This was the vital passage of our *assembly-line,* and the product had to flow through it smoothly or the whole plant would falter. (Italics added.)

. . . Once diners enter the fast-food restaurant, the process continues to appear to be efficient. Parking lots are adjacent to the restaurant and parking spots are readily available. It's a short walk to the counter, and although there is sometimes a line, food is usually quickly ordered, obtained, and paid for. The highly limited menu makes the choice of a meal's components quite easy. This contrasts to the many choices available in many of the alternatives to the fast-food restaurant. With the food obtained, it is but a few steps to a table and the beginning of the "dining experience." The fare almost always involves an array of finger foods (for example, Chicken McNuggets and french fries) that can be popped into the diner's mouth with the result that the entire meal is ordinarily consumed in a few minutes. Because there is little inducement to linger, the diners generally gather the leftover paper, styrofoam, and plastic, discard them in a nearby trash receptacle, and are back in their car and on their way to the next (often McDonaldized) activity.

Not too many years ago, those in charge of fast-food restaurants discovered that there was a way—the drive-through window—to make this whole process far more efficient for both themselves and the consumer. Instead of the "laborious" and "inefficient" process of parking the car, walking to the counter, waiting in line, ordering, paying, carrying the food to the table, eating, and disposing of the remnants, the drive-through window offered diners the choice of driving to the window (perhaps waiting in a line of cars), ordering, paying, and driving off with the meal. It was even possible to engage in the highly efficient act of eating while driving, thereby eliminating the need to devote a separate time period to dining. The drive-through window is also efficient from the perspective of the fast-food restaurant. As more and more people use the drive-through window, fewer parking spaces, tables, and employees are needed. Further, consumers take their debris with them as they drive away, thereby eliminating the need for additional trash receptacles and employees to periodically empty those receptacles. . . .

■ ■ ■ "HOME-MADE" FAST FOOD AND THE STAIRMASTER

Given the efficiency of the fast-food restaurant, the home kitchen has had to grow more efficient or it might have faced total extinction. Had the kitchen not grown more efficient, a comedian could have envisioned a time when the kitchen would have been replaced by a large, comfortable telephone lounge used for calling Domino's for pizza delivery. The key to the salvation of the kitchen was the development and widespread adoption of the microwave oven. The microwave is simply a far more efficient means than its major alternative, the convection oven, for preparing a meal. It is usually faster than the old oven and one can prepare a wider array of foods in it than the old-fashioned oven. Perhaps most importantly from the point of view of this chapter, it spawned the development of a number of microwavable foods (including soup, pizza, hamburgers, fried chicken, french fries, and popcorn) that permit the efficient preparation of the fare one usually finds in the fast-food restaurants. For example, one of the first microwavable foods produced by Hormel was an array of biscuit-based breakfast sandwiches "popularized in recent years by many of the fast-food chains," most notably McDonald's and its Egg McMuffin. Banquet rushed to market with microwavable chicken breast nuggets. In fact, many food companies now employ people who continually scout fast-food restaurants for new ideas for foods that can be marketed for the home. As one executive put it, "Instead of having a breakfast sandwich at McDonald's, you can pick one up from the freezer of your grocery store." As a result, one can now, in effect, enjoy fast food at home without venturing out to the fast-food restaurant. . . .

Another factor in the continued success of the fast-food restaurant is that it has many advantages over the "home-cooked" microwave dinner. For example, a trip to the fast-food restaurant offers people a dinner out rather than just another meal at home. For another, as Stan Luxenberg has pointed out in *Roadside Empires,* Mc-Donald's offers more than an efficient meal, it offers fun—brightly lit, colorful, and attractive settings, garish packaging, special inducements to children, give-aways, contests—in short, it offers a kind of carnival-like atmosphere in which to buy and consume fast food. Thus, faced with the choice of an efficient meal at home or one in a fast-food restaurant, many people are still likely to choose the fast-food restaurant because it not only offers efficiency but a range of other rewards.

The microwave oven (as well as the range of products it spawned) is but one of many contributors to the increasing efficiency of home cooking. Among other obvious technological advances are the replacement of the hand beater by the electric beater; slicers, dicers, and even knives by the Cuisinart; and the presence of either stand-alone freezers or those that are an integral part of the refrigerator.

The large freezer has permitted a range of efficiencies, such as a few trips to the market for enormous purchases rather than many trips for small purchases. It has permitted the storage of a wide range of ingredients that can be readily extracted when needed for food preparation. It has allowed for the cooking of large portions which can then be divided up, frozen, and defrosted periodically for dinner. The widespread availability of the home freezer led to the expansion of the production of frozen foods of all types. The most notable frozen food from the point of view of efficiency is the "TV dinner." People can stock their freezers with an array of such dinners (for example, Chinese, Italian, and Mexican dinners as well as a wide variety of "American" cooking) and quite readily bring them out and pop them into the oven, sometimes even the microwave. . . .

The McDonaldization of food preparation and consumption has been extended to the booming diet industry. Diet books promising all sorts of efficient shortcuts to weight loss are often at the top of the best-seller lists. Losing weight is normally difficult and time-consuming, hence the lure of various diet books that promise to make weight loss easier and quicker, that is, more efficient.

For those on a diet, and many people are on more or less perpetual diets, the preparation of low-calorie food has been made more efficient. Instead of needing to cook diet foods from scratch, they may now purchase an array of prepared foods in frozen and/or microwavable form. For those who do not wish to go through the inefficient process of eating those diet meals, there are the diet shakes, like Slim•Fast, that can be mixed and consumed in a matter of seconds.

A fairly recent development is the growth of diet centers like Nutri/System and Jenny Craig. Nutri/System sells dieters, at substantial cost, prepackaged freeze-dried food. All the dieter need do is add water when it is time for the next meal. Freeze-dried foods are not only efficient for the dieter but also for Nutri/System, because they can be efficiently packaged, transported, and stored. Furthermore, the dieter's periodic visit to a Nutri/System center is efficiently organized. A counselor is allotted ten minutes with each client. During that brief time the counselor takes the client's weight, blood pressure, and measurements, asks routine questions, fills out a chart, and devotes some time to "problem-solving." If the session extends beyond the allotted ten minutes and other clients are waiting, the receptionist will buzz the counselor's room. Counselors learn their techniques at Nutri/System University where, after a week of training (no inefficient years of matriculation here), they earn certification and an NSU diploma.

There is a strong emphasis on efficiency in modern health clubs, including such chains as Holiday Spas. These clubs often offer, under one roof, virtually everything needed to lose weight and stay in shape, including a wide array of exercise machines, as well as a running track and a swimming pool. The exercise machines are highly specialized so that one may efficiently increase fitness in specific areas of the body. Thus, working out on running machines and the StairMaster—one kind of exercise machine—increases cardiovascular fitness, whereas using various weightlifting machines increases strength and muscularity in targeted areas of the body. Another efficiency associated with many of these machines is that one can do other things while exercising. Thus, many clubs have television sets throughout the gym allowing people to both watch television and exercise. The exerciser can also read, listen to music, or even listen to a book-on-tape while working out. The exercise machines also offer a high degree of calculability, with many of them registering miles run, level of difficulty, and calories burned. All of this in the kind of clean, sterile environment we have come to associate with McDonaldization.

■ ■ ■ "SELLING MACHINES" AND L. L. BEAN

Shopping has also grown more efficient. The department store obviously is a more efficient place in which to shop than a series of specialty shops dispersed throughout the city or suburbs. The shopping mall increases efficiency by bringing a wide range of department stores and specialty shops under one roof. Kowinsky describes the mall as "an extremely efficient and effective selling machine." It is cost-efficient for retailers because it is the collection of shops and department stores ("mall synergy") that brings in throngs of people. And it is efficient for consumers because in one stop they can visit numerous shops, have lunch at a "food court" (likely populated by many fast-food chains), see a movie, have a drink, and go to an exercise or diet center.

The drive for shopping efficiency did not end with the malls. In recent years, there has been a great increase in catalogue sales (via L. L. Bean, Lands' End, and other mail-order companies), which enables people to shop while never leaving the comfort of their homes. Still more efficient, although it may require many hours in front of the tube, is home television shopping. A range of products is paraded in front of viewers who may simply phone each time a product catches their eye and conveniently charge their purchase to their credit card accounts. The latest advance in home shopping is the "scan-fone," an at-home phone machine that includes "a pen-sized bar-code scanner, a credit card magnetic-strip reader, and a key pad." The customer merely "scans items from a bar-coded catalogue and also scans delivery dates and payment methods. The orders are then electronically relayed to the various stores, businesses, and banks involved." Some mall operators fear that they will ultimately be put out of business because of the greater efficiency of shopping at home.

■ ■ ■ ■ VIDEO RENTALS AND PACKAGE TOURS

With the advent of videotapes and video rental stores, many people no longer deem it efficient to drive to their local theater to see a movie. Movies can now be viewed, often more than one at a sitting, in one's own den. For those who wish even greater efficiency, viewers can buy one of the new television sets that enable viewers to see a movie while also watching a favorite television program on an inset on the television screen.

The largest video rental franchise in the United States is Blockbuster, which, predictably, "considers itself the McDonald's of the video business." Blockbuster has more than 2,000 outlets. . . . However, there may already be signs that Blockbuster is in danger of being replaced by even more efficient alternatives. One is pay-per-view movies offered by many cable companies. Instead of trekking to the video store, all one need do is turn to the proper channel and phone the cable company. Another experimental alternative is an effort by GTE to deliver movies to one's home through fiber-optic cables. Just as the video store replaced many movie theaters, video stores themselves may soon be displaced by even more efficient alternatives.

. . . [T]ravel to exotic efficient locales has also grown more efficient. The best example of this is the package tour. Let us take, for example, a thirty-day tour of Europe. To make these efficient, only the major locales in Europe are visited. Within each of these locales, the tourist is directed toward the major sights. (In Paris, the tour would definitely stop at the Louvre, but perhaps not at the Rodin Museum.) Because the goal is to see as many of the major sights as possible in a short period of time, the emphasis is on the efficient transportation of people to, through, and from each of them. Buses hurtle to and through the city, allowing the tourist to glimpse the maximum number of sights in the time allowed. At particularly interesting or important sights, the bus may slow down or even stop to permit some picture-taking. At the most important locales, a brief stopover is planned; there the visitor can hurry through the site, take a few pictures, buy a souvenir, and then hop back on the bus to head to the next attraction.

There is no question that this is a highly efficient way of seeing the major tourist attractions of Europe. Indeed, the package tour can be seen as a vast people-moving mechanism that permits the efficient transport of people from one locale to another. If tourists attempted to see the major sights of Europe on their own, it would take more time to see the same things and the expense would be greater. There are, of course, costs associated with the package tour (for example, does the tourist ever really have time to experience Europe?), as there are with every other highly rational system, but we will reserve a discussion of them for later. . . .

■ ■ ■ CUSTOMIZED TEXTBOOKS, BOOKS–ON–TAPE, "NEWS McNUGGETS," AND DRIVE-IN CHURCHES

Turning to the educational system, specifically the university, one manifestation of the pressure for greater efficiency is the machine-graded, multiple-choice examination. In a much earlier era, students were examined on a one-to-one basis by their professors. This may have been a very good way of finding out what students know, but it was (and is) highly labor intensive and inefficient. Later, the essay examination became very popular. While grading a set of essays was more efficient from the professor's perspective than giving individual oral examinations, it was still relatively inefficient and time-consuming. Enter the multiple-choice examination, the grading of which was a snap in comparison to giving oral tests or reading essays. In fact, the grading could be passed on to graduate assistants, an act that was very efficient for the professor. Now we have computer-graded examinations that maximize efficiency for both professors and graduate students.

The multiple-choice examinations still left the professor saddled with the inefficient task of composing the necessary sets of questions. Furthermore, at least some of the questions had to be changed each semester because new students were likely to gain possession of old exams. The solution: Textbook companies provided professors with books (free of charge) full of multiple-choice questions to go along with the textbooks required for use in large classes. Professors no longer had to make up their own questions, they could use those previously provided by the publisher. However, the professor still had to retype the questions or to have them retyped by the office staff. Recently, however, publishers have been kind enough to provide their sets of questions on computer disks. Now all the professor needs to do is select the desired questions and let the printer do the rest.* . . .

***

*Some publishers also offer a "call-in testing service." A professor can call a toll-free number, specify the desired questions, and the publisher e-mails the test to the professor—all free.——Editor.

Publishers have provided other services to make teaching more efficient for those professors who adopt their textbooks. With the adoption of a textbook, a professor may receive many materials with which to fill class hours—lecture outlines, computer simulations, discussion questions, videotapes, movies, even ideas for guest lecturers and student projects. With luck, professors can use all of these devices and do little or nothing on their own for their classes. Needless to say, this is a highly efficient means of teaching from a professor's perspective, and it frees up valuable time for the much more valued activities (by professors, but not students) of writing and research. . . .

Another example of efficiency in publishing is the advent of books-on-tape. There is a number of companies that now rent or sell books recorded on audiotape. The availability of such tapes permits greater efficiency in "reading" books. Instead of doing nothing but reading, one can now engage in other activities (driving, walking, jogging, watching TV with the sound off) while listening to a book. Greater efficiency is also provided by many of these books-on-tape being available in abridged form so that they can be devoured far more quickly. Gone are the "wasted" hours listening to "insignificant" parts of novels. With liberal cutting, a book such as *War and Peace* can now be listened to in a sitting.

Most "serious," nontabloid newspapers (for example, *The New York Times* and *The Washington Post*) are relatively inefficient to read. This is especially true of stories that begin on page one and then carry over to one or more additional pages. Stories that carry over to additional pages are said to have "jumped," and many readers are resistant to "jumping" with the stories. *USA Today* eliminated this inefficient way of presenting and reading stories by starting and finishing most of them on the same page, in other words, by offering "News McNuggets." This was accomplished by ruthlessly editing stories so that narrative was dramatically reduced (and no words wasted), leaving a series of relatively bare facts. . . .

In the realm of religion, McDonaldization is manifest, among other places, in drive-in churches. Another is the widespread development of televised religious programs whereby people can get their religion in the comfort of their living rooms. A particularly noteworthy example of such religious rationalization occurred in 1985 when the Vatican announced that Catholics could receive indulgences through the Pope's annual Christmas benediction on TV or radio. ("Indulgences are a release by way of devotional practices from certain forms of punishment resulting from sin.") Before this development Catholics had to engage in the far less efficient activity of going to Rome for the Christmas benediction and manifesting the "proper intention and attitude" in order to receive their indulgences in person. . . .

■ ■ ■ [DESTROYING RELATIONSHIPS]

The fast-food restaurant offers its employees a dehumanizing setting within which to work. Few skills are required on the job. Said Burger King workers, "A moron could learn this job, it's so easy" and "Any trained monkey could do this job." Thus workers are asked to use only a minute proportion of all their skills and abilities.

Employees are not only not using all of their skills, but they are also not being allowed to think and to be creative on the job. This leads to a high level of resentment,
job dissatisfaction, alienation, absenteeism, and turnover among those who work in
fast-food restaurants. In fact, the fast-food industry has the highest turnover rate—
approximately 100 percent a year—of any industry in the United States. That means
that the average worker lasts only about four months at a fast-food restaurant; the
entire workforce of the fast-food industry turns over three times a year. . . .

   The fast-food restaurant is also dehumanizing as far as the customer is concerned. Instead of a human dining experience, what is offered is eating on a sort of
moving conveyor belt or assembly line. The diner is reduced to a kind of overwound
automaton who is made to rush through the meal. Little gratification is derived from
the dining experience or from the food itself. The best that can usually be said is that
it is efficient and it is over quickly.

   Some customers might even feel as if they are being fed like livestock in a highly
rationalized manner. This point was made a number of years ago on television in a
Saturday Night Live skit entitled "Trough and Brew," a take-off on a small fast-food
chain called Burger and Brew. In the skit, some young executives learn that a new
fast-food restaurant called Trough and Brew has opened and they decide to try it for
lunch. They are next seen entering the restaurant and having bibs tied around their
necks. After that, they discover a long trough, resembling a pig trough. The trough is
filled with chili and is periodically refilled by a waiter scooping new supplies from a
bucket. The customers bend over, stick their heads into the trough, and begin lapping
up the chili as they move along the length of the trough making high-level business
decisions. Every so often they come up for air and lap some beer from the communal
"brew basin." After they have finished their "meal," they pay their bills, "by the
head." Since their faces are smeared with chili, they are literally "hosed off" before
they leave the restaurant. The young executives are last seen being herded out of the
restaurant, which is being closed for a half-hour so that it can be "hosed down."
Saturday Night Live was clearly pointing out, and ridiculing, the fact that fast-food
restaurants tend to treat their customers like lower animals.

■ ■ ■ "GET LOST" AND *WHEEL OF FORTUNE*

Another dehumanizing aspect of fast-food restaurants is that they minimize contact
among human beings. Let us take, for example, the issue of how customers and
employees relate. The nature of the fast-food restaurant turns these into fleeting
relationships. Because the average employee stays only a few months, and even then
only works on a part-time basis, the customer, even the regular customer, is rarely
able to develop a long-term personal relationship with a counterperson. Gone are
the days when one got to know well a waitress at a diner or the short-order cook at
a local greasy spoon. Gone are the days when an employee knows who you are and
knows what you are likely to order.

   Not only are the relationships with a McDonald's employee fleeting (because
the worker remains on the job only a short period of time), but each contact between

worker and customer is of a very short duration. It takes little time at the counter to order, receive one's food, and pay for it. Both employees and customers are likely to feel rushed and to want to move on, customers to their dinner and employees to the next order. There is virtually no time for customer and counterperson to interact in such a context. This is even more true of the drive-through window, where thanks to the speedy service and the physical barriers, the server is but a dim and distant image.

The highly impersonal and anonymous relationship between customer and counterperson is heightened by the employees having been trained to interact in a staged and limited manner with customers. Thus, the customers may feel that they are dealing with automatons who have been taught to utter a few phrases rather than with fellow human beings. For their part, the customers are supposed to be, and often are, in a hurry, so they have little to say to the McDonald's employee. Indeed, it could be argued that one of the reasons for the success of fast-food restaurants is that they are in tune with our fast-paced and impersonal society. People in the modern world want to get on with their business without unnecessary personal relationships. The fast-food restaurant gives them precisely what they want.

Not only are the relationships between employee and customer limited greatly, but also other potential relationships. Because employees remain on the job for only a few months, satisfying personal relationships among employees are unlikely to develop. . . .

Relationships among customers are largely curtailed as well. Although some McDonald's ads would have us believe otherwise, gone are the days when people met in the diner or cafeteria for coffee, breakfast, lunch, or dinner and lingered to socialize with one another. Fast-food restaurants are clearly not conducive to such socializing. If nothing else, the chairs are designed to make people uncomfortable and interested in moving on to something else. The drive-through windows are a further step toward McDonaldization, by completely eliminating the possibility of interacting with other customers. . . .

Fast-food restaurants also tend to have negative effects on other human relationships. There is, for example, the effect on the so-called "family meal." The fast-food restaurant is not conducive to a long, leisurely, conversation-filled dinnertime. The family is unlikely to linger long over a meal at McDonald's. Furthermore, as the children grow into their teens, the nature of fast-food restaurants leads to separate meals as the teens go at one time with their friends, and the parents go at another time. Of course, the drive-through window only serves to reduce the possibility of a family meal. The family that gobbles its food while driving on to its next stop can hardly be seen as having what is called these days "quality time" with each other. Here is the way one journalist describes what is happening to the family meal:

> Do families who eat their suppers at the Colonel's, swinging on plastic seats, or however the restaurant is arranged, say grace before picking up a crispy brown chicken leg? Does dad ask junior what he did today as he remembers he forgot the piccalilli and trots through the crowds over to the counter to get some? Does mom find the atmosphere conducive to asking little Mildred about the problems she was having with third-conjugation French verbs, or would it matter since otherwise the family might

have been at home chomping down precooked frozen food, warmed in the microwave oven, and watching *Hollywood Squares?*

There is much talk these days about the disintegration of the family, and the fast-food restaurants may well be a crucial contributor to that disintegration.

In fact, as implied above, dinners at home may now not be much different from meals at the fast-food restaurant. Families tended to stop having lunch together by the 1940s and breakfast altogether by the 1950s. Today, the family dinner is following the same route. Even when they eat dinner at home, the meal will probably not be what it once was. Following the fast-food model, people are growing more likely to "graze," "refuel," nibble on this, or snack on that, than they are to sit down to a formal meal. Also, because it is now deemed inefficient to do nothing but just eat, families are likely to watch television while they are eating, thereby efficiently combining two activities. However, the din, to say nothing of the lure, of dinnertime TV programs such as *Wheel of Fortune* is likely to make it difficult for family members to interact with one another.

A key technology in the destruction of the family meal is the microwave oven and the vast array of microwavable foods it helped generate. It is striking to learn that more than 70 percent of American households have a microwave oven. A recent *Wall Street Journal* poll indicated that Americans consider the microwave their favorite household product. In fact, the microwave in a McDonaldizing society is seen as an advance over the fast-food restaurant. Said one consumer researcher, "It has made even fast-food restaurants not seem fast because at home you don't have to wait in line." As a general rule, consumers are demanding meals that take no more than ten minutes to microwave, whereas in the past people were more often willing to spend about a half hour or even an hour cooking dinner. This emphasis on speed has, of course, brought with it poorer taste and lower quality, but people do not seem to mind this loss: "We're just not as critical of food as we used to be." . . .

■ ■ ■ FAST FOOD [AND HOMOGENIZATION]

Another dehumanizing effect of the fast-food restaurant is that it has contributed to homogenization around the country and, increasingly, throughout the world. Diversity, which many people crave, is being reduced or eliminated by the fast-food restaurant. This decline in diversity is manifest in the extension of the fast-food model to all sorts of ethnic foods. The settings are all modeled after McDonald's in one way or another and the food has been rationalized and compromised so that it is acceptable to the tastes of virtually all diners. One cannot find an authentically different meal in any of these ethnic fast-food chains.

The expansion of these franchises across the landscape of America means that one finds little difference among regions and among cities throughout the country. Tourists find more familiarity and predictability and less diversity as they travel around the nation, and this is increasingly true on a global scale. Apparently exotic settings are likely to be overrun with both American fast-food chains as well as indigenous varieties. The new and world's largest McDonald's and Kentucky Fried Chicken in Beijing are but two examples of this. . . . The spread of American and indigenous fast food throughout much of the world means that there is less and less diversity from one setting to another. The human craving for new and diverse experiences is being limited, if not progressively destroyed, by the national and international spread of fast-food restaurants. The craving for diversity is being supplanted by the desire for uniformity and predictability. . . .

■ ■ ■ CONCLUSION

Although I have emphasized the irresistibility of McDonaldization, my fondest hope is that I am wrong. Indeed, a major motivation is to alert readers to the dangers of McDonaldization and to motivate them to act to stem its tide. I hope that we are able to resist McDonaldization and can create instead a more reasonable, more human world.

McDonald's was recently sued by the famous French chef, Paul Bocuse, for using his picture on a poster without his permission. Enraged, Bocuse said: "How can I be seen promoting this tasteless, boneless food in which everything is soft." Nevertheless, Bocuse seemed to acknowledge the inevitability of McDonaldization: "There's a need for this kind of thing . . . and trying to get rid of it seems to me to be as futile as trying to get rid of the prostitutes in the Bois de Boulogne." Lo and behold, two weeks later, it was announced that the Paris police had cracked down on prostitution in the Bois de Boulogne. Said a police spokesman, "There are none left." Thus, just as chef Bocuse was wrong about the prostitutes, perhaps I was wrong about the irresistibility of McDonaldization. Yet, before we grow overly optimistic, it should be noted that "everyone knows that the prostitutes will be back as soon as the operation is over. In the spring, police predict, there will be even more than before." Similarly, it remains likely that no matter how intense the opposition, the future will bring with it more rather than less McDonaldization. . . . [F]aced with Max Weber's iron cage imagery of a future dominated by the polar night of icy darkness and hardness, the least the reader can do is to follow the words of the poet Dylan Thomas: "Do not go gentle into that good night. . . . Rage, rage against the dying of the light."

How Many Sexual Partners Do Americans Have?

Robert T. Michael, John H. Gagnon,
Edward O. Laumann, and Gina Kolata

introduction ■ ■ ■ ■ ■

Human sexual behavior is one of the many fascinating aspects of social life that sociologists study. This aspect of social life is significant because it involves not only social relationships but also a central part of our personal identity—our feelings of self, of who we are. Yet when sociologists investigate this vital area of human behavior, they meet resistance and suspicion. Resistance comes from people who feel that human sexuality is solely a private matter and no prying sociologist should examine it. Suspicion is generalized, coming from a great number of people who feel that the sociologist's motives are somehow impure and improper. If sociologists do research on teenage sexuality, they are thought to harbor secret fantasies. If they do research on prostitutes, they are thought to visit prostitutes under cover of night. If they gather data on homosexual behavior, they are thought to be closet homosexuals. No matter what area of sexual behavior they investigate, they are suspected of fantasies, secret longings, and various forms of deviating from the sexual norms.

This risk to reputation and relationships (which often comes with snide remarks and smirking) is not faced by sociologists who investigate voting behavior or changes in food preference. These researchers do not come under suspicion or derision as people who may covertly want to undermine democracy or who harbor secret food longings. With this risk to reputation, few sociologists investigate human sexual behavior, despite its high significance for understanding social life. Some do, however, and this selection by Robert Michael, John Gagnon, Edward Laumann, and Gina Kolata provides an update on changing human sexual behavior.

Thinking Critically

As you read this selection, ask yourself:

1. In the introduction to this selection, the editor says that unlike those who do research on political behavior, sociologists who study human sexual behavior risk reputation and relationships. Why do you think this is so?

2. This selection underscores the significance and influence of marriage. What evidence do you find for this statement?

3. Based on this reading, how has the sexual behavior of Americans changed? Why?

Sometimes, the myths about sex contain a grain of truth. The common perception is that Americans today have more sexual partners than they did just a decade or two ago. That, it turns out, is correct. A third of Americans who are over age fifty have had five or more sexual partners in their lifetime. But half of all Americans aged thirty to fifty have had five or more partners even though being younger, they had fewer years to accumulate them.

Still, when we ask older or younger people how many partners they had in the past year, the usual reply is zero or one. Something must have changed to make younger people accumulate more partners over a lifetime, yet sustain a pattern of having no partners or only one in any one year. The explanation is linked to one of our most potent social institutions and how it has changed.

That institution is marriage, a social arrangement so powerful that nearly everyone participates. About 90 percent of Americans have married by the time they are thirty, and a large majority spends much of their adulthood as part of a wedded couple. And marriage, we find, regulates sexual behavior with remarkable precision. No matter what they did before they wed, no matter how many partners they had, the sexual lives of married people are similar. Despite the popular myth that there is a great deal of adultery in marriage, our data and other reliable studies do not find it. Instead, a vast majority are faithful while the marriage is intact. . . .

So, yes, many young people probably are having sexual intercourse with a fair number of partners. But that stops with marriage. The reason that people now have more sexual partners over their lifetimes is that they are spending a longer period sexually active, but unmarried. The period has lengthened from both ends and in the middle. The average age at which people have their first sexual intercourse has crept down and the average age at which people marry for the first time has edged up. And people are more likely to divorce now, which means they have time between marriages when they search for new partners once again.

To draw these conclusions, we looked at our respondents' replies to a variety of questions. First, we asked people when they first had heterosexual intercourse. Then, we asked what happens between the time when people first have intercourse and when they finally marry. How many partners do they have? Do they have more than one partner at any one time or do they have their partners in succession, practicing

From *Sex in America: A Definite Survey,* by Robert T. Michael, John H. Gagnon, Edward O. Laumann, and Gina Kolata. Copyright © 1994 by CSG Enterprises, Inc., Edward O. Laumann, Robert T. Michael, and Gina Kolata. Reprinted by permission of Little, Brown and Company, Inc.

serial monogamy? We asked how many people divorced and how long they remained unmarried. Finally, we asked how many partners people had in their lifetimes.

In our analyses of the numbers of sex partners, we could not separately analyze patterns for gay men and lesbians. That is because homosexuals are such a small percentage of our sample that we do not have enough people in our survey to draw valid conclusions about this aspect of sexual behavior.

If we are going to look at heterosexual partners from the beginning, from the time that people first lose their virginity, we plunge headfirst into the maelstrom of teenage sex, always a turbulent subject, but especially so now, in the age of AIDS.

While society disputes whether to counsel abstinence from sexual intercourse or to pass out condoms in high schools, it also must grapple with a basic question: Has sexual behavior among teenagers changed? Are more having sexual intercourse and at younger ages, or is the overheated rhetoric a reaction to fears, without facts? The answer is both troubling and reassuring to the majority of adults who prefer teenagers to delay their sexual activity—troubling because most teenagers are having intercourse, but reassuring because sexual intercourse tends to be sporadic during the teen years.

We saw a steadily declining age at which teenagers first had sexual intercourse. Men and women born in the decade 1933–1942 had sex [for the first time] at an average age of about eighteen. Those born twenty to thirty years later have an average age at first intercourse that is about six months younger, as seen in Figure 1. The figure also indicates that the men report having sex at younger ages than the women. It also shows that blacks report a younger age at first intercourse than whites.

Another way to look at the age at first intercourse is illustrated in Figure 2. The figure shows the proportions of teenagers and young adults who experienced sexual intercourse at each age from twelve to twenty-five. To see at what age half the people had intercourse, for example, follow the . . . horizontal line that corresponds to a cumulative frequency of 50 percent. It shows that half of all black men had intercourse by the time they were fifteen, half of all Hispanic men had intercourse by the time they were about sixteen and a half, half of all black women had intercourse by the time they were nearly seventeen, and half the white women and half the Hispanic women had intercourse by the time they were nearly eighteen. By age twenty-two, about 90 percent of each group had intercourse.

The patterns are crystal clear. About half the teenagers of various racial and ethnic groups in the nation have begun having intercourse with a partner in the age range of fifteen to eighteen, and at least four out of five have had intercourse by the time their teenage years are over. Since the average age of marriage is now in the mid-twenties, few Americans wait until they marry to have sex. . . .

It's a change that built up for years, making it sometimes hard to appreciate just how profound it is. Stories of what sex among the unmarried was like decades ago can be startling. Even people who were no longer teenagers, and who were engaged, felt overwhelming social pressure to refrain from intercourse before marriage. . . .

In addition to having intercourse at younger ages, many people also are marrying later—a change that is the real legacy of the late 1960s and early 1970s. This period was not, we find, a sexual revolution, a time of frequent sex with many

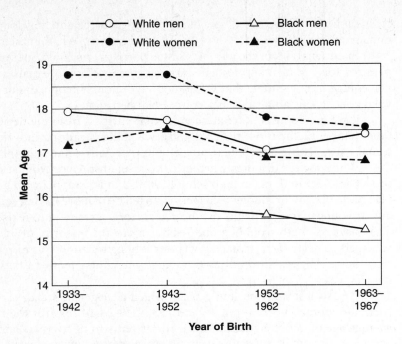

FIGURE 1   Mean Age at First Intercourse

Note: This includes respondents who had vaginal intercourse no later than age twenty-five and who have reached their twenty-fifth birthday by the date of the interview. [There were an] insufficient number of cases [to show Hispanics]. Whites computed from cross-section sample; blacks computed from cross-section and the over-sample.

partners for all. Instead, it was the beginning of a profound change in the sexual life course, providing the second reason why Americans have accumulated more partners now than in decades past.

Since the 1960s, the route to the altar is no longer so predictable as it used to be. In the first half of the twentieth century, almost everyone who married followed the same course: dating, love, a little sexual experimentation with one partner, sometimes including intercourse, then marriage and children. It also was a time when there was a clear and accepted double standard—men were much more likely to have had intercourse with several women before marrying than women were to have had intercourse with several men.

At the dawn of the millennium, we are left with a nation that still has this idealized heterosexual life course but whose actual course has fragmented in the crucial years before marriage. Some people still marry at eighteen, others at thirty, leading to very different numbers of sexual partners before marriage. Social class plays a role, with less-educated people marrying earlier than better-educated people. Blacks tend to marry much later than whites, and a large number of blacks do not marry at all.

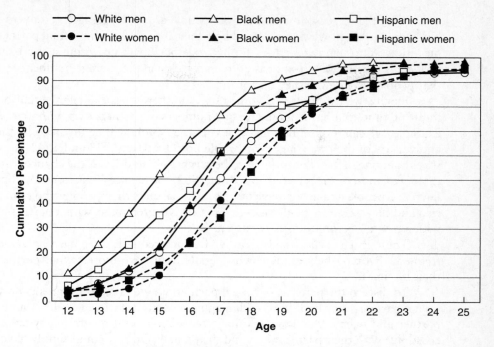

FIGURE 2   Cumulative Percentage Who Have Had Intercourse [by Age 25]

Note: Cumulative percentage indicates the proportion of respondents of a given group at a given age. This figure only includes respondents who have reached their twenty-fifth birthday by the date of the interview.

But a new and increasingly common pattern has emerged: affection or love and sex with a number of partners, followed by affection, love, and cohabitation. This cycles back to the sexual marketplace, if the cohabitation breaks up, or to marriage. Pregnancy can occur at any of these points, but often occurs before either cohabitation or marriage. The result is that the path toward marriage, once so straight and narrow, has begun to meander and to have many side paths, one of which is being trodden into a well-traveled lane.

That path is the pattern of living together before marriage. Like other recent studies, ours shows a marked shift toward living together rather than marriage as the first union of couples. With an increase in cohabitation, the distinctions among having a steady sexual partner, a live-in sexual partner, and a marriage have gotten more fuzzy. This shift began at the same time as talk of a sexual revolution. Our study shows that people who came of age before 1970 almost invariably got married without first living together, while the younger people seldom did. But, we find, the average age at which people first move in with a partner—either by marrying, or living together—has remained nearly constant, around age twenty-two for men and twenty for women. The difference is that now that first union is increasingly likely to be a cohabitation. . . .

With the increase in cohabitation, people are marrying later, on average. The longer they wait, however, the more likely they are to live with a sexual partner in the meantime. Since many couples who live together break up within a short time and seek a new partner, the result has been an increase in the average number of partners that people have before they marry. . . .

Finally, we can look at divorce rates, another key social change that began in the 1960s and that has led to increasing numbers of partners over a lifetime. . . . For example, we can look at how likely it is that a couple will be divorced by the tenth anniversary of their marriage. For people born between 1933 and 1942, the chance was about one in five. For those born between 1943 and 1952, the chance was one in three. For those born between 1953 and 1962, the chance was closer to 38 percent. Divorced people as a group have more sexual partners than people who remain married and they are more likely, as a group, to have intercourse with a partner and live with a partner before they marry again.

These three social trends—earlier first intercourse, later marriage, and more frequent divorce—help explain why people now have more sexual partners over their lifetimes.

To discern the patterns of sexual partnering, we asked respondents how many sexual partners they had. We could imagine several scenarios. People could find one partner and marry. Or they could have sex with several before marrying. Or they could live with their partners first and then marry. Or they could simply have lots of casual sex, never marrying at all or marrying but also having extramarital sex.

Since our respondents varied in age from eighteen to fifty-nine, the older people in the study, who married by their early twenties, would have been married by the time the turbulent 1960s and 1970s came around. Their premarital behavior would be a relic from the past, telling us how much intercourse people had in the days before sex became so public an issue. The younger people in our study can show us whether there is a contrast between the earlier days and the decades after a sexual revolution was proclaimed. We can ask if they have more partners, if they have more than one sexual partner at a time, and if their sexual behavior is markedly different from that of the older generations that preceded them.

Most young people today show no signs of having very large numbers of partners. More than half the men and women in America who were eighteen to twenty-four in 1992 had just one sex partner in the past year and another 11 percent had none in the last year. In addition, studies in Europe show that people in the United Kingdom, France, and Finland have sexual life courses that are virtually the same as the American life course. The picture that emerges is strikingly different from the popular image of sexuality running out of control in our time.

In fact, we find, nearly all Americans have a very modest number of partners, whether we ask them to enumerate their partners over their adult lifetime or in the past year. The number of partners varies little with education, race, or religion. Instead, it is determined by marital status or by whether a couple is living together. Once married, people tend to have one and only one partner, and those who are unmarried and living together are almost as likely to be faithful.

Our data for the United States are displayed in Table 1.

TABLE 1 Number of Sex Partners in Past Twelve Months and Since Age Eighteen

	SEX PARTNERS PAST TWELVE MONTHS				SEX PARTNERS SINCE AGE EIGHTEEN					
	0	1	2 to 4	5+	0	1	2 to 4	5 to 10	10 to 20	21+
Total	12%	71%	14%	3%	3%	26%	30%	22%	11%	9%
Gender										
Men	10	67	18	5	3	20	21	23	16	17
Women	14	75	10	2	3	31	36	20	6	3
Age										
18–24	11	57	24	9	8	32	34	15	8	3
25–29	6	72	17	6	2	25	31	22	10	9
30–34	9	73	16	2	3	21	29	25	11	10
35–39	10	77	11	2	2	19	30	25	14	11
40–44	11	75	13	1	1	22	28	24	14	12
45–49	15	75	9	1	2	26	24	25	10	14
50–54	15	79	5	0	2	34	28	18	9	9
55–59	32	65	4	0	1	40	28	15	8	7
Marital status										
Never married, noncohabiting	25	38	28	9	12	15	29	21	12	12
Never married, cohabiting	1	75	20	5	0	25	37	16	10	13
Married	2	94	4	1	0	37	28	19	9	7
Divorced, separated, widowed, noncohabiting	31	41	26	3	0	11	33	29	15	12
Divorced, separated, widowed, cohabiting	1	80	15	3	0	0	32	44	12	12
Education										
Less than high school	16	67	15	3	4	27	36	19	9	6
High school graduate or equivalent	11	74	13	3	3	30	29	20	10	7
Some college, vocational	11	71	14	4	2	24	29	23	12	9
Finished college	12	69	15	4	2	24	26	24	11	13
Master's/advanced degree	13	74	10	3	4	25	26	23	10	13
Current Religion										
None	11	68	13	7	3	16	29	20	16	16
Mainline Protestant	11	73	13	2	2	23	31	23	12	8
Conservative Protestant	13	70	14	3	3	30	30	20	10	7
Catholic	12	71	13	3	4	27	29	23	8	9
Jewish	3	75	18	3	0	24	13	30	17	17
Other religion	15	70	12	3	3	42	20	16	8	13
Race/Ethnicity										
White	12	73	12	3	3	26	29	22	11	9
Black	13	60	21	6	2	18	34	24	11	11
Hispanic	11	69	17	2	4	35	27	17	8	9
Asian	15	77	8	0	6	46	25	14	6	3
Native American	12	76	10	2	5	28	35	23	5	5

Note: Row percentages total 100 percent.

The right-hand portion of Table 1 tells how many sexual partners people had since they turned eighteen. Very few, just 3 percent, had no partners, and few, just 9 percent, had a total of more than twenty partners.

The oldest people in our study, those aged fifty-five to fifty-nine, were most likely to have had just one sexual partner in their lifetimes—40 percent said they had had only one. This reflects the earlier age of marriage in previous generations and the low rate of divorce among these older couples. Many of the men were married by age twenty-two and the women by age twenty.

The left-hand portion of Table 1 shows the number of sexual partners that people had in the past twelve months. These are the data that show how likely people are to remain faithful to their sexual partner, whether or not they are married. Among married people, 94 percent had one partner in the past year. Couples who were living together were almost as faithful. Seventy-five percent of people who had never married but were living together had one partner in the past year. Eighty percent of people who were previously married and were cohabiting when we questioned them had one partner in the past year. Two-thirds of the single people who were not living with a partner had no partners or only one in the past year. Only a few percent of the population had as many as five partners for sexual intercourse in the past year, and many of these were people who were never married and were not living with anyone. They were mostly young and mostly male. . . .

One way to imagine the patterns of sexual partners is to think of a graph, with the vertical axis showing numbers of partners and the horizontal axis showing a person's age. The graph will be a series of blips, as the person finds partners, interspersed with flat regions where the person has no partners or when the person has just one steady partner. When the person marries, the line flattens out at a height of one, indicating that the individual has only one partner. If the marriage breaks up, the graph shows a few more blips until the person remarries, and then it flattens out again.

For an individual, the graph is mostly flat, punctuated by a few areas of blips. But if we superimposed everyone's graph on top of each other, we would have a sort of supergraph that looked like it was all blips. That, in essence, is what has led to the widespread impression that everyone is having lots of partners. We see the total picture—lots of sex in the population—without realizing that each individual spends most of his or her life with only one partner.

These findings give no support to the idea of a promiscuous society or of a dramatic sexual revolution reflected in huge numbers of people with multiple casual sex partners. The finding on which our data give strong and quite amazing evidence is not that most people do, in fact, form a partnership, or that most people do, in fact, ultimately get married. That fact also was well documented in many previous studies. Nor is it news that more recent marriages are much less stable than marriages that began thirty years ago. That fact, too, was reported by others before us. But we add a new fact, one that is not only important but that is striking.

Our study clearly shows that no matter how sexually active people are before and between marriages, no matter whether they lived with their sexual partners before marriage or whether they were virgins on their wedding day, marriage is such a powerful social institution that, essentially, married people are nearly all alike—they are faithful to their partners as long as the marriage is intact. It does not matter if the couple were high-school sweethearts who married after graduation day or whether they are in their thirties, marrying after each had lived with several others. Once married, the vast majority have no other sexual partner; their past is essentially erased. Marriage remains the great leveler.

We see this, for example, when we ask about fidelity in marriage. More than 80 percent of women and 65 to 85 percent of men of every age report that they had no partners other than their spouse while they were married. . . .

The marriage effect is so dramatic that it swamps all other aspects of our data. When we report that more than 80 percent of adult Americans age eighteen to fifty-nine had zero or one sexual partner in the past year, the figure might sound ludicrous to some young people who know that they and their friends have more than one partner in a year. But the figure really reflects the fact that most Americans in that broad age range are married and are faithful. And many of the others are cohabiting, and they too are faithful. Or they are without partners altogether, a situation that is especially likely for older women. . . . We find only 3 percent of adults had five or more partners in the past year. Half of all adult Americans had three or fewer partners over their lifetimes.

Name Index

Subject Index